ANGELA MERKEL

The Chancellor and Her World

Stefan Kornelius

Translated by Anthea Bell and
Christopher Moncrieff

ALMA BOOKS

ALMA BOOKS LTD
3 Castle Yard
Richmond
Surrey TW10 6TF
United Kingdom
www.almabooks.com

First published in German by Hoffmann und Campe Verlag in 2013
This translation, based on a revised German text including the additional
chapter 'The British Problem', first published by Alma Books Limited in 2013
This mass-market edition first published by Alma Books Limited in May 2014
Reprinted September 2014, January 2016

**The translation of this work was supported by a grant from the Goethe-
Institut which is funded by the German Ministry of Foreign Affairs.**

Printed and bound by CPI Group (UK) Ltd, Croydon, CR0 4YY

ISBN (PAPERBACK): 978-1-84688-318-7
ISBN (EBOOK): 978-1-84688-308-8

CONTENTS

Angela Merkel

The Chancellor and Her World

Merkelmania

The Chancellor's New Power

In the eighth year of her chancellorship, Angela Merkel has reached the zenith of her power – again. She has now been at the head of the greatest and richest economy in Europe for two parliamentary terms. She is the undisputed leader of her party and faces almost no opposition. She presides over a cabinet of mostly loyal and obedient ministers. She has tamed her second coalition partner, putting to rest the initial negative impression of her government. She treats the opposition with disdain. Publicly, she enjoys a great deal of respect – no chancellor before her had been able to call on such high approval ratings in their seventh year of government. Economically, her country is not in a bad shape – compared to its neighbours. Nor is Germany troubled by any major problems at home.

Angela Merkel has risen to a position of power and worldwide influence. She is one of a small group of heads of state who can look back on a similarly long period in office. In the European Union she is the last of her generation of leaders: apart from that perennial, the Prime Minister of Luxembourg, no one has been in power longer than she has. The President of the European Commission took office the year before her – but only with her help. Merkel is working with the second American President of her time in office, and she had dealings with their predecessor. She is engaged in a kind of hare-and-tortoise race with the President of Russia as to who will stay in office longest. In China Merkel has so far seen only one change of leadership: she eagerly anticipated her meeting with the new leaders, wishing to compare the new politicians in power with their familiar predecessors.

She has contributed to the peace process in the Middle East. She has an intense and sometimes even emotional relationship with Israel, partly because of German history of course, but also because of the kind of personal feelings that she seldom allows to interfere with international relationships. The intensity of the events in the Arab world also caught her off guard. With a certain degree of sceptical apprehension, she is monitoring the developments in the Middle East and in those societies, now in turmoil, that wanted freedom but ended up being cut off from power. Merkel knows something about freedom: she has a story of her own to tell on that subject, although she seldom does, because she dislikes any excess of emotion. In her view, freedom is a very individual matter: the yearning for unfettered development, a wish to push one's limits, discover new ground, understand and master a subject – all of which can be used to describe the personal quest for freedom of a woman who had to hide her ambitions and her talent for thirty-five years. And it seems as if her hunger is not yet satisfied.

It has been said at various points that she has reached the peak of her career. But Merkel does not believe in linear progression. To her, politics is a zero-sum game – an accumulation of positives and negatives, a constant stringing-together of success and failure.

And this is where the problem begins: success and failure are measured not only by a coalition's stability, voter satisfaction or

4

the frequency of international visits. Those are the wrong parameters. The right parameters are events: asked by a journalist what could throw a government off track, the British prime minister Harold Macmillan once replied, "Events, my dear fellow, events." Angela Merkel also carries a historical burden, the economic crisis – and it is this event alone that will determine the success or failure of her chancellorship.

She did not seek out the crisis: it was the crisis that came to her. It came first in the form of the banking crisis, then mutated into a full-blown world economic crisis – and finally it became the euro crisis. There are several problems lurking in its shadow that could do untold damage: a debt crisis, problems with growth and competitiveness and, ultimately, the collapse of the euro. The possible consequences are terrifying: a run on the banks, insolvency, the demise of entire sectors of the economy, a fall in exports, high unemployment, social tension, the rise of radical parties – and the political disintegration of Europe. When we look at these scenarios, we can appreciate the historical significance of the crisis.

Angela Merkel has been forced to confront this event and try to avert its potentially destructive effects. Unlike Helmut Kohl, she does not have the advantage of governing during a relatively easy period in German history. Kohl made the most of the favourable circumstances and the positive dynamics of European movements of political emancipation, and with a sure instinct led Germany to unification and Europe to a new era of prosperity. Merkel, on the other hand, is fighting a defensive war: she is battling against potential ruin. She cannot promise flourishing landscapes – she can only strive to prevent Europe from becoming a place of desolation.

The defining theme of Merkel's chancellorship, then, is Europe's crisis. Konrad Adenauer firmly anchored the Federal Republic in the West, and he carried through a political model which provided social reconciliation and a market economy. Willy Brandt began to ease the country's relationship with the East. And Helmut Kohl has gone down in history as the chancellor who achieved the reunification of Germany. Merkel has now found her own historical mission, and this makes her position stronger. It must be admitted that the crisis has been beneficial to her career. Without it, her chancellorship would be considerably less relevant from a historical point of view. She now has the opportunity of joining the ranks of the great heads of state. Her decisions are momentous not just for Germany, but for Europe as a whole.

This elevation in her stature is not felt so much in Berlin as in the European political arena – for example in Brussels, at summits with the French President, or on visits to Athens. She is now a towering European figure – but in the process she has become something of a political loner.

There has been an increased focus on her personality, as if it were only up to her whether or not the Continent can overcome its problems. Her new status is confirmed by the many visitors to Berlin, the attention paid to her in Washington or Beijing, as well as the distortions and demonization that she has to endure.

Merkel became the protagonist of the current-affairs magazines during four crisis-ridden years. "The Mystery of Angela Merkel", "The Lost Leader", "Frau Europe", "Mother Discourage", "Achtung, It's Angela" – no caricature, no cliché went unused. Sometimes she laughs at the headlines or the cartoons – for instance the one in *The Economist*, which shows a ship called

The World Economy sinking far below the surface and onto the seabed, while a plaintive voice on the bridge enquires, "Please can we start the engines now, Mrs Merkel?"

Such gentle humour, however, is the exception. As a rule the cartoons show Merkel with a Hitler moustache; Merkel topless, suckling the Kaczyński twins; Merkel with blood dripping from her shoulders; Merkel as a dominatrix treading the Spanish premier under her boots as he pleads for mercy. The imagery reached new heights on the cover of the *New Statesman*, where the Kanzlerin was given the face of a Terminator and a robotic eye. The story inside – besides containing the predictable comparisons with Hitler – described her as a greater danger to the stability of the world than Kim Jong-un of North Korea or President Ahmadinejad of Iran. Merkel was either depicted as a bully or as Nero fiddling while Europe burned.

The conservative French newspaper *Le Figaro* suggested the following scenarios: either France would join the German-dominated north of Europe, or it would "become part of the peripheral countries derided by the pan-Germanists as PIGS". By pan-Germanists the paper presumably meant Germany and its vassals. The socialist economist Daniel Cohen called Germany "the China of Europe". And the Spanish writer Javier Cercas made sure that Merkel became the pantomime villain in southern Europe: "The economic terms she is forcing on us cannot be met, and arouse feelings of resentment and humiliation comparable to those aroused in Germany after the First World War, when the victorious Allies dictated its economic programme."

So Versailles all over again, but with the roles reversed? Germans underestimate the degree to which the economic strength of their country and Merkel's political power are resented by its neighbours. The American financial guru George Soros, a particularly vocal opponent of the German euro-rescue policy, warned Merkel that the rest of Europe would not love or admire Germany as an imperial power: "There will be hatred and resistance, because it will be perceived as an oppressor." And that has been one of the less severe warnings. Far more dangerous was the revival of old conspiracy theories: it was claimed that after unification Germany threw all its weight behind the euro because it planned to rule the Continent through its monetary policy. What had failed twice in military terms was now to succeed in peacetime with the aid of the euro and the cent – Teutonic imperialism, a brilliant master plan.

Is all of this just ideological hyperbole? Or fanciful hysteria? Chancellor Merkel was sure to be at least aware of the tensions. The mismatch within Europe in terms of economic capacity and competitiveness had given Germany an unbeatable advantage. In addition, its exports machine ran so well because the Federal Republic profited from the vast single market and because Germany's powerful industry allowed no chance to competitors from southern Europe for instance, where the cost of labour was higher. Thanks to its economic strength, Germany also enjoyed the favour of the financial markets: credit had never been so cheap, and it had never been so easy to find takers for government bonds. Germany was seen as profiteering in a time of crisis, and Merkel as the orchestrator of an unprecedented master plan. Thanks to the Schröder government's rigorous social reforms and a moderate wage-scale policy, Europe's economy had shifted to the middle of the Continent. New markets were opened up in Asia and Russia.

France had lost its traditional political and economic balancing role: in a Europe of twenty-seven nations, the political centre of power had shifted from Paris to Berlin.

The crisis gave Angela Merkel many advantages. Firstly, from the German viewpoint her rescue policy was both urgent and conclusive, so she encountered very little resistance from the opposition at home. Secondly, she was governing at a decisive moment for the executive. It was a time when heads of government in Europe – not the European Commission or national parliaments – were taking the lead. And thirdly, no road can bypass the Chancellor of the strongest economy in Europe; anyone wishing to save the euro would have to do so in conjunction with Merkel. Initially, therefore, the crisis put Merkel in a winning position, but she also bore a heavy responsibility. If the rescue operation went wrong she would be deeply implicated, even if she had done everything in her power to avert disaster. All eyes in Europe were focused on her. If Europe failed, then Merkel would have failed.

The Chancellor's special position was something entirely new in the history of the Federal Republic. Never before had a chancellor played such an important role in foreign policy. Even in Helmut Kohl's time it was accepted that he was steering the ship in Germany's interests at a favourable moment in history – but no more than that. Inadvertently, unintentionally, Germany has acquired an international significance that is alien to its nature, and which over the past few decades it has declined to assume.

History teaches us that Europe doesn't gladly tolerate the presence of a loner in its midst. The instant revival of ancient prejudices shows how delicate the Federal Republic's special position in Europe actually is. The country was ready and willing to share its power in Europe and fit into a post-national collective. The German Constitution and the history of its global alliances since the Second World War are evidence of the many safeguards that have been put in place to control this colossus. This was why Helmut Kohl gave a guarantee that Germany would be firmly anchored in Europe in return for unification. The Maastricht Treaty was signed in 1992 and the Deutschmark abandoned in favour of a European currency for the same reason. Suddenly the constants of post-war European history changed. The emphasis shifted.

It was at this moment that Angela Merkel became the focus of attention. Who was this woman who for so long had kept quiet, and who in only a few years had taken control of Germany's conservative party? Who was this politician who rose almost unnoticed to lead the leaders of Europe? The Germans have been pondering over the mystery of Merkel for many years, trying to interpret her character and the inner workings of her mind. But now the whole world wants to know: how did she get into politics? What is her worldview? What are her values, her yard-sticks? Merkel enjoys an interest in her as a person that rarely wanes – yet another reason why she has once more conquered the summit. This time she has come under scrutiny in her capacity as a stateswoman, a foreign-policy expert. What will she do if Germany's objective increase of power is perceived as a threat? She has managed to make Germany's dominance seem tolerable so far – but will it stay that way?

Yes, Merkel bears a heavy burden – and naturally she relishes this new-found assertiveness, because she is convinced that the blend of regulations and structural changes she has prescribed will be good for Europe. But she has not yet found an answer to the dilemma described by Bismarck: Germany is too small to exercise hegemony in Europe, and yet too large for its equilibrium. Or, to rephrase this in modern terms: Germany is too strong to be absorbed into the structures of Europe, and too weak to impose what it believes are the right policies on other nations. Historians refer to this as semi-hegemony – not a comfortable position for any country.

So here she is, catapulted into the leadership of Europe, constantly fending off the accusation that her sole aim is to make Europe more German. The future of the historical European project, the overcoming of former hostilities, is in her hands. Perhaps these thoughts crossed her mind as she sat in the City Hall in Oslo and watched as the Nobel Peace Prize was awarded to Europe.

Arnold Schwarzenegger, who has seen better days, once called her the most powerful woman on the planet. If further evidence of the German Chancellor's new power were required, this was provided by the Mattel toy company, who designed a Barbie doll modelled on her – claiming that Merkel was a role model for girls who dreamt of being able to become "whatever they wanted". Merkel herself doesn't much care for role models. In her office there is only one picture: a silver-framed portrait of Sophie von Anhalt-Zerbst, later known as Catherine the Great. As ruler of Russia, Catherine pursued policies very much in the spirit of the Enlightenment, but she was also assiduously imperialist. She loved to play with power, converted to the Orthodox Faith, took a Russian first name, made use of men – all with the aim of expanding her authority. Merkel was given the picture by a journalist, and it has been in her office ever since. She tends to dismiss excessive interpretations – she admires Catherine as a woman and a reformer, nothing more. Not only that, the Tsarina ruled for thirty-four years – a period of time that will not be granted to Angela Merkel.

Another World

A Sheltered Life in the GDR

Young Angela Kasner's world was quite straightforward. It consisted of her mother, father, brother and sister, the Waldhof and its various businesses, and the road outside. Sometimes Angela crossed the road to go to the nearby shop and wait for her father, who was usually out and about. "I didn't venture any farther," she said. As a little girl she didn't go to a crèche or kindergarten, and was afraid of horses – these are Angela Merkel's earliest memories. The Waldhof, a complex of residential and farm buildings, storehouses and workshops, was like an island in the idyllic little town of Templin. In 1957 her father, Horst Kasner, was asked to set up a college for Church administration, later known as the Pastoral College, and act as its head teacher. Curates and pastors would visit the Waldhof for several weeks to train or attend seminars on preaching. The Waldhof was an important institution for the Protestant Church in the State of Berlin-Brandenburg – it could be claimed that every pastor in the Church at the time would have been taught by Horst Kasner at some point in his life.

Herlind and Horst Kasner had married in Hamburg, where their first child, Angela, was born on 17th July 1954. Her mother's parents, Gertrud and Willi Jentzsch, also lived in Hamburg, having moved there from Danzig after the war. Grandmother Jentzsch seems to have come from Glogau in Silesia, known today as Glogow, and Grandfather Jentzsch from the area of Bitterfeld. Merkel's mother Herlind was born in 1928 in Danzig, at the time known as the Free City of Danzig and under the aegis of the League of Nations. Why nearby Elbing is frequently mentioned as Herlind's birthplace is a mystery. Merkel's grandparents had lived there for only a few years.

Her father, Horst Kasner, was originally from Berlin. His family background is more complex, and his forebears were quite severely affected by the troubled history of the area, where the borders of Germany and Poland were constantly shifting. Horst's father Ludwig, Angela's grandfather, was born in Posen in 1896 – although not as Ludwig Kasner, but Ludwig Kazmierczak. Like most inhabitants of the province of Posen, the Kazmierczaks had Polish roots, and since the second partition of Poland, the city and surrounding region had seen several boundary changes and various different rulers. At the time of Ludwig Kazmierczak's birth, Posen was part of the German Empire, so Merkel's grandfather was officially a German citizen. The family nonetheless had remained faithful to its Polish origins, although Ludwig clearly didn't share those sentiments. As a result he made a decision that was to have far-reaching consequences. In 1919, after the First World War and the Treaty of Versailles, Posen once again became part of Poland. In the years that followed, much of the German minority emigrated from the region – including those who didn't want to return to Poland. Ludwig Kazmierczak was one of those who left his native land and part of his family behind and set off for Berlin, where he met his future wife Margarethe. Their son Horst was born in 1926. But it wasn't until 1930 that Ludwig Kazmierczak decided to adopt the German version of his surname and began calling himself Kasner. Having worked as a police officer in the Pankow district of Berlin, he died in 1939. Angela, who was five at the time, has no clear memories of him. However, young Angela would often visit her grandmother Margarethe, who aroused her interest in art and music.

In 1995, at a Church congress in Hamburg, Angela Merkel said that one of her grandfathers was originally from Poland. She repeated the statement in 2000, describing herself as "one quarter Polish". There was great excitement over this apparently new revelation – especially in Poland, where a Friends of Angela Merkel group was immediately set up.

While little is known about her grandparents, more research has been done into her parents' background. A few weeks after Angela's birth in 1954, young Pastor Kasner and his family left Hamburg and moved to East Germany – his first parish was the village of Quitzow, in the Prignitz district of Brandenburg. Three years later the family moved to Templin. This was to be Angela Merkel's childhood home, the centre of her early life, the place which defined her youth. Templin is an hour and a half's drive north of Berlin, a hidden gem of the Uckermark district. Lakes, rivers, canals, the vast sky above, the old buildings – Templin retains its charm to the present day. The Waldhof had been founded in 1852 as a home for young people with learning difficulties, and had seen much upheaval – it was in a particularly bad state in the year when Pastor Kasner was setting up his seminary. It ceased to operate as an educational establishment under the East German Social Services. Instead, the Church used the large complex to house mentally disabled people, who could work in the vegetable garden and the forge, weave baskets or pursue one of the other crafts or trades. It was a remarkably modern concept for its time: the mentally disabled lived freely as part of society; they could take up gainful employment and were encouraged to do so. For Angela Merkel, mixing with them was part of everyday life.

There are few accounts of the Kasners' home life, but there is little doubt that Angela Kasner grew up in a politically engaged and open-minded household. For all the restrictions of the GDR system, Pastor Kasner and his wife still preserved their intellectual freedom, and their daughter Angela reaped the benefits. Her interest in the world was aroused and stimulated early in life, and the pastor's household provided protection from the regimentation of the system. Years later, in an interview with the photographer Herlinde Koelbl, Merkel said that "no shadow had darkened her childhood", that the Waldhof was an environment that a child could easily absorb and understand. Merkel said she had always been fascinated by people "who were at peace with life", such as the gardener who became a friend and confidant when she was a child, and who was a model of self-confidence and composure compared to her father. All her childhood memories are of security and intimacy. Horst Kasner, who died in 2011, said in one of his rare interviews: "The GDR itself was enough of a constraint. At home we gave the children space." Even in the 1970s, Kasner himself made use of this freedom to travel to London and Rome.

And yet there is something of a veil over Merkel's past – because many in the West find it difficult to imagine her early life in East Germany as picturesque and peaceful. Even the name Waldhof – forest court – has a fairy-tale ring to it, suggesting the good old days. Life in the parsonage, the sheltered idyll, intellectual brilliance – this conjures up the German intellectual bourgeoisie of the Biedermeier period, the rapid industrial expansion of the late nineteenth century in Germany, evoking safety and security.

Even if the political system sometimes disturbed the peace of the parsonage, Angela Kasner was never really aware of it. She enjoyed the luxury of not having to identify with the State. "I never felt that the GDR was my natural home," she told Herlinde Koelbl, "but I always made use of the opportunities that it provided." She was a fervent supporter of Lokomotive Leipzig football club, but to this day she can still get in a rage about the deciding goal scored by Sparwasser in the defeat of West Germany by East Germany in the 1974 World Cup – or so she says. Sparwasser's shirt now hangs in the Museum of German History in Bonn.

Among the more exotic aspects of Templin was the Soviet garrison stationed in Vogelsang, just outside the town. After Wünsdorf, Vogelsang was the largest Soviet military base outside the Soviet Union. The 25th Armoured Division and many other units were based there. Members of the garrison often came into Templin, and Angela Kasner took the opportunity to practise her knowledge of Russian on the occupying troops. She probably inherited her gift for languages from her mother Herlind, who had been a Latin and English teacher, but wasn't allowed to exercise her profession in the GDR because she was married to a Protestant pastor. After the fall of the Wall, however, she returned to teaching and found a job at the Berlin Mission House for church workers. Her daughter did not wish to become a teacher, as she did not want to be a conduit for ideology of the regime.

Angela was unrivalled at school in Russian and mathematics, and even in her early teens was good enough to compete in the national Russian-language Olympiad, which was intended for pupils at the Polytechnic Secondary School two years above her. Despite her young age, she was selected as the third-best Russian-language student in the GDR, winning a trip to Moscow, where – irony of ironies – she bought her first Beatles record and, as she later confessed, was asked about her views on German unification. That was something she hadn't expected. Two years later, when she was in Year Ten, she won the Russian competition. It was already clear that she would go on to study at a senior grammar school and take the Abitur, the German equivalent of A Levels.

Angela Kasner was an excellent pupil and naturally got top marks in the Abitur. Later, the journalist Evelyn Roll found a telling comment on Merkel's attitude to Russian language and literature in the Stasi file on her: "Although Angela tends to see the leading role of the Soviet Union as something of a dictatorship to which all other socialist countries are subordinated, she is enthusiastic about the Russian language and the culture of the Soviet Union." The same thing can essentially still be said of her today.

Angela Kasner already had a great passion for travel and meeting new people. As a child she spent part of her school holidays with her grandmother in Berlin. "Those were wonderful times, complete childhood happiness. I was allowed to watch television until ten in the evening, and I rushed out of the house at nine o'clock every morning and systematically visited all the museums one by one." The family hardly ever watched GDR television,

Merkel would later claim, "except for sports programmes". In Berlin, too, Angela was on a journey of discovery – and seems to have been especially fascinated by foreigners and their lives. "I met Bulgarians, Americans and British people – at the age of fifteen I went out for a meal with some Americans and told them everything I knew about the GDR." But she was honest enough to admit that she "wouldn't be quite so trusting today". Unfortunately, the people with whom she had that conversation have yet to be traced. Presumably the girl who was to become Chancellor must have made quite an impression.

Until she was in Year Ten, the Kasners – Angela's brother Marcus was born three years after her, and her sister Irene was ten years younger – always went on holiday together. Merkel remembers two trips in particular. Just before the 13th of August, the day the building of the Berlin Wall began, the family were on their way back from Bavaria. Angela's maternal grandmother from Hamburg was also with them in their VW Beetle – it was to be her last holiday with her daughter, son-in-law and grandchildren. As they were driving home on the Friday, Horst Kasner saw that large quantities of barbed wire were being stored in the woods, and noticed that there was an unusually large number of soldiers around. He was filled with feelings of unease. On the Sunday the border was closed and construction of the Wall began. Angela Merkel has vivid memories of that 13th of August. Her mother cried all day, prayers were said in church, and young Angela was overcome by a sense of powerlessness – she wanted to help, but there was nothing she could do.

Although the Kasners now shared the fate of so many Germans, and the extended family was split between the two countries – the first time Angela went to the West was in 1986 – the spirit of a united Germany remained alive within the family. Angela's parents were unable to come to terms with the partition of their country, and as a child she wanted nothing to do with the new State. She followed West German politics with passionate enthusiasm, and remembers listening to the election of Gustav Heinemann as President of the Federal Republic on her transistor radio in the school toilets. She knew the names of the West German cabinet off by heart, and at home in the Waldhof they always watched the news on Western television.

But there was a price to be paid for this way of life: silence and discretion were a precondition for survival in a nation of State informers. The dangers were discussed openly in the parsonage, and although Horst Kasner's political role in the church hierarchy has been interpreted in markedly different ways by her biographers, Angela Merkel has always said that she had little to do with the system. When she had finished her physics studies and Stasi agents tried actively to recruit her, she reacted as she had learnt to do at home: she put on a show of innocence, pretending to be frank and claiming that she couldn't keep secrets. These tactics soon put an end to any attempt to enlist her services. If there is one thing that Merkel is particularly good at, even to this day, it is keeping quiet. "Yes, learning when to keep quiet was a great advantage in the GDR period. It was one of our survival strategies," she said many years later.

In another trip, in the summer of 1968, which was to have a great impact on Angela's political world view, the Kasner family visited Czechoslovakia, staying in Pec pod Sněžkou at the foot of the Sněžka mountain on the border with Poland. Leaving their children with the owners of the rooms they were renting in the Krkonoše mountain range, her parents went to Prague, where they witnessed at first hand the mood of change and open discussion in that year of the Prague Spring. For once there was a sense of freedom in the air. But on 21st August the Red Army moved in and crushed the democratic movement. Angela was just fourteen at the time, and remembers the fervent debates that she helped organize at her school in Templin. Not that the school authorities showed any interest in debating the matter, as she soon realized; Dubček's proposed reforms never came to anything, and Angela Kasner knew that it was best to keep a low profile.

The consequences of that journey manifested themselves more than thirty years later, when the reunified Germany was involved in an acrimonious debate over past events in its Western half, brought about by the publication of some photographs of Joschka Fischer. Fischer was Foreign Minister at the time, and was confronted with pictures showing him wearing a helmet and attacking a police officer during a student riot in Frankfurt. As leader of the opposition, Merkel denounced his behaviour and demanded an apology for his stone-throwing, as a form of act of repentance in which Fischer would confess to his formerly subversive views. The crowning moment for Merkel was when she suggested the exact phrase which Fischer should recite for his apology: "This was not the right approach, and I must recognize that and atone for it."

Merkel is still annoyed with herself for using the word "atone", but she must nonetheless be thankful for what she learnt from the rest of this episode. The country was outraged at her angry outburst, and SPD and Green politicians who had taken part in the riots of 1968 refused to comment on the internal affairs of the West. They could do without these history lessons from a woman from the East. Merkel suddenly found herself isolated, even within her own party. She thought that as an East German one could feel a sense of grief for 1968, because all hope for freedom and an open society had been crushed. And that it was ideologically questionable for a generation in the West to praise these actions, which had been carried out in the name of social-ism or even communism.

In the East, however, the section of the population who longed for freedom didn't regard the student movement as helpful. The leader of the opposition was unable to understand why it was considered a good thing in the West to embrace socialism and attack democracy simply as a way of publicly distancing oneself from the state and its authoritarian post-war structures. Merkel valued the Western system too much for that, with its constitu-tion rooted in freedom.

Merkel wasn't able to impose her views, however, and had to endure a fair amount of spiteful criticism from the Red-Green coalition government. For her, 1968 represented a departure from the ossified post-war system, even a break with the Nazi past of her parents' generation. West Germans who had taken part in the 1968 riots refused to accept that someone could take their symbolic date and connect it in a much stronger way with a quite different historical event – in other words, the Prague Spring. Deep down, they too had the scent of freedom in their nostrils, but it was associated with freedom from the very ideology for which people in the West were demonstrating.

Merkel has rarely been out of line with the march of history, which is why she was accused of having accepted the historical narrative of the West in order to further her political career, to ease herself neatly into the system. It was also suggested that she was ignoring her past in the East. In one sense the accusation is justified, while in others – as the episode with the 1968 protesters demonstrates – it was not. Later she would admit rather ruefully, "I used to believe that the 1968 movement was a total disaster for Germany. But there came a time when I discovered, to my astonishment, that there were people in the CDU who opposed the 1968 contingent in the Party, and now think there ought to be a monument to Rudi Dutschke [a leader the of student movement]. This threw me off balance, but today I can understand their attitude."

She felt the same about other major social movements in West Germany, such as the anti-nuclear campaign and the peace movement. Once again, Merkel had to learn from experience. "One day I heard Joschka Fischer speaking about 'the fucking plutonium economy'. And I said to myself: 'The what?' Only then did I realize that for many people there are close associations between a nuclear power station and the production of nuclear weapons, and thus with NATO and our alignment with the West. I understand those sensitivities far better now."

She also had intensive discussions with her colleagues on why, among all of Germany's European relationships, so much importance was attached to that with France. The West German CDU's Francophile Rhineland notion of Europe didn't immediately appeal to her. But, in the spirit of a united Germany, the Kasner household had always kept a watchful eye on Western democracy. This is the only explanation as to why, as a woman from the East, Merkel didn't find herself at odds with the West German narrative of the past more often.

From Year Ten onwards, young Angela Kasner travelled with her school friends, by train and with rucksacks on their back, to Prague, Bucharest and Sofia – the Central European equivalent of Interrail. She said later that Batumi on the Black Sea was her favourite resort, and that in Budapest she had dreamt of London, imagining that the British capital must be similar. She was regarded as someone with a keen appetite for life, ready to try anything, outgoing and positive. Angela Kasner was filled with curiosity for life outside her own world: she compared and adapted to these different environments, testing herself and her intellectual capacity.

She countered the narrow world of the GDR by using the GDR's own methods. This is exemplified by one episode in Angela Kasner's life, when she was about to leave school. The pupils in the final year at the Hermann Matern Grammar School in Templin held a meeting to organize a cultural festival. After much hesitation – after all, they already had their Abitur and were probably in a rebellious mood – a small group decided to stage a performance with an international flavour. It must have been quite a striking performance, because the school authorities, intent on toeing the party line, were quick to real-ize its hidden meaning: the final-year pupils were collecting money as specified, but not for a Vietnamese resistance group that was fighting the USA. Instead they were collecting for the Mozambique freedom movement Fremilo, which certainly had socialist credentials, but their opposition to the colonial-ists inevitably brought them into conflict with the Portuguese occupiers. It was easy to see a parallel with Soviet troops in the GDR. Then the students performed the poem 'Mopsleben' ('Life of a Pug Dog'), by the nonsense poet Christian Morgenstern, which warns us:

> Go carefully, Mankind, when you decide to stand tall,
> Or you'll end up as a pug dog, hanging on a wall.

They closed the performance by singing the 'Internationale' in English, the language of the class enemy.

But this was all too obvious: the performance went beyond what was permissible, creating difficulties for the school authorities and for the pupils themselves, who risked losing their university places through such an act of rebellion. Horst Kasner intervened on his daughter's behalf, using Church channels to gain access to the highest authorities – and so Angela was able to begin studying physics at the Karl Marx University in Leipzig in 1973.

This anecdote shows that Merkel had developed a marked tendency for irony quite early in life, and has always possessed a mischievous sense of humour. Friends at the time found her open and positive. She has retained her love of double meanings and cutting remarks. Even today no one would deny that she has a sharp sense of humour, although she rarely displays it in public. What is surprising is that Merkel is regarded as being extremely serious, sometimes even grouchy. She keeps her facial expressions under strict control – but the mask sometimes slips and she makes a face that betrays what she is actually thinking.

In the early years of her chancellorship, when she was less cautious, she would sometimes imitate people she had met – the Pope, the Prime Minister of China, the French President – thereby revealing their weaknesses. "For her," *Die Zeit* magazine once wrote, "comedy is what is left unsaid." She has been quoted as saying that her favourite political satire is Heinrich Böll's short story 'Dr Murkes gesammeltes Schweigen' ('The Collected Silences of Dr Murke'). With dry wit, she transfers the favourite law of physics into everyday political life: "There is no depth without mass." Even now she assesses people according to whether they have a sense of humour or not. Her favourite jokes are full of biting social satire. One of the Chancellor's regular observers once wrote, "She has mastered the art of silent mockery." Her taste for irony and finely judged humour has seldom been clearer than during a newspaper interview in which she was asked the loaded question: "And so what strikes you most about Germany today?" Back came the answer, "Nice draught-proof windows."

Her studies in Leipzig, followed by the Academy of Sciences in Berlin, soon created a distance between her and the family home in Templin. Once again Angela achieved excellent results – she found her studies easy, enjoyed life in the capital, and was happy to join in with and organize events among her circle of friends. As a student in the big city she had an amusing experience while working in a laundry, when she had to iron Russian Army shirts ("Ironing never hurt anyone," she said). More appealing were all the new opportunities to discover the world.

She went to Prague again, as well as to Russia. She made several trips to the Heyrovský Institute in Prague to do research, some-times for months at a time. She has remained friends with her tutor, Rudolf Zahradník, and visits him whenever she is in Prague. On a recent visit, in April 2012, she was reminded of the legend-ary Vindobona express that ran on the Berlin-Prague-Vienna line and was notorious for always being late. The paternal Zahradník had advised her to keep calm. "'You're aware that we're taking part in an experiment that will never succeed, called socialism,'" she said, quoting him. "'The two of us know that already, but the others haven't realized yet.'"

In 1974 she went with some fellow students on an exchange programme to the Soviet Union, travelling to Leningrad and Moscow to meet Russian physics students. Among the group was the man who would become her first husband, Ulrich Merkel. Two years later they moved in together. Like so many GDR students looking for somewhere to work and, above all, live, Angela Kasner married the physicist Ulrich Merkel at the end of her time at university. This allowed them to be allocated a shared home, and the State would not separate a couple who were looking for work.

The wedding took place in the Chapel of St George in Templin. Angela took her husband's name, which has now become a household name in international politics. It was 1977 and she was twenty-three years old. Four years later the marriage broke down: husband and wife had grown apart. Almost overnight Angela Merkel moved out of the couple's apartment in Berlin, leaving behind a shocked Ulrich Merkel. They divorced in 1982.

After the divorce, Merkel set off on what was probably her most adventurous journey so far – with some friends she hitch-hiked through southern Russia to Armenia, Georgia and Azerbaijan; in Tbilisi she spent the night in the railway-station hostel. They avoided any brush with the police by claiming to be in transit to Romania or Bulgaria. Merkel could talk herself out of any difficulty. Her command of Russian was a great help, but she also managed to practise her English during this period by reading technical literature or the *Morning Star*. This mouthpiece of the British Communist Party could be found at certain news-stands in East Berlin once a week, and those who were up early enough were able to get a copy.

In the working group on quantum chemistry at the Central Institute for Physical Chemistry, to begin with Merkel was the only woman in that field. Women mostly worked elsewhere, usually in administration. She had no opportunity to go to the West – only twenty-four scientists at the Institute were issued with travel permits that allowed them to leave the GDR. The numbers were increased in 1988–89, and more scientists joined the group. One of them, Dr Joachim Sauer, was given permission to leave the GDR at that time. His name first appeared in connection with Merkel's in the acknowledgements to her doctoral thesis in 1984. She would marry him fifteen years later.

Angela Merkel fulfilled her passion for travel in other ways: with the help of the travel bureaux of the Free German Youth organization FDJ, Youth Tourist, she obtained a visa for Poland, where she managed to find propaganda material produced by the trade-union movement Solidarność – a dangerous activity, since martial law had been in force in Poland since 1981 and the borders were closed. Former colleagues at the Academy later spoke of her deep interest in political discussions. Even though the Stasi had its eyes and ears everywhere, the scientists were obviously aware of their special position and felt they could allow themselves to take some small risks.

Merkel generally describes the bond between her colleagues as being strong and close. It was nothing unusual for them to spend leisure time together – the GDR set great store by close links within the working environment. Exchange programmes at the Academy took Merkel back to the Soviet Union. Officially, long-distance journeys could only be made as a group and for professional purposes; anything else had to remain as pipe dream and wishful thinking. Ten years later the journalist Hugo Müller-Vogg asked her how she had coped with not being able to travel to the West. "I do rather wonder now how I managed," she replied, "particularly living here in Berlin."

Even while still a child Merkel had developed a strategy for dealing with restrictions: she made comparisons. Anyone who met her as a young woman spoke of the need she felt for a yardstick. She used the same method time and again, for example when she produced her famous tables during the euro crisis and showed her colleagues on the European Council comparative curves to illustrate the course the crisis was taking. Merkel compares systems, political procedures, solutions. Her computer-like brain is always comparing different models, testing intellectual capacity, making judgements. "Whenever I had contact with people from the West," she told Müller-Vogg, "I was always trying to find out if I could keep up with them intellectually. And the fact that I could made it easier for me to come to terms with not being able to go to the Mediterranean." Here we see her again, the analyst systematically dealing with what could have been an inferiority complex. Did she also manage to overcome her desire to travel, which obviously concealed dreams of freedom? The answer lies in a notable journey that she made during the final years of the GDR.

She was given permission for this unusual trip in 1986; the occasion was the wedding of a female cousin in Hamburg. Merkel hadn't been to the West since the building of the Berlin Wall. Yet she lived with the firm conviction that when she was sixty she would be able to realize her dream and fly to the United States. Sixty was the pensionable age, when the GDR allowed women to travel anywhere in the world. At home in Templin there had been family discussions: should Angela make an official application for an emigration permit? The older she grew, the more pressing it became, but her parents didn't like the idea. Her friend Joachim Sauer, now her partner, had a quite different view. He is described by those who know the couple as the main source of support for her inner convictions; although he sometimes loses his temper, he can also have a calming role. She always listens to his opinions, and when it came to her wish to go to the West his advice was this: if you can't stand it here any longer, then do whatever you want.

In the end Merkel didn't apply for an emigration permit. She once said that only the certainty that she could get a permit whenever she wanted made the GDR more tolerable. The first thing she did now was to board a train for her native city of Hamburg. We have no details of the cousin's wedding, but afterwards she went on to Karlsruhe to visit a professor in her field of study, and then to see a colleague in Konstanz, on the border with Switzerland. She never said much about the journey, apart from a few anecdotes about the cleanliness of West German Intercity trains. But there is one remark that Merkel likes to repeat: "It was at that wedding that I realized that the socialist system wasn't going to last." The journey from Hamburg to Karlsruhe would also have provided good reasons to reach such a conclusion – the railway line near Kassel had a marvellous view of the watchtowers on the border and the area known as the Death Strip, where armed guards were posted, although this time on the Western side.

The system lasted for another three years, and then Angela Merkel was catapulted out of her leisurely life at the Institute and into another orbit. For thirty-five years she had lived in the GDR as if in a cocoon: she had adjusted to it, and could live and work there with as much intellectual freedom as was possible. The parsonage was an oasis within the system, while the Uckermark and its isolated landscapes formed a peaceful backdrop. As a child the highly intelligent Angela Kasner was given every encouragement and also learnt how to motivate herself. Her enthusiastic and sociable nature helped her to overcome adverse conditions, while her family bolstered her self-confidence. And then there were the parcels of jeans from the West – presents sent regularly by family members there.

Angela Merkel was no freedom fighter, not cut out for revolution, although she was in touch with Church circles in Berlin. She lacked the courage for open revolt, and yet she wasn't prepared simply to accept the Regime. She didn't want to expose herself. This was the reason she chose – just like her brother – to study physics: because the subject offered the most freedom and opportunities for self-development. She was among the best in her age group, and was shrewd enough not to get involved with the Communist Party – although, conversely, as a pastor's daughter and emerging young scientist, the Party gave her scope to do as she liked. Within strict limits she was allowed to see the world. Now it was time for the world to open up to her. And her exploratory journeys through the landscape of political parties in the final days of the GDR in the late autumn of 1989 came at just the right moment.

When the Berlin Wall came down on 9th November that year, Angela Merkel was in the sauna with a friend, something that would earn her much mockery later. And yet nothing could have been more typical of her: working out the plan in advance, checking out the lie of the land, not rushing things. After her sauna she went to the Bornholmer Straße crossing to the West, and at one point found herself in an apartment belonging to total strangers, where there were drinks and a telephone. After that she went home. The next day she and her sister Irene set off again, this time to the Kurfürstendamm, the shopping street that in the GDR had always represented the glamour of the West. But then the politics began.

Merkel could have ended up in the SPD, the Social Democratic Party of Germany, or Bündnis 90, an organization of three non-communist groups that later merged with the West German Green Party. She was interested in all the political parties, but her instincts were sound. She could appreciate the warm companionship of the SPD, but there was too much egalitarianism for her liking. Bündnis 90 didn't suit her basic convictions, especially where nuclear power and questions of pacifism and defence were concerned. In those first chaotic weeks many things happened by chance, and it was chance that brought her into contact with Pastor Rainer Eppelmann, whom she knew through the Church. In turn this led her to the DA (Democratic Awakening) party. She liked the name, and the fact that she found so much there that was incomplete, waiting to be shaped. During those weeks the Democratic Awakening Party needed one thing above all else: people with sound principles, an overview of what was happening and who were capable of organizing. Angela Merkel was a good organizer, so she took leave from the Academy, and by February 1990 was installed on the third floor of the new offices of the House of Democracy, on the corner of Friedrichstraße and Französische Straße.

Anyone who was in East Berlin at the time and followed politics will remember the young woman typing press releases and writing notes just inside the door. Quite by chance, Merkel became the press officer for the Democratic Awakening Party, because the chairman Wolfgang Schnur wasn't able to meet Western journalists on a particular day and sent her instead. The GDR was collapsing, the first free elections to the People's Chamber were to be held in March, politics in Germany was racing ahead. In February the East German section of the CDU (Christian Democratic Union), the DA and the German Social Union merged into the Alliance for Germany. When the final election to the People's Chamber came down clearly in favour of the CDU and its chairman Lothar de Maizière, it was clear that the DA, as a small centre-right party, would either have to attach itself to the great tanker of the West German CDU party, or sink beneath the waves of these stormy times.

Angela Merkel didn't like the idea of being submerged. She was now working politically with all her might, and had three aims. She wanted the country to be reunified as soon as possible, she wanted a market economy, and she wanted to sit in the Bundestag, the parliament of West Germany and soon to be the parliament of a reunified Germany.

Then one day the phone rang, and Hans-Christian Maaß asked whether she would like to act as the spokesperson for Lothar de

Maizière. Maaß was one of the Western advisers who could be seen everywhere in East Berlin at the time. They had been sent by the sister parties in the West with the task of giving guidance to politicians in the GDR – and, from the perspective of the CDU, the ruling party in the Federal Republic, to introduce as smoothly as possible decisions that would be welcomed in Bonn, the seat of the West German government. Reunification was to go ahead; in West Germany it was now recognized that timing was important. The situation was becoming volatile: there might be unrest or civil resistance in the grass roots of the country. Partners in the Alliance or supporters might try to put obstacles in the way of unification. So there had to be a government soon, and the party had to act.

While the new East German government was being formed, it became clear that there should be someone from the DA working closely with the first freely elected Prime Minister of the GDR. When Merkel was offered the post of deputy government spokeswoman by Maaß, she discussed it with her partner Joachim Sauer, who had just fulfilled a long-held ambition by taking up an academic post in California. After some thought, Merkel agreed to take the job – and then flew to Sardinia with Joachim Sauer. When she got back from holiday the government was already installed; the coalition treaty was signed on Maundy Thursday 1990: the Prime Minister and the twenty-three ministers took their oaths, and the cabinet held its first meeting on 18th April, although she didn't receive her official appointment until later. She skipped her swearing-in ceremony.

In her new role, Merkel was deputy to Matthias Gehler, de Maizière's government spokesman. So she wasn't one of the inner circle, but witnessed many of the historical decisions that were made almost daily during the last six months of the GDR. Her job brought her into constant contact with journalists, but she also kept a watchful eye on her position within the Democratic Awakening party. She had no illusions about its future: it would merge into the CDU. Every morning the spokesman or his deputy would brief the prime minister and his closest advisers about what was in the press. It wasn't long before de Maizière made it clear that he was more than satisfied with Merkel's precise manner of expressing herself in the so-called kitchen cabinet, her gift for grasping a point quickly, her efficiency and her powers of interpreting the political situation.

Although Merkel wasn't making political decisions, she participated in the debates on party policy that took place under the last government of the GDR. She had access to the Prime Minister, particularly during foreign trips. De Maizière travelled a great deal – much to the annoyance of the West German Chancellor, Helmut Kohl. Visiting foreign countries attracted attention and added to the East German Prime Minister's political clout. Since there were disagreements, even in the West, as to the conditions of the reunification of Germany, unexpected opportunities emerged, and de Maizière did his best to capitalize on them. Not only that, the new politicians in East Berlin were enjoying their role and the importance that they found they now had, particularly abroad. Kohl was especially unhappy about de Maizière's visit to the French President, François Mitterrand: he feared that this rapport between East Germany and France might cause unnecessary problems and undermine his authority.

Like the United Kingdom, France viewed the colossus now taking shape in Central Europe with suspicion. The French President had visited East Berlin in December, paying court to the last government of the East German Social Unity Party under Egon Krenz – an act regarded as outrageous, not just by West German politicians. As much as Mitterrand might claim it was the result of an invitation from Krenz's predecessor Erich Honecker, it was still a spurious reason.

Merkel disliked Mitterrand because of this earlier flying visit to the GDR, but nonetheless – like all visitors to the Élysée – she was impressed by its atmosphere and the President's quiet, superior way of speaking. Mitterrand and the British Prime Minister, Margaret Thatcher, were intent on trying to limit the power of Germany. Kohl, meanwhile, wanted the new Germany to be firmly anchored in the Western alliances, in the European Union and NATO. Merkel supported him strongly in this – not that he noticed, or that he would have seen it as relevant. However, as de Maizière remembered later, Merkel made no secret of her convictions to him.

The last GDR government wasn't a particularly professional outfit. Those serving in it had had little experience or few opportunities to become involved in politics. People wanted a single currency for both parts of Germany, and they wanted reunification. Yet in de Maizière's cabinet – a grand coalition consisting of a diverse mixture of civil-rights campaigners, members of the old regime, new politicians and people involved with the Church – grew a sudden determination to create a new political system. Its partner in the coalition, the SPD, was discussing alternative foreign-affairs strategies for what was being planned in Bonn for a united Germany. The main consideration was whether the new Germany should be part of NATO, or whether the end of the Warsaw Pact meant that there was a need for a new security policy in Europe.

The Organization for Security and Co-operation in Europe (OSCE) had a better image in the GDR than NATO – so why not try a new form of alliance based on that? Such questions of alliance played a major part in another, central decision: what should be the legal basis of reunification? If the East were not simply to adopt the constitution and the great sweep of West German treaties, Germany's position in international law would have had to be redefined – every international treaty would have had to be renegotiated, with all the unpredictable consequences that such a complex and expensive procedure would entail.

Merkel proved to be very firm in all these discussions. She had made up her mind, as de Maizière later acknowledged. The deputy spokeswoman also had a chance to contribute directly to the discussions: on her travels with the Prime Minister to the European Parliament in Strasbourg, to Paris and London, and finally in Moscow at the meeting of the foreign ministers of what was known as the Two-Plus-Four Group, in which the four victorious powers of the Second World War and the two Germanys gathered to discuss the consequences of reunification for foreign policy, questions of sovereignty, elections within the alliance, the stationing of troops and national borders. This was where she gained her first experience of international forums, with round after round of delegations, protocol and all the awkward questions that arise whenever sovereign states deal with each other. Voluble outbursts were inappropriate here; diplomacy demanded tact and sensitivity.

After the SPD left the coalition in August, de Maizière had taken on the role of Foreign Minister as well, and was thus representing the GDR at the last meeting of the Two-Plus-Four Group.

Angela Merkel went to Moscow with this party on 12th September 1990. De Maizière was aware of his colleague's linguistic skills and dispatched her into the streets with the idea – very characteristic of his approach – of getting her to sound out the ordinary people. Merkel picked up a few opinions on the underground – Russia was betraying its own interests, Gorbachev was selling out the Motherland – and took them back to the delegation. Her main task, however, was to look after the small group of journalists from East Berlin. Hans-Dietrich Genscher, who had come from Bonn, had a much larger retinue with him. Merkel remembered, with some surprise, how the heavyweight Genscher managed to cast a spell over the journalists with his quiet voice and dislike of all fixed arrangements. Whereas she, having organized a dinner in a Georgian restaurant, and with far more details and anecdotes about the negotiations at her fingertips, was considered less important by the media – in fact she was barely noticed. It was a lesson in how to punch above your weight in politics.

What the journalists did remember was that Merkel was wearing a new coat and shoes – later, de Maizière said she had been sent out to buy new clothes before the trip. The subject would haunt Merkel for quite some time. Her appearance, hairstyle, shoes, sloppy outfits – the young politician had to learn quickly what the public values besides sharp analysis and knowledge of detail. Merkel had particular difficulties with this aspect of the job, also because she suffered from it more than most female politicians. Her instincts must have been telling her: I'll show you that clothes and looks are of secondary importance – why don't you concentrate on what matters?

But it would take another ten years before public criticism of her style died down. Today she appears quite comfortable about the sartorial side of her job. In the morning she uses the time spent with her stylist, Petra Keller, to read newspapers, press releases and files. Her typical pose in a trouser suit with hands folded in front of her has become an iconic image. There was much applause and laughter when, on her official visit to the United States in 2011, Merkel presented a framed front page of the *Frankfurter Allgemeine* to another famous wearer of trouser suits. The photograph showed no faces, only the stomachs and hips of two women in trouser suits holding hands. Hillary Clinton was visibly amused.

In her early years in politics Merkel had struggled to come to terms with her public role. Even as press spokeswoman she preferred to let her boss Matthias Gehler take the stage. Later, at the beginning of her time in Bonn, she was regarded as being stubborn as well as shy in public. Appearances at election meetings were torture for her. Even today Merkel hates being given ovations at party conferences. She stands on the stage, knowing that she will have to stand there for minutes on end, because, as always, people are counting the minutes and it is expected that she will be greeted with record applause – but she would rather not be there at all. Large crowds are not her style.

So it is not surprising that Merkel developed qualities she had already shown as a child – such as mistrust and discretion. If anything, her experiences in life have tended to make her even more shy in public. It hurt her feelings when the West German media and opponents in her own party claimed that she had a murky past in the GDR: during her time at the Academy she had been involved with the Free German Youth organization. Merkel's version was that her role had simply consisted in promoting cultural events, getting theatre tickets and organizing trips. Her critics accused her of agitation and propaganda on behalf of the system. This was contradicted by witnesses, who provided solid evidence to support their accounts and argued that the special status of the Academy as an independent body proved that Merkel had always maintained a great distance from the system.

Merkel faced similar questions at the beginning of her political career, when she was Minister for Women and Youth. At an event in Schwerin she once talked jokingly about her ML thesis for her doctorate. ML stood for Marxism-Leninism, which was a mandatory subject in addition to the requirements of her physics studies. Making a funny anecdote out of it, she said that the essay had focused on the relationship of workers and farmers in a country known as the Workers' and Farmers' State, and wasn't given high marks because she had attached too much importance to the farmers. The journalists interpreted this quite differently, however, and trawled the university archives in search of a scoop – Merkel's thesis on Marxism-Leninism. But it had disappeared and has never been found.

Merkel was annoyed, thinking she was going to be burdened with a now toxic ideology. In the event there was a great deal of conspiratorial whispering. No one seemed interested in the fact that every student dutifully handed in his or her ML thesis and just secretly hoped for the best. There was a similar outcry when it was claimed that Merkel had studied in Moscow. It isn't true, but the rumour persists. All this has served to reinforce Angela Merkel's mistrust and discretion. She clams up, accusing her critics of muckraking and sensationalism. And it has to be said that they have never taken the trouble to consider the living conditions in the GDR at the time.

Even now there are problems of communication. In the debate over childcare allowances, Merkel pointed out that all women in the GDR had worked for a living. There was an outcry among female members of the West German CDU. Was the Chancellor criticizing their lifestyle and idealizing conditions in the former East? No, said Merkel, she hadn't meant to sound critical: in fact her mother had never had a job apart from bringing up the children, but only because she wasn't allowed to. Yet the episode demonstrated once again how little readiness there is in the old camps of East and West to confront the realities of life on the other side. But Angela Merkel had decided early on that she had no wish to contribute to that quarrel. She was weary of conflicts, so she kept quiet. Now, at the end of her second term as Chancellor, her attitude has changed slightly – presumably because after eight years in office she has softened her stance and is already thinking about her legacy.

In the period immediately after the fall of the Wall, Merkel described herself as being wary of conflict, or at least hating the vicious personal attacks that are often a feature of politics. "The only things that worry me are unjust and intentionally false claims. I loathe personal quarrels," she admitted in conversation with Herlinde Koelbl. Serious discussion and debate were more her thing. "I seek cooperation rather than confrontation in politics," she said, and then went on to provide an accurate self-assessment: "I find the tendency that certain male politicians have constantly to assert themselves rather unpleasant. Many people puff themselves up and try to drown out each other's voices in order to impose themselves. When that happens I feel almost physically oppressed and would prefer not to be there." Merkel studies her political opponents very closely, and while she has certainly not been a paragon of virtue over the years, at the time she had this to say: "When that happens it ceases to be an objective debate, it just becomes a question of who can take the wind out of the other person's sails. That isn't the way I work."

Twenty-two years later, anyone who wants to study Merkel's methods needs to look at what emerged at the time of the fall of the Berlin Wall. Angela Merkel has remained true to herself. Pastor Erhart Neubert, who was one of the founders of Democratic Awakening and knows all of Merkel's different facets, spoke of an "aesthetic of the honourable and good". This is somewhat sentimental, but even if many of the edges have been smoothed off Merkel the post-reunification politician, she has retained her image of the hard-working public servant, the dutiful pastor's daughter who wants to get to the heart of everything without any unpleasant ulterior motives. Of course, what becomes of these good intentions in the reality of politics may be quite a different matter. Her antagonists in the CDU and the opposition parties, in the EU or among her coalition partners, have their own opinions of the Chancellor's character and methods.

Order, structure, the ability to plan ahead – Merkel has brought many of her qualities from thirty-five years in the GDR into her new life. She has said that even as a child she had to think ahead, because problems with her physical growth and development meant that she had difficulty running and climbing stairs. According to her she was "clumsy in her movements", with the result that every unnecessary walk had to be avoided and each step planned in advance. Two months before Christmas she would already be thinking of presents. "I always wanted to know what I was getting, even if it spoilt the surprise. It mattered more to give structure to my life and avoid chaos."

Merkel has also retained her Prussian sense of duty and Protestant work ethic. As a child she soon grew accustomed to being industrious and proper, working harder than other people. The Lutheran passion for self-improvement, for doing things better, knowing things better, getting ahead, has never left her. That is also why she absolutely refuses to see herself as predestined for any role. Obviously she followed various people's examples, wanted to be like other girls – imagined being an actor, a dancer, an ice skater. But these were childhood dreams, fantasies about roles for which Angela Kasner wasn't suited. Years later, when asked if she had a particular role model, she cited the physicist Marie Curie, who grew up in Russian-occupied Poland in the 19th century, studied in Paris and determinedly made her mark as a female scientist. That impressed Merkel.

If asked today whether she has any political role models, she always answers, "None." She has coolly dismissed any comparison with Margaret Thatcher, and no one asks her any more (except in English-speaking countries, where memories of the Iron Lady have persisted for slightly longer). Ronald Reagan was something of a hero in her youth, but Merkel no longer mentions him. Not only has she discovered that the former US President has lost much of his positive image in the West, but it would probably also be against her principles to stand in the shadow of other politicians and compare her image with theirs.

There are thirty-five years of the GDR in Angela Merkel. That is a long time, and it has left its mark. The Merkel mystery is rooted in the failed East German republic. This explains the fascination for her as a person, especially in her second term as Chancellor and particularly abroad. Merkel doesn't open up to many people, because they are unable to understand her previous life, her completely alien other world. The influence of the GDR hovers around her like a secret that won't reveal itself. And how could it be otherwise for those who didn't share the same experience? As a result, public interest in Merkel has continued far longer than for politicians with similar careers but whose lives can be more easily imagined. She knows this, and handles the mystery with particular care.

In Search of New Frontiers

Breaking into Politics

In the last months of the GDR, Helmut Kohl was constantly in touch with Lothar de Maizière and his government. Yet Merkel had never met the West German Chancellor, only catching a glimpse of him in the summer of 1990. She wanted to change that now. Their first meeting was arranged during the CDU unification conference, a few days before the official celebrations at the beginning of October 1990. Kohl was sitting in the Hamburg Rathauskeller, where the CDU used to hold evening press briefings during its party conferences in the city. On these occasions the leader of the party held court, invited selected journalists to his table and urged them to try his favourite local dish of *Labskaus*, a casserole of beef, beetroot and potatoes with fried eggs. Merkel asked a mutual acquaintance from Dresden to introduce her – she was obviously keen to get to know him.

Kohl took her to another room so they could talk, and Merkel later described her excitement at this meeting. "I thought to myself, now you're going to meet the Chancellor of the Federal Republic and he'll ask you something really difficult. And then I got a very simple question." Merkel had clearly not expected Kohl to be so chatty, and had imagined high-level politics as something more profound and difficult. But the Chancellor must have been impressed as well: he asked Merkel to come and talk to him again in Bonn that November. He probably already had his eye on her as a minister in the first all-German cabinet.

After the general election in December, Merkel was offered the post of Minister for Women and Youth. Naturally she accepted, although a few days earlier she had admitted that she knew nothing about these subjects. But she was a woman, she came from the East and was a Protestant – so Kohl, the champion of proportional representation, chose her. She was sworn in to the Bundestag on 18th January 1991. After this meteoric ascent to the senior ranks of German politics, it was almost natural for her to rise in the hierarchy of the CDU as well. When her patron of many years, Lothar de Maizière, resigned from all his party functions in September 1991 – he was worn down by all the speculation over his involvement with the Stasi in the GDR – Merkel took on the role of deputy party leader in December. Along with Günther Krause, she now represented the East at the head of the CDU.

The Ministry for Women and Youth had evolved out of the former Federal German Ministry for Women, the Family, Youth and Health. Kohl had divided it into three. Merkel took on one of these units, and soon showed how she planned to go about leading: by appointing a team of loyal colleagues.

No one, however, was to become more important than the young woman who entered Merkel's life in 1992. At the time Merkel was in hospital, after breaking her leg while visiting a bookshop. She was looking for an aide to help her as she mastered her role in the party, and had been allocated, as deputy chairman, a part-time assistant. While she was in hospital, Merkel had a visitor – Christian Wulff, a politician from Lower Saxony. Wulff, whom she later appointed President of the Federal Republic, had just finished his time as a city councillor in Osnabrück, and was about to launch his career in regional politics. He had a good network in the Lower Saxony CDU, and wanted to introduce his hospitalized friend to a talented young woman whom he knew from the CDU youth organization, the Youth Union, in Osnabrück, and who would be suitable for the job: Beate Baumann.

So the two women who were to dominate the political landscape of the Federal Republic met. It turned out to be a unique symbiosis. Baumann soon became Merkel's personal adviser, and then, in 1995, her personal private secretary and office manager, a title she still bears today.

Baumann's role in the Chancellor's office defies any job description: she serves and commands in equal measure, and the two women lead parallel lives. "Such connections grow like hard wood," wrote the journalist Christoph Schwennicke, "very slowly, one ring every year." Baumann accompanied Merkel to the General Secretary's office, to party headquarters, moved with her to the parliamentary party offices, and finally to the Chancellor's office.

Except perhaps for her husband Joachim Sauer, no one knows Merkel better, no one else knows exactly where to find her or to keep track of her political activities so meticulously. Baumann is Merkel's most important adviser, and she has as elephantine a memory as her boss. According to Berlin rumours, the personal private secretary is the second most powerful person on the political scene – and feared accordingly.

If there is one thing that Baumann hates it is being the subject of scrutiny or commentary. It is her task to smooth the way for Merkel as much as possible, to see any dangers coming and stop them in their tracks. She is the ship's pilot in an ocean of appointments, questions, requests and demands – an ocean in which a host of dangerous mines are always drifting. She is, as Schwennicke has put it, "Merkel's mistrust." Baumann enjoys what Merkel has given up only reluctantly: the cover of objectivity, anonymity. She has perfected the art of the personal private secretary by serving and assisting without reducing her own power. In the early years her influence on Merkel was viewed with suspicion, and some people claimed that it was she who pulled the strings.

It is true that she has constant access to the Chancellor, can speak to her frankly and express her own opinions. Because Merkel trusts her implicitly, colleagues find it increasingly difficult to get past Baumann and put their views to the Chancellor. Only Ulrich Wilhelm, Merkel's first government spokesman and her close colleague for four and a half years in the Chancellery, fulfilled a similar balancing function.

Born in 1963 and nine years younger than Merkel, Baumann studied German and English and, like Merkel, joined the CDU more by chance than by design. The arms race and the stationing of medium-range American missiles in Germany in the mid-1980s were ultimately the deciding factors in her pursuing a political career. She detested the ideological narrowness of the Greens and the Social Democrats, something that also affected Merkel in her own search for the right party in East Berlin. Baumann shares a passion for foreign policy with her boss. As personal private secretary she is rarely able to travel with Merkel, but sometimes she is at the helm of government when the Chancellor is away – for example in Canada or the Middle East – and when things are quiet in Berlin. She was with Merkel in Sochi when Putin let his dog off the leash, and in Israel when she made her historic speech to the Knesset. She and Merkel both enjoy analysing the characters of their foreign guests, and like the Chancellor she has a quick mind and is visibly impatient when a speaker gets lost in an argument that she has already understood.

Besides a fondness for everything from the English-speaking world, above all else Baumann shares Merkel's attachment to Israel and her attitude towards the subject of the Holocaust. It was perhaps not entirely by chance that Israel was the second foreign country that Merkel visited as the newly appointed Minister for Women and Youth. The first was France – she had seen enough in her dealings with Kohl to know that particular attention must be paid to political counterparts in Paris. Also on board the government jet were the Federal Minister for Research, Heinz Riesenhuber, and the Secretary of State for the Security Services, Lutz Stavenhagen, who nine months later admitted responsibility for a secret delivery of tanks made from components belonging to the National People's Army to the Israeli Secret Service, and was forced to resign.

In foreign-policy terms, however, the high point in Merkel's first year as a minister ought to have been her visit to the USA in September 1991 with Helmut Kohl – that is, if Kohl had had his way. The then Chancellor first went to California, then travelled on to Washington. With him was his Minister for Women and Youth, as a kind of trophy from the days of reunification. But Merkel would have preferred the role of observer. She wasn't allowed to operate independently, and did not want to stand out, although she did shake hands with her childhood idol, Ronald Reagan, and was introduced to George Bush Sr at the White House.

Later, Merkel described the scene in the bus when Helmut Kohl, as was his wont, wanted to introduce her to everyone who was travelling with them. The Federal Chancellor told his young minister that she should tell them what they had really thought of him in the East. Merkel was at a loss. Everyone thought that she would have to admit that the pear-shaped Kohl had been as much a figure of fun in the GDR as he was in West Germany. Yet there was another reason for Merkel's hesitation. She didn't want to curry favour, because what she remembered more than anything about Kohl was his brilliant after-dinner speech during Erich Honecker's visit to Bonn in 1987. In line with what had been agreed between the two parties, the verbal joust between Kohl and Honecker at the Redoute in Bonn had to be transmitted on GDR television as well as in the West, and Kohl's speech had made the citizens of East Germany feel hopeful, because he made several emphatic references to German unity.

In her early years as a minister, foreign policy was of secondary importance to Merkel. It wasn't part of her responsibilities at the Ministry for Women and Youth. Later, while at the Ministry of the Environment, issues in European politics and the EU council meetings of environmental ministers became more urgent for her. Whenever she could, Merkel would travel privately with her partner Joachim Sauer. She told Herlinde Koelbl that they enjoyed spending time in California. In the summer of 1993 she went on a "wonderful" trip to the West Coast. "A holiday far from home helps me to escape. In those four weeks I managed to switch off." Four weeks in a row – a remarkable achievement for a cabinet minister, and evidence of Merkel's carefree attitude at the time. A year later she went to Provence, but she "felt like an unborn child", because she didn't speak French. Next time it was California again, but at Christmas. "Nothing troubles me there," she said.

In fact this period is notable for its mixed messages, as her long interview with Koelbl illustrates. Merkel struggled to come to terms with life as a politician at first, but less and less as time went on. "I still can't imagine that the rest of my life will be like it is now," she groaned in 1993. She reflected on how the profession could have a negative effect on some aspects of her personality that she had suddenly discovered and didn't much like: impatience, an unwillingness to listen to others, an inability to immerse herself in a book. "I find myself looking forward to the time when all this stress will eventually come to an end," she was still saying in 1997. "For me, quality of life means cooking meals at home and being able to fit in around other people's diaries." Merkel continued to give voice to her thoughts as to when would be the right moment to leave politics, probably to reassure herself that she could still do something else with her life. "I don't want to be a half-dead wreck when I leave politics," she said. "After a period of boredom I would rather find something else to do."

Even now she still toys with the idea of leaving political life. She seems to have been particularly taken with the possibility – although more so in the past than today – of being able to do something completely different. At the end of the 1990s she told an interviewer that she could imagine going with Joachim to a research institute somewhere, maybe in South Africa. At another time she expressed a desire to learn French after the end of her political career, or to live in the USA for a while, or to simply stay at home and then re-emerge, "to see what's available".

But these temptations never became too strong. Angela Merkel marched through the political landscape of the Nineties at a tearing pace, in November 1994 moving from her interim position at the Ministry for Women and Youth to the Ministry for the Environment; with the CDU's return to opposition in November 1998 she became General Secretary of the party, and two years later, after the expenses scandal and the retirement of Wolfgang Schäuble, was appointed Party Chairman. At this point foreign policy was less of a priority than securing power, fighting the opposition and, above all, surviving the most difficult crisis in the history of the Christian Democratic Union.

Yet there is another event that stands out even more in those years, one of which Merkel still speaks with a glint in her eye, and which must have been a formative experience in her understanding of international diplomacy: the 1995 climate summit in Berlin. Environmental policy was a relative newcomer on the global political stage. Representatives of almost every nation had met for the first time in Rio de Janeiro in 1992 to discuss the problems of climate change. This was enormous progress: the human race had finally recognized that the climate of the planet affects everyone, but no one could agree as to whether the changes were for the worse, or what could be done about them. And it was the first time a binding treaty with climate change at its heart had been signed under international law.

When the Federal Government invited its Environment Minister Angela Merkel to Berlin a year after the Rio convention came into force, the question was quite simple: how to give meaning to the Rio treaty. The Berlin conference was the test: if Rio was to live on, then it had to be taken further. If the efforts to protect the climate were already faltering at this stage, then the whole international project would probably fail.

The Federal Government was hosting this great event. In Rio, Helmut Kohl had generously offered Germany as the venue for the next summit, and he now called for commitment from his ministers. After all, he told them, this was "the most important international conference that would be held on German soil for the foreseeable future". The Foreign Minister and Vice-Chancellor Klaus Kinkel invited the delegations to a dinner – held beneath the dinosaur skeletons in the Natural History Museum in Berlin. Angela Merkel was chosen as chairman of the assembly, and presided over it in the large meeting hall of the International Conference Centre, beneath an enormous blue globe hovering in front of white waves.

Around 160 countries, as well as a similar number of non-governmental organizations, had accepted the invitation, and apart from the main conference there was an additional programme of related events and an environmental fair.

Merkel loved the atmosphere as, for the first time in her life, she was speaking in front of such a huge international audience: a thousand delegates, hundreds of other interested parties, a Babel of languages, a complex web of negotiations. "That's how I always imagined it," she said later. "160 states. I really came alive. For the first time I had the opportunity to get to know the different cultures of the world and their various ways of working."

As chairman, Merkel took on the role of broker: she had to mediate between the different factions. In the end she listened to the advice of her experienced Indian colleague, Kamal Nath. Nath had been his country's Environment Minister for several years, so he understood the complexities of the conference and took Merkel aside. Proceed with caution on the final evening, he advised; divide the delegations into developing countries and industrialized countries, and shut them up in two separate rooms. Merkel did as she was told: she divided the delegates, and went back and forth between the two, with the aim of preventing the whole event from collapsing, and at least drawing up a binding schedule as the basis for the next phase of climate-change policy.

At six in the morning, after a night of negotiations, there was a result: the Berlin Mandate. This was the name given to it by Tim Wirth, the American lead negotiator. The mandate stated that, by the time of the next-but-one conference, to be held in 1997 in Kyoto, the industrialized nations had to sign up to a binding timetable of CO_2 reductions. The more stubborn countries among them, particularly the USA, had thus bought themselves time, but were duty-bound to go along with the proposals. Merkel had made herself popular with the developing countries, and even today her reputation in the Third World is sometimes based on the climate conference of 1995. The Berlin summit revealed an interesting side to Merkel, one that is still characteristic of her approach and which may even define it: she is extremely pragmatic when there is the chance of reaching a compromise. Dogmatism is foreign to her; she always wants a result. She won't brook unnecessarily binding arrangements. After the Berlin conference she said, "Of course one can go on insisting on one's maximum demands for years, refusing to compromise. I often decide to move things forward at least a step or two, even if I know I won't get unanimous applause for it [...]. Perhaps a compromise only works when everyone involved ends up in a bad mood – then I just have to rejoice all by myself." Merkel regards politics as a linear process: negotiations follow a kind of scale. If she is arguing with an opponent over a particular position, Merkel draws a line and looks for the central point between the two positions. Even if the decision is only slightly in her favour, she still considers the compromise as successful. But most of all she prefers a result that doesn't conflict with her moderating style.

Berlin 1995 provides a good example of this process of weighing up different arguments, and her preference for the role of moderator, but also illustrates her sometimes naive enthusiasm for politics at this early stage. Merkel became a little less callow every year. A new characteristic emerged, one that she hadn't previously acknowledged: the pleasure of competition, the excitement of victory. As a politician of the immediate post-reunification era, Merkel had always concentrated on the matter in hand, relishing fact-laden debates, whereas Merkel the minister found herself increasingly enjoying the thrill of political success. She was more at ease with public life. She admitted to a liking for the cut and thrust of political argument and seeing through the tactics used by opponents. When she was shown up in public several times by the First Minister of Lower Saxony, Gerhard Schröder, over the question of the permanent disposal of nuclear waste, she at first reacted with unchecked anger. Schröder had been playing games with her; she felt she had been dragged into the limelight only to be tricked. As Environment Minister she became more and more of an Aunt Sally for the opposition. Schröder described her as "not commanding, just pitiful". And then, in her interview with Herlinde Koelbl, she made this feisty comment: "I told him that the time would come when I would get him in a corner too. I still need time for that, but the day will come. I'm looking forward to it." Schröder would have done well to take the warning seriously.

Merkel began to revel in competition: kill or be killed. Be better than the others in order to deprive them of the advantage. A few months before the CDU was defeated in the 1998 general election and Schröder became Chancellor, Merkel showed that she was ready for the fray. "I've promised myself not to put up with things so much," she said to Koelbl in an almost threatening tone. "And I'm enjoying it. It's rather like sinking a battleship – I feel great whenever I score a hit." Later she would put it even more clearly. Asked about the pleasures that come with power, she replied, "In the past I would have said it consisted of shaping policy. Now I would say it's about snatching the prey away from your opponent." And suddenly there she was, Merkel the huntress with a quite definite instinct, the ability to pick up the scent at exactly the right moment – and even, when things looked doubtful, a dash of courage.

In Germany, during the years spent serving one's political apprenticeship, the emphasis tends to be mainly on domestic issues. As a result, Merkel achieved very few foreign-policy milestones while she was coming to political maturity. As her party's General Secretary her first task was to attack – and since at the time the CDU was mostly fighting battles over itself and its past, involving party donations and illegal bank accounts, Merkel mounted the ultimate attack on Helmut Kohl himself by suggesting that the party might have to disassociate itself from its father figure. Yet she had no desire to abandon Kohl's foreign policies – nor was she in a position to do so, at this stage or later. She felt no urge to reshape the party's political complexion: it appeared that Helmut Kohl had left the CDU's foreign policy in good order.

It was only from 2002, as Chairman of the CDU Parliamentary Party and Leader of the Opposition, that she made a decisive return to foreign policy. So it was surprising when Merkel revealed some of her personal policies on the political stage for the first time, providing an inkling of her appetite for European politics. And a politician's appetite is particularly voracious when it comes to appointing people to important positions. 2004 saw the search for a President of the European Commission, in a demonstration of power politics. Between 10th and 13th June 2004, the European Parliament was elected for the sixth time. The majority of the votes went to the European People's Party, made up of the various conservative parties in the EU. After that the Commission would have to be formed again, with a President to head it, who had to be approved by the Parliament and its conservative majority.

For the European Socialists, which included the German Chancellor Gerhard Schröder, it was, in the light of the new balance of power in Parliament, almost impossible that one of their own candidates could win. But in the Liberal Premier of Belgium, Guy Verhofstadt, they found a candidate who was to their liking. As a candidate he had another great advantage: Verhofstadt was accepted by the conservative French President,

Jacques Chirac, because the previous year he had arranged the "chocolate-box summit" – a meeting of the heads of government of France, Germany, Luxembourg and Belgium – with the aim of creating a European security alliance, an alternative to NATO, something which in the shadow of the Iraq War was seen as a retort to the USA.

These ideas didn't suit Merkel at all. In her view the old structures of Germany's alliance weren't up for discussion, so she decided to put obstacles in Verhofstadt's way. Not only that, the conservatives wanted to demonstrate their new strength, so they had to have a candidate of their own to thwart the Belgian. Surprisingly, on the evening before the European Council meeting, Merkel appeared at the gathering of the heads of government and leaders of the European sister parties. She had already persuaded the British Tory leader, Michael Howard, to put forward the widely respected European Commissioner Chris Patten for the post. He was a strong rival contender, particularly since Tony Blair, the British Labour Prime Minister and supporter of the Iraq war, was bound to vote against Verhofstadt and for the British candidate. As usual when such blocking tactics are used, both candidates were sacrificed – and, as a compromise solution, out of the conjurer's hat came the Portuguese conservative Premier, José Manuel Barroso. He was hardly Merkel's preferred choice, but at least he was a conservative, and he also represented a considerable setback for Gerhard Schröder. In Brussels people rubbed their eyes in astonishment – so far no one in Europe had taken much notice of Angela Merkel.

Yet anyone who was looking more closely saw a quite different picture: a woman who knew exactly what she was doing.

As Leader of the Opposition Merkel was extremely active: she travelled Europe and made contact with the governments of Germany's neighbours. France's President Chirac was also on her list, but despite Helmut Kohl's advice she made no secret of her dislike of the French President's policies. And again, anyone looking more closely realized that here was a woman who had begun exactly where Helmut Kohl had left off. Merkel had a clear idea of Germany's role in the world, and of its friends and allies.

Questions of Belief

What Makes Merkel Tick?

Angela Merkel loves opera, particularly Richard Wagner and the tragic and fatalistic aspects of his music. Her favourite work is *Tristan und Isolde*, especially in the production directed by Heiner Müller, whose work Merkel, as a theatre-goer, would have been familiar with in East Berlin before the fall of the Wall. Müller's interpretation of Wagner's tale of doomed love was included in the Bayreuth programme six times, and Merkel believes that the production "verges on genius". Perhaps she is so fond of Tristan because the king's son could never hope to be rescued. Only death could bring release from his all-consuming love.

Nor is there any ambiguity in her view of *Der Ring des Nibelungen*. Here Merkel's interpretation is short and sharp: "If things go wrong at the start they can develop in a number of different ways, but they will never turn out well." Merkel doesn't believe in resigning oneself to one's fate, but she has emotive opinions about Wagner: "It grieves me to think that, even from the outset, the final outcome can't be avoided. So to do something properly you have to get it right from the start."

The Chancellor could not have chosen a more fitting motto for her own life. Getting it right from the beginning, step by step, methodically, calmly – that is her aim, or at least what she aspires to. Thinking things through by working back from the desired outcome is a basic principle that she shares with her Finance Minister, Wolfgang Schäuble. Merkel hates it when events become inevitable or inescapable. She doesn't want to be driven, she wants to control and influence the course of events. Yet Wagner's grandiose manner, his powerful music and the weighty subject matter of Romanticism don't suit her at all. Quite the opposite: in style and character Merkel is the precise antithesis of Wagner's operatic world. But perhaps that is why, in her passion for his music, she allows herself one last spark of the irrational – just as during her childhood she dreamt of role models who were particularly remote from her own life: ice skaters, dancers, film stars.

Anyone who spends time observing Merkel will soon be able to understand and categorize her. The Chancellor reveals her sensibilities and idiosyncrasies in a relatively open way. She doesn't indulge in role play, she is not glib or capricious, self-important or condescending, she doesn't rant and rave, she isn't whimsical. It is easy to say what Angela Merkel is not. But if none of this describes her character, then what does?

Most people see Merkel as being typically close to her roots and "normal". But perhaps this is where we discover why there has been so much interest in her personality: we suspect that there is another, different woman behind the Merkel that the public see. You don't get to be Chancellor if everyone can see through you. And so the same question comes up over and over again: what is she really like? What makes her tick?

The answer is hardly exciting: with Merkel, what you see is what you get. There are no great secrets behind her public image. This is a woman who has been quite closely studied by commentators as well as her long-standing entourage. A number of positive qualities can be attributed to Merkel: she is correctly described as a woman with an enquiring mind, always keen to learn. If she has to solve a problem she needs to identify all its elements first. Whether the question concerns the formula for calculating pensions, a housing bubble or the South China Sea, she insists on knowing the facts, she wants to understand the other side of the argument, even if it differs from her own opinion. Before she met the new French President François Hollande in Reims on 8th July 2012 to celebrate the fiftieth anniversary of the Franco-German reconciliation, she studied the history of the city and the relationship between the two countries. She dissects the CVs of foreign people she meets, looking for material that will help solve her own problems.

She has formed a particularly close bond with the Indian Prime Minister, Manmohan Singh: she is impressed by his political career, but even more so by his calm, serene manner and fatherly composure. If a day comes when Merkel can no longer marvel at new experiences, then, as someone close to her said: "It will be over." Even those who plan her schedule take account of this tendency and know how to accommodate it. Merkel hardly ever travels abroad without visiting a scientific institution. In Indonesia she visited a tsunami early-warning centre, in Canada a marine research institute.

Merkel shapes her world view in an analytical way. She weighs up arguments, industriously collects facts, considers the pros and cons. The problem with this dialectical approach is that Merkel would rather find a compromise than give her personal opinion. She is far from impulsive as a politician, and no ideologist. In this she is the opposite of Gerhard Schröder, who frequently made decisions based on personal feeling. The ability to do that impresses Merkel, but it is not one of her qualities. She has developed a great respect for Schröder – she once described him as "a man of infinite ability" – but always with a sense of quiet triumph at the back of her mind, knowing that she defeated him at the polls. Schröder is a master of the moment, one of Germany's most instinctive politicians. Appreciative words for her predecessor come easily to Merkel: she sees herself as being engaged in a sporting contest with him.

In general, she admires people with qualities that are not her own, but prefers to work her way steadily forward. Herein lies Merkel's problem: if her opponent doesn't use rational arguments, then the logical framework ceases to function, arguments cannot be weighed against each other and compromises cannot be reached. The almost endless process by which Greece was supposed to find a way to save twelve billion euros while ushering in reforms drove Merkel to despair. She spelt out the arguments in favour of the reforms and the logic of thrift at countless Council meetings, as well as to the Greeks themselves. Counter-arguments were increasingly thin on the ground. But then the politics developed into petty haggling, something that she finds deeply distasteful. One of her favourite maxims is a simple one: "If you say you are going to do something, then you must do it."

Merkel likes discretion, and is discreet herself. "We tend to be rather sparing with discretion in society, which has become quite loud," she said in an interview with presenter Anne Will. For her there are times when there is something distinguished about keeping quiet – in fact, it can often be a political imperative, such as on the eve of the general election in 2005 when, during a televised debate between the party leaders, Gerhard Schröder worked himself up into a rage and predicted that she would never become Chancellor, not with her small lead, and not against his party. If Merkel had answered back in the same vein it would probably have been all over, and the debate would have ended in a duel that neither could have survived. As it was, come the election Schröder was defeated and, despite its poor showing at the polls, the CDU pulled itself together – so in the end she did become Chancellor. So there it was: discretion, silence – "To me it has great beauty."

This is not always the case – because Merkel is a sociable person who likes a good natter. Those who travel with her – her spokesmen and advisers – need more than just knowledge in their particular field: they need to know about other things, such as football, music, opera, art, history. Merkel values well-educated people who stimulate her mind.

But her approach varies according to the company, particularly when it comes to being able to speak openly. Merkel can be extremely frank, very direct in judging others when she is among close confidants. "Close" means the inner circle in the Chancellery – her private office, her advisers, government spokesman, those who give her morning briefings. These confidants also include colleagues such as Volker Kauder, Chairman of the CDU Parliamentary Party, the Ministers Wolfgang Schäuble and Thomas de Maizière. These trusted individuals have something in common: they all know how to be discreet. Discretion is a mark of loyalty. At the beginning of her time as Chancellor, Merkel would often seek advice from elsewhere; there would be dinners to which experts in particular fields were invited. But after a while these occasions became less and less common. There was far too much chatter. Quite recently, a professor was invited to one of these evenings, in which Europe was the subject of discussion. By the next morning half of Berlin knew that the professor had had dinner with Merkel. It will be a long time before he is invited again.

When someone doesn't live up to her expectations, Merkel can be cold, cutting and sarcastic. Those who work in her private office know that she is most dangerous when she is perfectly calm. When she is quiet, there is an outburst waiting just around the corner. Merkel never shouts, she just gets sarcastic – and then she strikes. When something has been brewing inside her for a long time, when an irritating individual has been getting on her nerves, she withdraws into her lair like a moray eel, only to shoot out when the time is right. This hard, unyielding side of her is usually only witnessed by close colleagues or collaborators whose political future depends on her, and whom – to put it bluntly – she no longer needs. Her latest prominent victim was the Environment Minister, Norbert Röttgen, who did not want to resign after losing the local elections in North Rhine-Westphalia, and whom she abruptly dismissed. Röttgen had refused to accept that this defeat in the polls meant that he had become a liability to the Cabinet and his Ministry.

With those whose careers are not in her hands, and whom she needs – such as the leaders of the coalition parties and the heads of foreign governments – Merkel behaves quite differently. She doesn't allow herself to lose her temper with them, nor does she openly show any preference. She would never say that she gets on better with Rainer Brüderle, the parliamentary leader of the Free Democratic Party, than she does with Philipp Rösler, the party's chairman. On a list of people she likes, she would never allow herself to rank George W. Bush higher than Barack Obama. Things are as they are: she can't change them, so she accepts them.

Merkel divides her political colleagues and opponents into two categories: those who know when to keep quiet and those who don't. On several occasions at the height of the euro crisis, the Chancellery invited the various party leaders to exchange ideas with her. Merkel was very frank about the seriousness of the crisis, which hadn't always been obvious, even to experts. Discretion was of utmost importance, because the markets – as everyone had now realized – would react instantly to the slightest rumour. In matters of discretion, Merkel has had variable experiences with her opponent in the 2013 election, Peer Steinbrück of the SPD. During the 2008 banking crisis, when Steinbrück was Finance Minister in the Coalition and, in an unusual show of strength, the Government decided, almost overnight, to guarantee all savings, they both preferred to keep quiet. But there were also periods of mistrust between them.

Merkel's relationship with the parliamentary leader of the SPD, Frank-Walter Steinmeier, and Jürgen Trittin, leader of the Green Party, runs more smoothly. Others senior politicians are regarded by the Chancellery as less trustworthy. However, Merkel's confidential meetings are dangerous for the opposition parties as well: she expects her opponents to understand that they are duty-bound to be discreet – but the political responsibilities and benefits are not shared equally. In the CDU-FDP Coalition there is a climate of trust between her and the FDP Foreign Minister Guido Westerwelle. Even in her own party it isn't always possible to speak openly. In the past, when aspects of foreign policy had to be agreed with the former Defence Minister, Karl-Theodor zu Guttenberg, many details found their way into the media. Since Guttenberg's resignation, however, things have been calmer.

For all her openness, Merkel is very careful about the people she takes on as friends. Almost nothing is known about her social circle. Klaus von Dohnanyi, an SPD politician from Hamburg, is said to be one of them; others are described as "opera friends". But members of her circle never talk about their friendship with Merkel. The Chancellor maintains a professional distance between herself and those who work for her; she even addresses her personal private secretary, Beate Baumann, by her surname and uses the formal address *Sie* when talking to her. However, with a few of her colleagues, such as Guido Westerwelle, Edmund Stoiber and Horst Seehofer, Merkel uses the informal *du*.

Within the CDU there are other friends on informal terms with her, but there is also one particularly tricky case in which relations have remained on *Sie* terms: the Finance Minister Wolfgang Schäuble. Her predecessor as Party Chairman is probably not really that formal, but they have continued to maintain a slightly wary distance from one another. During a European election, Schäuble and Merkel once let themselves be photographed together. Schäuble chose the caption: "Not always of the same opinion, but always on the same side." At least it was honest. He had perhaps not forgotten that when she published a letter in the *Frankfurter Allgemeine,* publicly distancing herself from Helmut Kohl, she didn't tell him first. Or a year earlier, when she had quietly announced her marriage to Joachim Sauer, Schäuble had known nothing about it (nor indeed had the couple's parents and siblings). That hit him hard. In private, Merkel can sometimes behave oddly.

In the spring of 2012, however, there was a private meeting between them that only gradually became known to the public, thus producing an even greater effect. Merkel asked Schäuble if he would like to go to the cinema with her to see the French film *Les Intouchables*, released in Germany under the title of *Ziemlich beste Freunde*, which can be translated along the lines of *Almost Best Friends*. It is the acclaimed and touching story of a wealthy aristocratic paraplegic, Philippe Pozzo di Borgo, who is confined to a wheelchair, and his rather unconventional black carer. Jokingly, Schäuble wondered whether he ought to go to the cinema with a woman who wasn't his wife. But in the end he and Merkel slipped almost unnoticed into a cinema on the Potsdamer Platz. The Chancellor and the Finance Minister – almost best friends. But only almost. Afterwards they went for a drink and watched football.

There was a time when Merkel talked fairly openly about her inner life, and so we know that she not only holds the word humility in high regard, but also its meaning. If someone is too forceful with her, she will say to her colleagues: "He needs a little more humility." Every fibre of her being makes it clear that she sees her role as one of service, duty, structure. Discipline is a key concept in her working life, punctuality is important: she will drive herself hard, almost to the point of torment, sit in endless meetings and manage on only a few hours of sleep. She gives an impression of utter sobriety, of being free of ideology, but also comes across as a consummate tactician. Merkel restricts herself to what she does best: debate and discussion.

She keeps to the facts, uses them to wrestle with opinions and win. She knows she has to work hard to justify her claim to power, and cannot take her unassailable position for granted. Asked about her relationship with power, she took a noticeably aggressive line: "I'm not a defeatist; one must never simply fall into line with other people. I like to keep my head above water. I'm no good at drifting." Asked whether she enjoys power, Merkel replied, "If ones approaches it in the right way then it's just part of the job. It's not something one should talk about."

At the beginning of her rise to prominence, it was to her advantage to be underestimated. She always appeared less formidable than she was. Politicians like Schröder or Kohl would never have made light of their achievements. Unlike Merkel, who once said, "I know that fear you get when things are going too well. I take the view that bad luck more or less tends to cancel out the good luck. In other words, when I've been lucky, when I've been through a good period, I'm always afraid that it will be followed by a bad one."

Yet at the end of her second term, she seems more relaxed. Although Merkel has been under enormous pressure and the euro crisis raised existential concerns, she has proved that she is at peace with the world. She has twice been elected Chancellor, and has made it through two parliaments, hardly a foregone conclusion after an uneasy start with a slim majority for the CDU in a Grand Coalition. Still less was it to be expected that in her second term the coalition with what had looked like her ideal partner, the FDP, would turn out to be so fractious – and yet manage to continue for so long.

Merkel seems to be at ease with herself because she has managed to rise above the pettiness of everyday politics in what are difficult circumstances. She now rules largely unchallenged, particularly in foreign policy. While her first election in 2005 put her under an enormous amount of pressure, physically as well as mentally, she looks forward to the run-up to her potential second re-election in an intriguingly relaxed mood. She has nothing more to prove. She wants to be seen as a safe harbour in stormy seas. The PR strategists and spin doctors are lucky: at last they can use their candidate's qualities to their advantage.

In this disregard for the duties of electioneering, Merkel appears almost dull. And yet that has been the secret of her success for at least eight years. Perhaps needs will change and people will yearn for a voluble, exuberant chancellor. That would not be Merkel's style. No one can imagine her being photographed in a victorious pose, like Gerhard Schröder, with all the trappings of success, such as a cigar and a long, flowing coat. The most important thing is self-control, keeping things in check, moderation. Money is not important to her, and she dislikes ostentation – whether in her predecessor or the former President of France, Nicolas Sarkozy. All she needs is the privacy of her country cottage and her rented apartment in Berlin.

At the centre of this private world is Joachim Sauer, one of the best quantum chemists in the country, and renowned as such throughout the world. If in spite of the public exposure Merkel still exudes a certain mystery, Sauer really does live in a different world. This is exemplified by the way he greets any unwanted enquiries about himself: "I made the decision to have no conversations with journalists that are not about my work as a university lecturer and researcher, and which concern only my wife's political activities."

This leaves one with no choice but to respect his decision, because Sauer shuns all publicity. His political views are unknown: it is impossible to estimate what influence he might have on his wife's work. His scientific CV is nonetheless impressive, bearing witness to considerable creative powers. For example, he might be happy to talk about the interaction between gold atoms and thio-aryl-ligands on a gold surface.

Angela Merkel has hardly ever mentioned the part played by Joachim Sauer in her political life. If we remember her preference for calm, analytical men who keep their distance, men like the Indian Prime Minister Singh, then her husband embodies all these qualities. She once called conversations with him "vital" in her life, and has described him as a "very good adviser".

Because of the code of discretion they impose upon their lives, as a couple Merkel and Sauer have set new standards for political relationships. In doing so they have also brought the diplomatic protocol of international statesmanship into the twenty-first century. Long gone are the days when a politician and his wife had to go on foreign trips together. One reason for this might be because the politician is no longer necessarily a man, and the politician's partner not necessarily of the opposite sex. During Merkel's time as Chancellor the requirements of protocol have decreased even further, particularly regarding the antiquated tradition of "first ladies' entertainment", which is now called "spouses' agenda" – if it still exists at all.

Merkel's G8 summit in Heiligendamm in 2007 was Joachim Sauer's first and last attempt to conform to protocol. Everywhere in the world, like-minded partners of both sexes have all followed his example. No president is now automatically accompanied by his or her spouse – Hillary Clinton put an end to that. Merkel makes only a small number of state visits, choosing to leave this highest honour to the President of the Republic. As Chancellor she prefers rigorously organized working trips, when anything that needs saying is said in the space of a few hours.

On the few trips he does make with Merkel, Sauer will sometimes engage in minor diplomacy. He has twice been on tour with her: in 2006, soon after she first took office, he went with her to Vienna, although probably just for the music. And then he accompanied her when she was presented with the Presidential Medal of Freedom by Barack Obama. Like the Chancellor, he feels a great affinity for the United States, and his work often takes him across the Atlantic. At the state dinner in the White House he managed to shake hands with 208 guests without appearing overwhelmed. He had travelled separately, arriving late – a conference in Chicago took precedence. He had decided where his priorities lay, not American protocol. Besides, as he says himself, "I'm of no interest to the public."

Merkel's Concept of Freedom

If Joachim Sauer holds the key to Merkel's personality and values, the inner world of her ideas is often revealed by people with whom she is less closely connected, such as the football managers Vicente del Bosque and Jürgen Klinsmann. Merkel thinks very highly of both of them. Firstly because she likes football and admires both men's work, and secondly because they embody attitudes and beliefs that she regards as exemplary. If there is such a thing as a popular version of Merkel's articles of faith, then these two football managers provide access to it.

Merkel was an enthusiastic fan of Jürgen Klinsmann well before he produced the magical summer of 2006 – the World Cup euphoria that swept through the entire country and even allowed politicians to share in the national high spirits. What Merkel admires about Klinsmann is his logical approach to putting his ideas into practice, the way he returned from exile in California to run the national team, the way he shook up the German football league with his modern tactics and training methods, eventually creating a side that was a model of effortless strength and performance.

It is much the same with the Spanish national manager, Vicente del Bosque, whom Merkel doesn't know personally. Del Bosque has not only made the Spanish team virtually unbeatable, but he has also united the players (who are traditionally loyal to their own regions) by giving them a sense of nationality and community, imbued them with a philosophy based on freedom and respect.

In studying Merkel's values, sooner or later we have to talk about freedom, because it is the driving force behind them. "Values" is a much used term in an era when political correctness has a whole catalogue of ready-made beliefs and convictions at its disposal, where we can expect to be given a lecture on tolerance and human dignity by members of our local council, where every import-export firm publishes its ethos and mission statement on its website. So when politicians put on their best clothes and talk about values, voters usually take little notice. They know that they are living in a post-ideological age in which politicians have to be prepared to tone down their convictions if they want to win elections. Angela Merkel would not have become Chancellor if she had rigidly stuck to one position and had not shown flexibility in adapting to the views of both left and right.

Nonetheless, there is a big difference between talking about values and values themselves. Perhaps convictions can only be tested once they have settled, rather like sediment. So are values just a form of fossilized convictions? Heads of government like to talk about their values, especially when discussing foreign policy. Yet all these words mean very little unless they are tested in the real world and survive the rough-and-tumble of political decision-making. Early in her political career, Angela Merkel spoke frequently about her principles – but it is only now, after two terms as Chancellor, that a pattern begins to emerge.

At the top of Merkel's scale of values is freedom. In terms of pure credibility she has an advantage, having lived for thirty-five years under a regime in which there was no freedom. The only surprising thing is that it took almost ten years before freedom appeared as a verbal weapon in her vocabulary – almost surreptitiously at first, at the 2000 CDU Party Conference in Essen, where she was elected Party Chairman and no doubt deemed it wise to be more specific about principles. So she went through a catalogue of values – not her own, but those held by the CDU, around which the delegates could rally. Freedom, responsibility, security: one of the holy trinities that the CDU and other parties liked to use during the post-war era.

The word freedom reappeared in full force three years later, in perhaps the most programmatic speech that Merkel has ever made. "*Quo vadis, Deutschland?*" was the somewhat old-fashioned theme when, as leader of the opposition, Merkel called the conservative camp to arms on 1st October 2003, a year after the re-election of the Red-Green Coalition. She castigated the country's fossilized institutions, its stagnation, and produced something like a work schedule. Yet at the heart of it was her concept of freedom, or rather a combination of the values of freedom, solidarity and justice. What at the time sounded like a crowd-pleaser from the Ten Commandments of the CDU was to be repeated many times.

"Without freedom there is nothing!" declared the Chairman of the CDU to her audience in the German Historical Museum. "Freedom is the joy of achievement, the flourishing of the individual, the celebration of difference, the rejection of mediocrity, personal responsibility." This was the sermon that Merkel preached as a politician dealing with domestic issues – and who wanted to shoehorn her party into modern values. According to her, democracy and the social market economy are the offspring of freedom. "If we are to be able to live in justice and solidarity again, freedom must be restored to our hierarchy of values, written clearly on every line."

In 2005 freedom hit the headlines again, when Merkel took her oath as Chancellor and delivered her first policy speech from the podium in the Bundestag. "Let us dare to want more freedom" was a nod to Willy Brandt as well as a tactical move to dominate her SPD coalition partner. As in her *quo vadis* speech, she used the motif of freedom mainly with reference to domestic politics – stressing the individual's role in society and the need for everyone to take responsibility for his or her own life.

To Merkel, values are something very personal, so it is not surprising that – given that she is always sparing with details of her private life – she has never tried to capitalize on her GDR past. It is also worth noting that the idea of Merkel as a symbol of freedom has largely been imported from abroad. President George W. Bush was the first to fall under the spell of this tale of Cinderella from Eastern Europe. Merkel's life has been quite dramatic, so it seems only natural that she should be more readily understood in the land of Hollywood and political celebrities.

When Barack Obama awarded her the Presidential Medal of Freedom, it wasn't to recognize the fact that she had decided to phase out Germany's nuclear programme, but for her own life story, which had deeply touched the Americans. Yet for Merkel, freedom has clear boundaries. She does not want to be an icon of liberty, refusing to carry the banner of freedom that she has been handed. But to an observer this is only visible on closer inspection. For instance, the daughter of the former Ukrainian Prime Minister, Yevhenia Tymoshenko, asked to meet Merkel, hoping to play on the theme of freedom in order to persuade her to plead her mother's cause. Merkel declined: she felt she was being manipulated. The fate of Yulia Tymoshenko is one thing, her own past is another. On this occasion Merkel was the Chancellor of Germany rather than a sister in the struggle for freedom.

Yet it is striking to see how successful a narrative this association between herself and freedom is, particularly outside Germany. When she is abroad, Merkel is less disinclined to use her story to break the ice. When a new head of government is elected somewhere, or she wants to make a personal connection, she will talk about her early life – receiving a personal reminiscence or some other disclosure in return. All these things help forge bonds.

Now, after over seven years as Chancellor, freedom is more than ever the leitmotiv of her foreign policy. Freedom, she said in one of her early variations on the theme, is above all else the chance to discover one's own limitations. Translation: as a young physicist, Angela Merkel was prevented from realizing her potential by the restrictive GDR system. Only the fall of the Wall allowed her to discover and develop her abilities. And she has now risen to the position of Chancellor. Even now, this experience of freedom in itself represents fulfilment to Merkel: "Freedom is the happiest experience of my life. There is nothing that fills me with more enthusiasm, drives me farther, makes me feel more positive than the power of freedom."

There is an important message to the world in this experience: a system that prevents men and women from developing freely is neither free nor just. Individuality – within the context of the rule of law – is the driving force behind democracy. Only those who have fulfilled themselves are free. It is convenient that this message also suits the CDU's core values. In the last few years, however, the party has had to take second place to the international audience to whom Merkel is now performing. Her message of freedom suits China as well as Latin America or Russia. It is directed both at indebted countries, whose restrictive regulations are an obstacle to freedom and creativity, as well as at the European Commission, which smothers diversity in Europe in its obsession with the community.

To Merkel, freedom is less a political dogma than a personal experience. Yet the Chancellor sees it as one of the most powerful driving forces in the world. Whenever there is an effort to make reforms – she said just before her election in 2005 – freedom must play a central role in political decisions, even in international conflicts. And later she said: "It was an incredible victory for democracy to stand up to the Soviet Union and thus put an end to the Cold War. And I would like to make my own contribution by helping freedom and human rights to spread throughout the world. We have the tools to do it."

"We" in this case means the West, with its understanding of the values of freedom. The tools consist of democracy, a belief in emancipation, self-fulfilment, openness – all products of the Enlightenment. Indeed, if – after seven years as Chancellor, six visits to China, numerous conflicts over war and peace, violent arguments with the President of Russia, ideological disagreements with Turkey over questions of tolerance, after all her experience of revolution, oppression and injustice – one idea has taken root in the Chancellor, it is this: Angela Merkel cares about the West.

She fears that the free systems of government might not survive, that democracy and the market economy might ultimately prove to be too weak. Merkel, who adores comparisons and studying systems, has a clear message: the hardest test of freedom is something that the West has yet to undergo. The supremacy of its values is not guaranteed. Everything could yet degenerate into a war of values. "I am afraid that open societies in the post-Cold War world are in more danger than we realize," she once said.

Merkel seldom speaks of her concern for the system. In fact she has never dwelt on it at length. There are occasional clues, such as in her speech after the signing of the reunification treaty twenty years ago. "Sometime my greatest fear is that we have somehow lost the inner strength to stand up for our way of life. To which one can only say: if we have lost that, then we might also lose our prosperity and success."

On another occasion she acknowledged her "responsibility to recognize when systems are going to collapse". She later said in an interview: "It is very important for us not to deceive ourselves. The current situation in Germany and Europe is not a law of nature." Or, to put it in more positive terms: "We must move away from a bipolar world, based on mutual deterrence, towards a multipolar world. In this new world there will be stability if there is international agreement on basic values and we respect each other on that basis."

If we unpack this phrase, Merkel is saying that the world faces a clash of values, a conflict for the superior political system and way of life. This conflict could become unpleasant or – in political terms – create instability. Perhaps water and raw materials will be at stake, perhaps zones of influence, trade regulations or property: it will be a conflict between systems that are free and systems that are not. Because, as Merkel says, "We have no inherent right to democracy or to lasting prosperity." Threats are always possible, history is an ongoing process.

On her trips abroad, the Chancellor likes to assemble the journalists accompanying her in the conference cabin of the Luftwaffe airbus. They meet once on the flight out, once on the flight home, and they sit on sofas arranged in a rectangle round a coffee table attached to the cabin floor. They have to sit close together, knees bent, because there is never quite enough room. The Chancellor squeezes herself in among them: it is pointless to try and avoid touching. Meanwhile the large monitor in the cabin shows the pictures taken by a camera mounted on the tail fin: you can see the plane in flight, the fuselage shooting along above the clouds like a torpedo, the earth far below. It is a time for fundamental, strategic thinking. Merkel's colleagues can recognize the moment when she looks far into the future – ten, twenty years ahead. What she says publicly remains in your memory. "For thirty-five years I lived in a dictatorship that followed in the footsteps of the previous one. So I am always sceptical when people say: it can never happen again."

Merkel shares this experience with many other heads of government from Eastern Europe, and during the euro crisis she never tired of telling the group of EU leaders: "I know what living in a collapsing system feels like, and I don't want to go through that again." There are times when Merkel turns her East German gaze on the Western model that she has always admired. On one occasion she said: "The market economies have used the economic struggle to their advantage, but that doesn't mean that they have won the competition between the different systems once and for all."

She will examine the rapid growth of the Asian countries, compare demographic data; she can describe the age distribution in Germany and Europe from memory. She knows the growth targets that must be achieved if European prosperity is to be at least maintained, and asks, "Can we keep up in a global environment, or do we have to learn to live with the weaknesses caused by our demography and lack of growth?" She complains about the decision-making processes in Europe, the atrocious length of time it takes to discuss propositions, and embrace or reject them, whereas on the other side of the globe an autocratic machine hungry for growth sets about gobbling up the world.

An exaggerated prediction? Slightly, perhaps, but geostrategists all agree that the next great ideological confrontation after the struggle between capitalism and communism will be between open and closed systems, liberty and autocracy. "We can see gradual processes of transition ahead," Merkel once said. "Twenty years is not a long time. The different forces are still developing. Ways in which states can co-exist are only just beginning to form." She might also have said: I want democracy to win.

These new conflicts between states are only just appearing. During the recent currency crisis, for instance, the International Monetary Fund asked its members to raise their contributions in order to boost its holdings of securities. Ethiopia and many other states did so, but the United States did not. That kind of thing hurts Merkel, because she sees that here, of all places, the emphasis is shifting. At some point the relationship between contributions will turn into voting blocs, and states other than the USA will determine the policy of the IMF. Sometimes Merkel would like to listen in on the discussions of the Permanent Committee of the Politburo of the Communist Party of China, when the eight men at the head of that mighty land are making decisions. Or she would like to be present at discussions of the Arab League. She would also probably have no objection to travelling back in time to the Politburo of the Social Unity Party of the GDR.

Whenever Merkel goes to China or other newly prominent states with minimal levels of democratic representation or none at all, she always leaves them with a warning: you are doing well, but human beings require freedom. In her experience, freedom is the prize that comes with prosperity and growth. In her view it is a prize worth having.

In 2010 Merkel awarded a media prize to Kurt Westergaard, the artist who drew the cartoons of Muhammad. She gave a speech entitled "The Secret of Freedom Is Courage". Joachim Gauck, who was not yet President of the Federal Republic, but knows a thing or two about freedom, presented the prize. In her address Merkel tried to define freedom – so that no one present could presume to stretch this elastic concept to suit their own personal criteria. Freedom, said Merkel, is concerned first and foremost with responsibility. "On one side stands freedom from something; on the other, freedom to do something. So when we speak of freedom we are always really speaking of someone else's freedom." Tolerance is required. In Merkel's value system, tolerance comes just below freedom and next to responsibility.

In this system, responsibility is mainly concerned with politics and the economy. She doesn't like her freedom to be taken lightly. In the financial crisis, as Merkel saw it, the banking economy did just that – it behaved irresponsibly. Merkel can get very annoyed about bankers who come cap in hand to the State after paying themselves enormous bonuses. She not only felt that a blow had been dealt to her understanding of values, but that her authority had been challenged. So she put it in writing for all to read: "The State protects the order of our social market economy." Merkel feels that the authority of the State was challenged, and she has sworn to restore her own idea of values and order.

Another item related to freedom in Merkel's value system is courage. "The secret of freedom is courage," she said, quoting the general and politician of the ancient world, Pericles of Athens. Or, to echo the dissident East German songwriter Wolf Biermann, whom she admires: "Courage begins with overcoming our own despondency." We have all experienced that, even if we haven't lived in the GDR. Merkel clearly belongs to the club of those who speak their minds – when the moment is right, when she has weighed up the consequences and exhausted all the alternatives, Merkel can be brutally direct.

In the case of the cartoons of Muhammad, it was about the universal nature of values. It was about who would win in the end – those who are free or those who are not. In her address at the award to Westergaard, she concluded with another statement of principle. To those who ask themselves, "Are we allowed to do it?" she said, "It isn't presumptuousness on our part. Anyone who questions these rights isn't concerned about the good of humanity. No cultural difference can justify disregard for those rights." Merkel is not a pessimist, she believes in the West as she sees it, and in her own values, although they are sometimes slow to make themselves heard. She also says: "I believe that free societies are more creative, and in the long term develop more workable solutions."

Once, during the euro crisis, the Bulgarian Prime Minister, Boyko Borisov, visited the Chancellery and held the usual joint press conference with Merkel. He was clearly still somewhat overwhelmed by what his host had been telling him, in vivid terms, about the nature of the crisis, and told the world: "Frau Merkel quite rightly pointed out that the Maya and many other civilizations have disappeared from the face of the earth." Is Europe as a civilization threatened by extinction? The Bulgarian Prime Minister looked very serious, the Chancellor looked rather contrite. Obviously she had made the gravity of the situation a little too plain. As usual, however, not many German journalists were at the conference, and so his historic statement went unnoticed.

Necessary Evils

The Chancellor and Her Coalitions

As I mentioned before, Angela Merkel prefers foreign politics to domestic politics. She said so shortly before she was first elected Chancellor, and would say the same today. "Foreign policy is my thing," she confided to anyone who cared to listen. Or: "Foreign policy is easy."

It isn't difficult to find reasons for this enthusiastic openness to the world. Most heads of government prefer foreign policy because it raises their profile: in no arena does a chancellor or prime minister have more creative power, freedom, figure more prominently in the public eye than in his or her dealings with foreign countries. On the domestic front, Merkel has to deal with a coalition partner who can be uncooperative to say the least, a CSU (the Bavarian sister party to the CDU) that has a mind of its own, the Bundestag and the interests of hundreds of MPs. She has to think about the structure of the cabinet, and must never lose sight of the interests of the *Länder*, or regions: you never know when the Bundessrat, the legislative body that represents the regions, will want to have its say. All this takes place on an increasingly small political playing field, in an over-regulated system where there are laws for everything – and in which the Constitutional Court has the deciding vote.

By comparison, foreign policy is unhampered. Business between countries is booming, the world wants to be governed and coordinated, natural disasters and revolutions clamour for the attention of government leaders – who are delighted to accept the task. In France and the USA, the President is always the leading figure in foreign policy, steering the ship of state single-handedly. In Germany, however, the head of government doesn't have a comparable level of power. But constitutional reality is catching up, as the national media spotlight focuses on the Chancellor rushing from summit to summit, attending more and more bilateral meetings, presiding over more and more governmental consultations. On top of that, European Union summits are piling up as well. "European policy is domestic policy," Merkel always says – but she treats it like classic foreign policy, as the prerogative of the country's leader. Politics in Germany is becoming presidential, hierarchical, centralized.

There are no guidelines for this area of politics, and coalition agreements are traditionally thin on foreign policy. As a result, people feel a need to pad things out. The fundamentals have to be established: what are the Chancellor's aims, how does she see the world, what is her country's position? Before he became Foreign Minister, Joschka Fischer wrote a book in which, over 340 pages, he laid out his world view, the current state of affairs in Germany as far as foreign policy is concerned, as well as touching on the history of ideas. In Great Britain, France and the United States it is taken for granted that the head of state should make declarations about their country's foreign-policy aims. Strategy and vision go together; in the United States they are studied as part of the National Security Doctrine.

Merkel has never done this. Nor has she ever made a speech on foreign policy that would do justice to these lofty ideals. She has certainly made many speeches, some of them detailing her own plans and beliefs. Anyone who studies them carefully can piece the jigsaw together – a major document on transatlantic politics here, a range of opinions on European policy there – but never a complete blueprint.

This doesn't mean, however, that when Merkel moved into the seventh floor of the Chancellery she didn't have any plans in this area. Far from it. She is constantly thinking about Germany's precise position on foreign policy, has devoted long sections of her speeches to the subject, collected research from all over Europe and the rest of the world, and created a network of contacts during her travels as Leader of the Opposition. But when she came to power, at first nothing happened. In Merkel's initial statement as Chancellor in 2005, foreign policy was mentioned on page fifteen of an eighteen-page speech. With some reluctance, Merkel included comments on foreign policy in a series of statements on domestic policy. Yet it is worth noting that what she said about Europe, the USA, security and the international institutions aroused very little enthusiasm. The German public still had Schröder's strident voice ringing in their ears. Merkel openly admitted: "I'm not going to fight the battles of the past all over again. Those conflicts have been decided."

A hackneyed phrase, but along with a few symbolic acts it should have been enough to restore German foreign policy to its position at the top of the agenda. With his fierce opposition to the Iraq War and President George W. Bush, Gerhard Schröder had already caused enough resentment. Europe was still having to cope with the gaping fault lines that had been opened up by the conflict. And in the east there was Vladimir Putin, the President of Russia, who had taken Chancellor Schröder on a sleigh ride and negotiated new gas-pipeline agreements while the Poles feared yet another German-Russian stranglehold.

For Merkel, the international political climate was ideal for adapting the circumstances to suit her ideas within the space of a few weeks. George Bush had just been elected for a second term, but he had to contend with a hostile Congress, while public support for his blustering foreign policy was collapsing. Very few of his predecessors had had to face such a bleak prospect of reaching agreement. In Europe, Merkel also met two heads of government whose power was on the wane – Tony Blair and Jacques Chirac. The British Prime Minister had been damaged by his close relationship with Bush; Chirac was coming to the end of his second and final term. The timing of the French presidential election and the political timetable were both in Merkel's favour: in her second year in office, Germany held two revolving presidencies, those of the G8 and the European Union. Something could be made of this situation. With that in mind, she had to spell out where Germany stood with herself as Chancellor.

The first opportunity to take up a position is always the best. So Merkel used her official visits to Brussels, Paris, Washington and Moscow to make some statements. The French were surprised that this Chancellor didn't immediately bow twice to the Tricolour – as had been the custom of her forebear, Helmut Kohl – but told the President that, with all due respect, she thought his European policy during the Iraq crisis had been divisive. She pulled off a considerable coup in Washington when, with a couple of remarks in an interview, she dispelled any fears that she was too uncritically close to the United States. Shortly before meeting George W. Bush she had served notice, in *Der Spiegel,* about the need to close Guantánamo and respect the rule of law: no previous Chancellor would have dared to do that in their first few weeks in office. And, since she had given Bush, who was now rather a lame duck, advance warning of her position, no real offence was taken.

But she sent out the clearest signal in Moscow, when she not only asked President Putin to provide an immediate explanation for what was obviously the politically motivated murder of the journalist Anna Politkovskaya, but also met opposition leaders and critics of the government one evening over vodka and wine. She had always found the testosterone-fuelled friendship of Putin and Schröder objectionable, so there was no mistaking the fact that a new note had been struck. The press was effusive in its praise. *Die Zeit* spoke of "a critical bow wave" and took stock of the new scope she had given herself. The report spoke of "small steps towards a new self-awareness", but most striking of all was the following conclusion: "The first secret of her success goes by the name of Schröder. In his last two years in office he brought German foreign policy to a standstill. Lasting damage was done to our relationship with the United States, and Germany was too close to Russia for any criticism to be effective."

The *Frankfurter Allgemeine* noted laconically that at the White House Merkel had made it clear that she belonged to "the school of Helmut Kohl". That could be read in any number of ways, but the basic message conveyed a sense of reliability and tradition. On the anniversary of Merkel's election – an appropriate distance in time from the event – *The Economist* wrote: "Merkel as a global star. German Chancellor wants Europe's powerhouse to play a bigger role on the world stage." And then it added, with a note of concern: "But is Germany ready for that?"

At this stage, all Merkel had to her credit was that she had restored the situation to what it was before. After his departure, Schröder had left a disgruntled – and intrigued – world behind him. Was this still the post-war Germany – an integral part of Europe and the Atlantic Alliance? Or was something else afoot – was the European giant in the process of reawakening? Merkel felt that Schröder had been excessively drawn to the hard men, while she had always preferred those with a more inconspicuous approach to governing. So she kept her distance from Vladimir Putin, was never really close to Nicolas Sarkozy and thoroughly disliked Silvio Berlusconi.

But the remarkable aspect of Merkel's realignment was that she didn't take Germany back to the almost homespun post-war order of previous administrations – such as Kohl's – which discouraged any form of criticism, out of fear for a dispute with the country's allies. The boldness with which Merkel acted was also remarkable, as was her personal interpretation of foreign policy. This approach was exemplified by the way in which she first dealt with the problem of Germany itself, in order to see the country play its part alongside other nations, and thus solve the problem of German identity. "If Germany can find its identity and stand by it, that will be good for democracy," she said after becoming Chairman of the CDU. "A great deal of damage is done by what remains unsaid, concealed. We must develop a sense of our history as a whole, and then say: we are glad to be German. The words come easily to us." "Glad" is trademark

Merkel – it is a declaration, but couched in relative terms: she avoids saying "proud".

When the CDU was once more struggling with the idea of identity, insisting that there should be a debate on the *Leitkultur* ("guiding culture") in Germany, she deftly evaded the issue during an interview with *Der Spiegel* – much to the annoyance of the conservative wing of her party. When she was accused of speaking lightly about her home and fatherland, she retorted, "You see it only from the West German perspective – but I see it from the point of view of all Germany. I have grappled inwardly with these concepts, because I couldn't speak openly about them in the GDR. When I use a word like fatherland I don't mean it in an elevated sense. I don't think the Germans are particularly bad or outstandingly wonderful. I am fond of kebabs and pizza, I think the Italians have a nicer al-fresco café culture, and I think there is more sunshine in Switzerland."

Then she recalled that in the nineteenth century it took the arrival of the Huguenots and their silkworms to get Prussia to abandon its uncomfortable, scratchy fabrics. But at the end of the interview she became more serious: "I use the term fatherland not to mean that we are the hub around which the whole world revolves. I use it in the sense that this is my language, these are my trees, that is my lake, I grew up here. I like living here. I have confidence in this country, I am part of its history, with all the pain and all the good things." A disarmingly down-to-earth statement.

Merkel's understanding of Germany is also reflected in the way she wants it to take its place in the world, as a more modern, more open country, at home within its international-alliance structures, led by its values and interests – and confident in itself. In a sense this sounds like a classic, one-size-fits-all definition; yet in another, Merkel was able to reassure more sensitive observers around the world. After all, she was only the second head of government since Kohl, the Chancellor who ushered in reunification. At a time when foreign affairs were more prominent than ever, his successor, Gerhard Schröder, had indicated that Germany's position in the world could change. Who could say with any certainty where this stronger Germany would channel its power? Merkel made it clear that one could not change the basic tenets of foreign policy over-night any more than one could reinvent those of health or pensions.

The most important principle of her foreign policy is that Germany cannot solve its problems alone: the country is part of several confederations and alliances. Europe and the European Union, the United States, the transatlantic alliance in the form of NATO, subordination to international law under the United Nations Charter and an acute sense of duty towards Israel – these are Merkel's main prerogatives. Everything else stems from them: friendship with France, the importance of Poland, the balance of interests in Europe, the euro and being prepared for military intervention as a last resort.

Regarding Germany's security policy, in 2011 she said in a speech to the Körber Foundation that "our partnership with the USA and the transatlantic alliance forms the basis of our foreign policy". Merkel often mentions the alliance with the USA before the EU in her speeches, as if she wants to establish an order of precedence – perhaps because she sees, with some anxiety, how America is drifting away from Europe and Germany. Her primary concern is not with guarantees of support or agreements for stationing troops in Europe. America occupies a central place in her world of alliances, because it shares its history, culture and values with Europe – and values are what ultimately hold countries together. In this alliance of values with the USA, in her darker moments Merkel sometimes suspects that America is ignoring its roots or, worse, fails to understand how globalization can sap even the resources of a superpower. Because that superpower could suddenly wake up one morning and realize that although it is large and heavily populated, it has slept through the process of modernization and failed to pay attention to some of its important friends.

During Merkel's first term of office there were few foreign-policy crises. She took positions, set things in motion, mediated. In fact she unexpectedly found herself playing the role of a mediator in the Middle East, because she had built up a good relationship with the Olmert administration in Jerusalem and the Siniora government in Lebanon, without neglecting the Palestinian and Arab camps. There was another surprise when Merkel brought Europe and the G8 to a new agreement on climate policy. At Merkel's summit in Heiligendamm, President George W. Bush recognized for the first time that there was actually some kind of climate-change problem, and that halving emissions by 2050 ought to be "seriously considered". That was progress.

Her first term of office would have been regarded as relatively unexciting, had it not been for the bankruptcy of Lehman Brothers the year before the general election – a year when the global financial system, its surveillance and regulation, became the central theme of every discussion of foreign policy, and when fears of economic collapse took precedence over everything else. The crisis in the financial markets in September 2008 was the turning point for Merkel as an international politician. From then on, her main preoccupation would be the economy, the stability of the banks, the survival of the single currency and, with it, a whole range of political setbacks that went hand in hand with the euro crisis. Had it not been for the demise of Lehman Brothers, Europe would have been spared the worst of the sovereign-debt crisis. The dramatic rescue of autumn 2008 was thus only the prelude to the currency disaster that gripped Europe two years later, and which was to be the central motif of Merkel's chancellorship.

Two ministers from her party play highly important roles in Merkel's foreign policy: Thomas de Maizière and Wolfgang Schäuble. She met de Maizière – a cousin of Merkel's first political boss, Lothar de Maizière – when he was his cousin's personal private secretary while he was Regional Prime Minister in Dresden. Merkel was impressed by his organizational skills and ability to work in a team, and she soon decided to have de Maizière at her side as a minister. But how exactly do you run a chancellor's office, how do you hold a government together? Her predecessor Schröder had not left behind an instruction manual: all chancellors develop their own particular strategies and structures, in accordance with their needs. Merkel took a methodical approach. She rang the British Prime Minister, Tony Blair, with whom she had a friendly, almost admiring relationship. Could the British lend a hand?

Blair offered to help, and de Maizière went to London to gain practical experience. For two weeks he accompanied Blair's chief of staff in the Cabinet Office in Downing Street, learning about the legislative process, the passing of laws, who was allowed to sign which documents, how to manage the secret services and the procedural rules. He took notes on who was included in which circle and had to be kept informed, who had access to the Prime Minister, how to run a head of government's schedule and how to find the right advisers. De Maizière's training paid off: he became an almost indispensable adviser himself, and remains one to this day – particularly in matters of foreign policy.

As mentioned before, the other person on whom she relies in terms of foreign policy, especially European policy, is Wolfgang Schäuble. He and Merkel have a special relationship. If there are two people in the cabinet who have similarly quick minds and penetrating intellects, they are the Chancellor and her Finance Minister. After many setbacks in his career, Schäuble has developed a self-confident composure that makes him unassailable. He has a natural authority that Merkel herself respects. In fact their relationship can best be described as "respectful". Schäuble respects the fact that his former General Secretary is fulfilling her duties as chancellor in the way he dreamt of doing himself. And Merkel respects Schäuble's influence and independence.

There have been a few times during the euro crisis when they found themselves in disagreement – for instance, Merkel insisted that the IMF should participate in any rescue plans, and was more mistrustful of the European Commission. But when it came to strategy and assessing events, Schäuble was always her main sparring partner. When he spent weeks in hospital during the first year of the crisis, plagued by doubts over his political future, the strength of their relationship was evident: Schäuble wanted to retire, but Merkel kept refusing to accept his resignation. In the end, the Chancellor rang Schäuble's wife and asked her to tell her husband that he should take time to recover and stop offering to resign. Perhaps then he would listen to her – and he did.

Foreign politics are also within a coalition's remit, which is why Merkel would never have fooled herself into believing that she would have more problems in dealing with the world in coalition with the Free Democratic Party (FDP) than with the Social Democratic Party (SPD). This had a lot to do with the personalities of the respective Foreign Ministers in her successive governments, but it was also due to the series of policies with which each coalition was concerned. Merkel had a good working relationship, albeit not a warm one, with her first Foreign Minister, Frank-Walter Steinmeier of the FDP. She felt closer to Franz Müntefering, her Vice-Chancellor and the chairman of her coalition partner, the SPD. Not only had Steinmeier always been too much of a Schröder supporter to show unreserved loyalty to the person who had defeated the former chancellor, but after a while, as Foreign Minister, he started to find fault with Merkel's foreign policy. He would calculatingly throw a spanner in the works without breaking the actual coalition agreement. In the same way he dissociated himself from her when a young Senator from Illinois wanted to stop off in Berlin on his way to the White House – right outside the Brandenburg gate. Steinmeier thought it was a wonderful idea – he regarded it as evidence of good international relations. He also knew that it was welcomed by a majority of the German population. But Merkel felt that she was being used by Obama: she did not believe it was right for a foreign politician to campaign for election in front of Germany's most important national symbol.

There was a more serious clash between Merkel and Steinmeier when the Chancellor received the Dalai Lama in September 2007

– an affront to the Chinese, who saw this as a show of support for Tibetan efforts to achieve independence. Steinmeier thought the gesture unnecessary and the recent history behind it embarrassing.

Their relationship became particularly difficult in the autumn of 2007, when Steinmeier took over as Vice-Chancellor from Franz Müntefering. Müntefering had decided to retire from politics to care for his terminally ill wife. It was clear to Steinmeier that he would have to position himself as a leading candidate for the next general election, and it was decided in September 2008 that he would be the one to challenge Merkel. How the two of them managed to work together more or less amicably for two years despite this rivalry is one of the Chancellor's most remarkable achievements.

The change of government in 2009 marked a genuine turning point for Merkel. No one expected such a difficult parliamentary term, in which events came almost as thick and fast as in the year of German reunification. No one expected the euro to face collapse – not only as a currency, but also as the glue that held Europe together. And no one would have thought that among the chaos one of the major areas of unrest would be German domestic policy: in particular the relationship between the coalition partners, the CDU/CSU and the FDP.

It is a commonly held opinion that years of crisis are good years for chancellors. It is undoubtedly true that Angela Merkel wouldn't have accumulated so much power, both for herself and her country, and would not have become the unchallenged leading figure in Europe if this multifaceted life-or-death crisis had not had so firm a hold on European and German politics. No politician wants to deal with crises. They take priority over everything else, dictating schedules and paralysing decision-making. The aim of politics is to change the speed of a crisis and force it to adapt to the political tempo. The crisis made Merkel strong.

During her second term in office, Merkel not only had to deal with the crisis, but also had to face a desperate struggle to control the coalition. From October 2009, with the change of coalition, the atmosphere became poisonous, gradually infecting the entire political body. It shook the political body by stages. In Europe, one piece of bad news followed the other: poor budget figures in Greece, the country virtually unable to pay its debts; a financial state of emergency in Ireland and Portugal; warning signals followed by panic in Spain and then later in Italy. Governments fell, political leaders changed.

Which strategy would work to solve the crisis? The time when it was solely a European problem was long gone. By now the whole world had been sucked in. And everyone was threatening, begging, raging – and heading in one direction, to Willy-Brandt-Straße and the Chancellor's office. Angela Merkel sat on the seventh floor, taking on the burden of everyone's hopes and expectations – as well as all their problems. Yet, as her halo grew brighter and brighter thanks to a strong German economy, the world's crises refused to go away. Then, in December 2010, a Tunisian street vendor burnt himself to death in protest against state autocracy: the Arab uprisings had begun.

First it was Tunisia and Egypt, then in February 2011 it was the turn of Libya: a civil war that NATO helped bring to an end, but without the Germans. The UN Security Council voted for a no-fly zone, and thus for intervention by a military coalition under NATO leadership. Germany abstained, and kept its own counsel. Merkel declined to vote with the other nations, as had her Foreign Minister and coalition partner, Guido Westerwelle, while the opposition parties in Germany vociferously expressed their dismay and pleaded for an intervention on humanitarian grounds.

But there was yet another major international disaster in store that year. On 11th March the coast of Japan suffered an earthquake and a tsunami flooded the country, leading to a nuclear catastrophe. As a physicist, Merkel's faith in the safety of nuclear technology was shaken, and she ordered an immediate U-turn on German nuclear policy. At the same time she had to cope with the defeat of the ruling coalition parties in important provincial elections in Baden-Württemberg and other regions. In the Chancellery they were already using the past tense to describe a parliamentary term that left everyone speechless.

Merkel's *annus horribilis* was not only the result of catastrophic events abroad, but of the weakness of the coalition. For at the same time as the euro zone and the Arab world were in turmoil, so was a domestic political pipe dream: the coalition of the CDU and the FDP. Guido Westerwelle and his party had won 14.6% of the votes in the election to the Bundestag, and as a result entered into coalition talks with confidence. As a matter of course, as well as the job of Vice Chancellor, the party chairman claimed the position that had traditionally been held by the FDP in previous coalitions with the CDU – the Foreign Ministry. Several miscalculations lay behind that decision. It later became clear that such a partnership wouldn't work: for years, the CDU and the FDP had believed that they were made for each other. Since the end of the Kohl government it was common opinion that a moderate coalition was almost a political duty. No one expected the FDP to be so unused to governing.

But eleven years are a long time. And during the two decades of his leadership of the FDP Westerwelle had been unable to acquire any experience in government. Heading a ministry with several thousand civil servants is a great deal more complicated than running the FDP party headquarters. The CDU, on the other hand, had returned to power four years earlier, and the Grand Coalition had made a much stronger mark on it than was previously thought. Not only that, Merkel and Co. felt they now had a head start when it came to the issues at hand. At the Foreign Ministry, painful as it was, Guido Westerwelle had to accept that the force field of foreign policy was now centred largely on the Chancellor's office.

Yet the truth is that Merkel and Westerwelle have a relationship of trust. During the time in which they were both in opposition a professional bond grew up between them that is closer and more open than most such relationships in the political corridors of Berlin. Working together they had made Horst Köhler Federal President, thus exposing the weakness of the Red-Green coalition then in power. They both hoped to rule one day. But now that the day had come, one disaster followed another.

In the Chancellor's office, the verdict on the FDP and especially Westerwelle's first year was unanimous: he could have done so much more, should have concentrated on fewer issues, his emphasis should have been on other things. Instead he seemed to be constantly overworked in his party and ministerial positions, harassed and lacking any plan of action. Yet he and the Chancellor trust one another. Westerwelle always asks colleagues to leave the room when he rings Merkel. And to her he is an important source of information at the heart of the FDP. She trusts him more than Philipp Rösler, who has taken over from Westerwelle as Vice Chancellor and chairman of the FDP.

In the first year of the euro crisis, after months of criticism of his handling of his responsibilities as Foreign Minister and party chairman, two incidents were instrumental in bringing about the putsch against Westerwelle: defeat in the provincial elections in the spring of 2011 and Germany's stance on Libya. The German government had not voted for the no-fly zone over Libya in the UN Security Council – thus distancing itself from its NATO partners. As a result, Germany found itself in the same camp as Russia and China, who had also abstained, and who are always reluctant about any intervention.

Merkel and Westerwelle had jointly agreed on the decision. They believed that Germany should keep out of Libya. But they had not reckoned with the storm of indignation in the country as well as among the Western alliance. In public, Westerwelle felt continually obliged to justify the abstention, which only made matters worse.

For two years, the coalition's problems also did damage to Germany's foreign policy. This led to the need for an unusual alliance: the civil servants in both the Chancellery and the Foreign Office came together to settle their differences. Their traditional rivalry disappeared. After all, they all knew each other, in particular Merkel's foreign-policy adviser Christoph Heusgen and the Foreign Office's most powerful woman, Minister of State

Emily Haber. The pair of them are on familiar terms, value each other's work and generally speak on the phone at least once a day. Furthermore, it is helpful that the office of the High Representative for Common Foreign and Security Policy in the European Union is run by a senior German civil servant: Helga Schmid, the Deputy General Secretary to Catherine Ashton. As Merkel's second term as Chancellor draws to an end, Heusgen, Haber and Schmid form the triad of German power at the most senior level of the civil service. It is rare that these representatives of the most important foreign-policy institutions are working together in such harmony.

Christoph Heusgen certainly deserves credit in this respect. Merkel's adviser on foreign affairs, he now has more experience than anyone else in government, and has been there from the start. Sometimes he describes himself as part of the furniture. Of course he is just teasing – besides, in his most famous picture Heusgen isn't standing like a piece of furniture but sitting down – crouching all alone at a conference table during a G8 summit at Camp David. Behind him stand the American and French Presidents, the British Prime Minister and the German Chancellor. Merkel looks strained, Cameron and Obama are jubilant, Hollande isn't sure what to do. And Heusgen? There is a look of sheer terror on his face. They are watching football, and Bayern Munich is just about to lose the legendary Champions League final against Chelsea on penalties. For Heusgen, a devoted Bayern Munich fan, it was probably the worst day of his career in the Chancellery.

Heusgen is the archetype of the sort of adviser with which the Chancellor likes to surround herself. Inconspicuous and unobtrusive, he cycles to the office. He does not have the big ego of his counterparts in Paris or Washington. He came to Merkel's attention when he was chief of staff to Javier Solana, the EU's High Representative for Common Foreign and Security Policy. Heusgen's greatest achievement from this period is a small pamphlet, the very first "EU Security Strategy", which he drew up and for which he led the negotiations.

Soon after the 2005 election Merkel invited Heusgen to Berlin. They talked for several hours, and found that they shared opinions in many areas. Then Merkel asked him to work out a schedule for her first few days in office. Heusgen suggested visiting Paris, Brussels and Warsaw on the same day to show that foreign policy was her priority. The Warsaw visit turned out to be impossible for scheduling reasons, but otherwise the plan worked. Thus began his career in the Chancellor's office, where he plays an essential role. Apart from her personal private secretary Beate Baumann, no one else has worked with Merkel for so long.

Pacific Dreams

Yearning for the USA

Angela Merkel has two kinds of relationship with the United States of America: one very private, the other very public. The public, professional world of America is the side she sees as Chancellor: it is the America of video conferences with the President, summits, high-level politics. This America stands like a monolith in the Chancellor's political landscape: it is firmly marked on her ideological map. Values, convictions, strategies – from a political point of view everything revolves around the USA. But sometimes this America is a stranger to Angela Merkel. The longer her Chancellorship lasts, the more she questions it. As she sees it, in this America there is a dysfunctional domestic policy, an inscrutable leader in President Obama and growing doubt in the country's ability to question itself.

The private America is an idealized America, a land of dreams and strong emotions. Angela Merkel got to know the country in her youth – as a focal point for her yearnings, a place of freedom and self-realization. As an adolescent she was convinced that she would not be able to go there until after her sixtieth birthday. But as it turned out, Angela Merkel did go to her dream destination when she was only thirty-six. In 1990, less than a year after the fall of the Berlin Wall, she and her partner Joachim Sauer boarded a plane for Los Angeles.

Joachim Sauer was in a position of great privilege at the time: the GDR Academy of Sciences had promoted him to the ranks of those who were allowed to travel. "I've been waiting a long time for this," said Sauer, in what is probably the only interview that has appeared in writing in his lifetime, published in the journal of the Humboldt Foundation. On the day the Wall came down he was in Karlsruhe, where he had been given a research grant. It was there he met some American scientists and was invited to work in San Diego for two years as deputy technical director of the software technology firm, BIOSYM. At the beginning of 1990 he took up his post in California, and that summer he was going to show Angela Merkel the Pacific Ocean.

Merkel described the trip almost two decades later, on 3rd November 2009, when she bore witness to her belief in America in the most distinguished surroundings imaginable. Only one other German chancellor had spoken to the assembled US Congress: Konrad Adenauer, in 1957 – when Angela Kasner was three years old and still learning to walk. As a child, she created her own America out of films and books, material that was sometimes smuggled into the Templin parsonage by West German relatives. That was where she developed her idealized view of the United States, which she described to Congress with unusual emotion many years later.

"What was I so enthusiastic about? The American Dream – the opportunity for everyone to succeed, to get somewhere by their own efforts," she said, her voice breaking. "And like many teenagers, I was also a fan of a certain brand of jeans that couldn't be bought in the GDR, but I had an aunt in the West who used to send them to me. I loved the vast American landscapes, where the air is full of the spirit of freedom and independence. In 1990 my husband and I flew to America for the very first time, to California. We will never forget that first view of the Pacific Ocean. It was nothing short of magnificent."

"Magnificent" – such was the image that appeared to Merkel and Sauer on a summer's day at the end of their long transatlantic flight. In Los Angeles they boarded another plane for San Diego. On the flight south a view of the Pacific opened up on the right-hand side of the aircraft. Merkel was fascinated to think that on the other side lay Asia. That same evening they went to the beach.

Today, Angela Merkel would still like to go on holiday to California, but the time-zone difference and the distance from Berlin make it impossible. Nine hours between her office and holiday destination – out of the question for a head of government who has to be contactable at all times.

However, traces of her nostalgic feeling for the United States come up again and again in the Chancellor's everyday life, and she allows an extraordinary number of American visitors to go straight up to the seventh floor of the Chancellery. Merkel's colleagues know which of these must be given a slot in her diary: from New York there is naturally Henry Kissinger, the foreign-policy oracle. He never stays longer than an hour, and thirty minutes are usually enough. And she always likes to see Condoleezza Rice, Hillary Clinton and Bob Kimmitt. The discreet Kimmitt was the United States Ambassador in Bonn when Merkel was first a Minister. The diplomat had asked to meet her because he was fascinated by the story of this woman from the former East Germany. Not many ambassadors came to the Ministry for Women and Youth, and that impressed Merkel enormously. She is still in private contact with Kimmitt.

She was also impressed by the two former US Secretaries of State, Clinton and Rice. It is not usual for the German head of government to receive foreign ministers, but Clinton and Rice were exceptions. Merkel values strong women who have made their way in the tough political world of Washington. She has always felt close to Hillary Clinton – although she has never said as much in public, she would have liked to see her win the presidency in 2008. Condoleezza Rice's previous career was also of interest to her. Before entering politics, Rice was a lecturer in politics at Stanford, specializing in Russia and Eastern Europe. In 1995 she co-wrote *Germany Unified and Europe Transformed*, which is still a work of reference on that subject. Like Merkel she speaks Russian, and that is an additional bond between them.

Merkel is fascinated by the style of American politics, which often throws caution and tactical manoeuvring to the wind, and rewards those who relish vigorous argument and confrontation. America is a conservative country, in no way comparable to Germany and Europe in terms of social policy. Merkel knows that the political centre ground in the USA lies much farther to the right than it does in Germany. And while she doesn't draw parallels, she admires the clarity of argument and keen combativeness of the American system. She is fascinated by how the sheer radicalism of a presidential candidate, or a major political movement like the Tea Party, can call the basic consensus of society into question, and how fundamental concepts like the very notion and purpose of social security can be thrust aside. Does the state really have to be responsible for pensions? Is medical care the government's business? How much personal responsibility can be expected of a citizen? How much of a sense of community does a state need? How much injustice will it tolerate?

Merkel loves comparing systems, and travels the world with these criteria in mind: how do they do this or that compared with the way we do it? What can we learn? Where are we better? America repays such curiosity and asks the Germans, in particular, some challenging questions: at first sight the country is so like Germany, so European, imprinted with the history and culture of the Old World. But Europeans regularly despair of the USA because Americans can be so ruthless, so radical.

Merkel herself has been on that typically European journey of discovery, which had begun in her youth, when she knew the United States only from Western television. During her studies at the Academy of Sciences she would follow the mind games played by the superpowers over the question of armaments. Yet at one point her belief in America was called seriously into question – when Mikhail Gorbachev and Ronald Reagan began their conference on disarmament in Iceland. The cause was Reagan, who in October 1986 initially turned down Gorbachev's offer of a drastic reduction in strategic nuclear weapons. He was unwilling to do what Gorbachev wanted and give up his planned anti-ballistic missile shield in outer space (known in the West as the Strategic Defence Initiative or "Star Wars"). Discussions in the white wooden house in Iceland ended inconclusively, without even a statement. Reagan appeared to be a hardliner, ready for conflict. Had he gambled away his great chance of reconciliation? Was this the beginning of a new and terrifying phase of the Cold War?

The Party interpreters in East Berlin were quick to give their own analysis of the summit. Gorbachev's course had always been too soft for the Socialist Unity Party, so the version that landed on Merkel's desk in the Academy of Sciences was that they had to expect the worst – perhaps even war. Angela Merkel's faith in the USA and Reagan's wisdom began to waver – but this weakness lasted only a few hours. At home that evening, Joachim Sauer managed to restore her faith in the West.

Her professional rapprochement with the USA began in September 1991, when Chancellor Helmut Kohl set off with an impressive retinue for a wonderful six days in the USA – there are few official foreign trips these days that would last a week. Kohl flew first to California, then on to Washington. As Minister for Women and Youth, Merkel was part of the delegation. Kohl wanted to introduce her as one of his reunification discoveries, his political foster-child. He also wanted to do her a favour by showing her America – Kohl could be overzealous at times. Others on the trip remember Merkel trying to escape this constant coddling and the attentions of Kohl's wife Hannelore and his personal private secretary, Juliane Weber, who were always pushing her into the front row, which was where protocol demanded that she should stand. The Kohl entourage apparently even made sure that the young minister's wardrobe was suitable for the occasion.

On a visit to a national park, Kohl was quite offended when he went to show Merkel the natural wonders of America, but "his girl", as he called her, replied coolly that she had already been here with her partner and knew all about it. But at least the trip gave Merkel an opportunity to meet Ronald Reagan, who by then was already suffering from Alzheimer's. In her GDR days she had revered him for his clarity of mind and unshakeable will. The meeting took place at Reagan's ranch in Santa Barbara, and Nancy Reagan was also there.

These days Merkel rarely talks about the hero of her youth. Reagan's image in the West differs from the perception that people have of him in the former Warsaw Pact countries, who admired the President's sharp mind and plain speaking, and Merkel herself would probably give more credit to the penultimate US President during the Cold War. But, as so often, she avoids describing herself as the heir to any particular political role model.

Unlike Kohl's image of the United States, Merkel's is not so obviously coloured by gratitude. At the centre of Kohl's America are its role in the liberation from Nazi barbarity and Washington's unwavering support for German reunification. Kohl was forever expressing his gratitude. When Merkel speaks of gratitude, it sounds more as if she is paying lip service to the conventions of transatlantic rhetoric. She prefers to speak of friendship. It tends to disturb her that every time she travels to Washington, anxious questions are asked about whether her relationship with the President is a good one – whether Germans, or Europeans in general, still have something to offer, or whether America hasn't long turned its back on its former allies. Such questions betray a lack of self-confidence, an inability for independent action. In Merkel's view, friendship means equal rights, a level playing field.

Such self-confidence doesn't come naturally to Merkel, however. It has been achieved through sheer hard work. Her political image of America centres around a single event: the Cold War, with its competing systems and the struggle of slavery against freedom. To her, America is the incarnation of freedom and, ultimately, she owes her own freedom to the steadfastness of the United States. Initially, Merkel's America was above all else the repository of Western values as laid down in the Declaration of Independence and the United States Constitution. "What brings us Europeans and Americans together, and holds us together, is our common values," she said on Capitol Hill. "It is the image of the inalienable dignity of mankind that we hold jointly, a joint understanding of freedom in responsibility."

Freedom in responsibility: this is the Chancellor's private code for a relationship between equals: you are my partner, but I am also your partner – so if you behave like a partner, we will do the same. Or, to put it even more forcefully: transatlantic relations lie at the heart of German foreign policy. They are not negotiable, whether the President is George W. Bush or Barack Obama. No President can be so bad that the relationship with his country has to be sacrificed on his account. For Merkel, relations with the USA, as well as with the European Union and Israel, are the cornerstones of German foreign policy. She sometimes speaks of reasons of state, particularly in the case of Israel. But she always means the same thing: German policy must never oppose the European Union, Israel or the United States.

For this reason, just before the invasion of Iraq in 2003, Angela Merkel the party politician encountered what was her most serious foreign crisis to date when, unlike the parliamentary majority in Germany led by Chancellor Gerhard Schröder and contrary to public opinion, she refused to brand the then US President,

George W. Bush, as Satan's representative on earth. Seldom had the country seen more debate about foreign policy than during the period from the summer of 2002 to the beginning of the Iraq War on 20th March 2003.

Nine months after the attack on the Twin Towers in New York and the Pentagon in Washington, it became apparent that the Bush administration might have more in mind than simply driving the Taliban out of Afghanistan as a display of American power: in other words, revenge for those who died on 9/11. Chancellor Gerhard Schröder got wind of public opinion early on in the run-up to the general election of 2002, and decided to put foreign policy at the heart of his campaign. On 5th August he began his bid for re-election in the streets of Hannover, with a speech on the Opernplatz. It was this shift towards foreign policy – after a long period during which the emphasis had been on social and educational policy and other domestic reforms – that electrified the public. Schröder spoke about the new dangers that the world was facing, about terror, and then added: "I say that we are ready to show solidarity, but under my leadership this country will never take part in adventures."

This was a swipe at George W. Bush and rumours of a possible invasion of Iraq. The public reaction was one of strong approval. Schröder noted this with satisfaction – he had found the right topic to please his audience. "Playing at war or military intervention – I can only warn against that," said the Chancellor in another variation on the theme, encouraged by the applause. "It is not the sort of thing we do."

The CDU and CSU, led by their candidate Edmund Stoiber, were caught on the back foot by these remarks. Even today, those close to Merkel say that from a competitive point of view Schröder was extremely shrewd in his understanding of the mood of the nation. Stoiber's inability to engage in a debate on the subject, as well as his mishandling of the emergency caused by the flooding of the River Oder, cost him the Chancellorship. But as leader of the Christian Democratic Union, Angela Merkel found her most strongly held convictions – never to act against America, never to act against Europe – under attack. For that was exactly what Schröder caused by describing Iraq as an adventure: a divided Europe. Suddenly there were hawks and doves among the European powers: the group of five and the group of ten. There were states who distanced themselves openly from the USA and a faction which favoured putting military pressure on Saddam Hussein or, at least from a tactical point of view, wanted to avoid falling out with the United States.

Merkel clearly belonged to the more cautious faction. She was anxious to prevent a clash with the United States and to preserve European unity. She said later in interviews that, with the help of a united European front, she would have hoped to persuade Bush not to invade in the spring of 2003, or at least to postpone the invasion for six months. That might have given the US the time to overthrow Saddam without resorting to military intervention. Another consideration was central to Merkel's argument: she never understood why the United States wanted to prove, and on such a dubious basis, that Iraq had weapons of mass destruction. She thought that Secretary of State Colin Powell's appearance before the UN Security Council was unworthy of the man. In what was a most peculiar performance,

Powell alleged that Saddam Hussein had a mobile chemical-weapons laboratory.

In Merkel's view, the matter was quite clear: the United Nations had passed almost two dozen resolutions against Iraq. But Saddam Hussein had refused to comply with the demands of the international community, which was therefore justified in asserting its authority, up to and including the threat of force. "I really suffered during the months before the Iraq war, because I know how dictators think and what makes an impression on them," she said in an interview for a book by the journalist Hugo Müller-Vogg. "It was difficult just to stand by and see so many people making fools of themselves. Seventeen UN resolutions had failed to have any effect. And when the latest one was passed we were unable to agree on a time limit. And then the Chancellor of Germany stands in a marketplace and says: 'Never mind what the UN does, we're not going along with it.' That really took the biscuit!"

It was in those weeks in the autumn of 2002 and the spring of 2003 that Angela Merkel's attitude to foreign policy was forged. After her party lost the general election she took over as chairman of its parliamentary group from Friedrich Merz, thereby making an early declaration of her candidature for the Chancellorship at the next election. She also needed the support of the conservative wing of her Party, which up till then had gone to Merz and Roland Koch, Prime Minister of the region of Hesse. And she needed to enhance her foreign-policy profile. In the party, she was surrounded by a number of experts who were keen to share their personal opinions on international affairs with the prime ministers of the different regions. Friedrich Pflüger, the parliamentary-party spokesman on foreign policy, supported the thesis that Iraq had weapons of mass destruction. In March, he was to accompany Merkel on a visit to Washington, which increased in significance thanks to a newspaper article.

The weeks before the trip were marked by nervousness. The Security Council was working non-stop on the question of Iraq, troops were being assembled, the threat of war was increasing, the tone became more and more strident. Shortly after Christmas the then Foreign Minister, Joschka Fischer, said in an interview with *Der Spiegel* that he could envisage Germany agreeing to intervention in Iraq if the UN Security Council gave its approval for war. Fischer thus positioned himself clearly against the line taken by Chancellor Schröder. There was fierce infighting in the governing coalition. Schröder was clearly not going to allow his Foreign Minister's insubordination to go unheeded: the Chancellor had to have the last word. He gave his reply on 21st January – this time in the marketplace in Goslar during the election campaign in Lower Saxony. No, said Schröder, Germany would not back intervention, even if the United Nations voted in favour of it.

Schröder's remarks sent shock waves through the alliance. So where did Germany stand? The US Secretary of Defence, Donald Rumsfeld, who had a gift for cynicism, made disparaging comments about the old and the new Europe. Fischer flung the fury of old Europe back in his face, whispering in his ear at the Munich Security Conference in February: "Mr Secretary, we are not convinced."

In fact very few people in Europe were convinced, but deep inside Merkel knew that this war couldn't be allowed to lead to a transatlantic rift or cause damage to Europe. Her answer to the problem appeared on 20th February – of all places on page 39 of the *Washington Post*.

Once again she was giving her opinion to a newspaper. Rarely is Angela Merkel deliberately courageous, and rarely does she choose to expose herself to danger. On only two or three previous occasions had she been known to make bold decisions. When she was Environment Minister she visited the nuclear-waste facility at Gorleben – a risky outing given that there were noisy demonstrations going on outside the plant. And in December 1999 she wrote a letter breaking with the father figure of the CDU, Helmut Kohl, which was published in the *Frankfurter Allgemeine Zeitung*. Already rocked by an expenses scandal, the party was shaken to its foundations and Merkel had taken a vital step towards becoming its leader.

"We don't know what it really feels like. We have to experience it ourselves." This is what Merkel usually tells colleagues in difficult situations where the outcome is uncertain. That was the case on 20th February 2003, when the *Washington Post* published a guest contribution by the leader of Germany's opposition party on its opinions page. "Schröder Doesn't Speak for All Germans" was the title of the article. In it, Merkel took the Chancellor to task for his policy on Iraq – something quite unheard of. It is an unspoken rule never to attack the government of your own country abroad, and certainly not in a newspaper. The author of such an article risks being accused of currying favour in the cheapest possible way, perhaps even of cowardice. In her guest column, Merkel accused Schröder of adopting a position out of "electoral tactics". She also condemned the French government for attacking new Eastern European candidates for membership of the EU "simply because they have declared their commitment to the transatlantic partnership". And she conjured up the nightmare scenario of German foreign policy: of being once again alone and isolated in history.

These were the opposition leader's greatest fears: that Germany might distance itself from the Western alliance of values, Schröder might break with America, the nation to which Germany owed its rebirth after the Second World War, as well as its acceptance into the Western alliance. And back would come the poison that, so often in German history, had driven the nation into isolation and eventually to its downfall.

The article provides a true illustration of Merkel's core sensibilities. She had no intention of punishing Schröder: she just wanted to dispel, via an American newspaper, any doubts that Germany might not be a reliable ally. Where foreign policy was concerned she refused to give up her deeply held convictions.

In the Chancellor's closest circle today, the view is that the news-paper article was not really necessary. Nowadays she wouldn't lay it on quite so thick. As Leader of the Opposition she had already made her position clear in speeches in the Bundestag. This may be true, but as a statement on foreign policy, the *Washington Post* article came across as the most authentic one she made during her time in opposition – accordingly, it brought her strong criticism. Yet more than anything it established the image of Angela Merkel as a true supporter of transatlantic relations and an obedient ally for years to come. What the Leipzig party conference had achieved for social and economic policy, her *Washington Post* article did for foreign policy. In a mixture of self-assertion within her party, genuine indignation at Chancellor Schröder and fear that the foundations of her world would be overturned, Merkel chose to stay close to the United States, and thus in the eyes of her critics, pro-war. She had to become Chancellor before she could be able to correct this image of her position on foreign policy.

At that time it wasn't difficult to despise President George W. Bush. Bush had only been elected in 2000 because, after heated legal battles, the US Supreme Court stopped a recount of the votes in Florida and awarded the Republican candidate victory in that state. Bush was a president appointed by the court rather than the people. Liberal Western Europe reacted with outrage. Al Gore was the natural winner, not this ignorant provincial politician from Texas whose only merit was being the son of George Herbert Walker Bush, the former President and Helmut Kohl's ally during German reunification.

It took George W. Bush some time to settle into the job. Then Al Qaeda terrorists flew two airliners into the Twin Towers, and the war began. As Angela Merkel was about to announce her candidature for the chancellorship in 2005, Bush was elected for a second term and insurgents were murdering people in Afghanistan and, particularly, in Iraq. The world was outraged by the Abu Ghraib torture scandal and the CIA's rendition flights. The POW camp in Guantánamo didn't conform to any standards based on the rule of law. The neoconservatives had lost their relevance, and America now seemed very foreign to most Germans. The Schröder administration had the worst relationship with Washington that was possible to imagine.

In her 2005 election campaign, Angela Merkel steered clear of foreign policy. Germany was discussing Schröder's "Agenda 2010" and social reform. Even the Red-Green coalition government had little appetite for including foreign policy in the election campaign – the decision to send German troops to Afghanistan had cost the coalition much energy and the loss of public confidence. Four years had passed since then, but no one wanted to revisit the war in any detail. Merkel herself avoided the subject of Iraq, and didn't make the usual visit to Washington as an electoral candidate. Images of solidarity are supposed to convey a sense of reliability and continuity in foreign policy. But this time it seemed that she could dispense with such a trip. Wolfgang Schäuble, the parliamentary party's *grand seigneur* on foreign-policy matters, went instead.

In November 2005, Angela Merkel finally became Chancellor. Her certificate of appointment still lay beside her desk in a rolled-up scroll, and the nation was surprised by the ease with which the new Chancellor handled foreign policy. In dealing with George W. Bush in particular, Merkel showed the skill of a judo black belt, using her opponent's weight to her advantage. In the case of the USA itself, the target of her attacks was Guantánamo. A few days before she flew to Washington, Merkel gave an interview to *Der Spiegel*. One sentence was enough to distance herself from Bush, establishing her reputation as a critical thinker. "An institution like Guantánamo cannot and must not continue in the long term," said Merkel. "Other ways and means of dealing with the prisoners must be found." That was all she said, but suddenly there was a chorus of agreement.

The delight over this act of daring was overwhelming. As if suddenly set free, the European Union joined in the criticism. Merkel had got the tone exactly right: a hard line on the war on terror, while rejecting the Bush administration's methods. There was only one drawback: criticism of Guantánamo had little credibility so long as the German government allowed German citizens to suffer under this unjust system. So Thomas de Maizière, Minister in the Chancellery, swiftly arranged for the German-Turkish Murat Kurnaz to be handed over. Kurnaz, who had been in the prison camp since 2002, and who had been subjected to two boards of inquiry and countless legal proceedings, returned to Germany after four and a half years in US custody.

By criticizing Bush, Merkel had given herself room to manoeuvre. The President, and especially his foreign-policy team, headed by Condoleezza Rice and security adviser Stephen Hadley, were very interested in re-establishing a good relationship with Germany. Washington was beginning to feel its isolation. Merkel offered the chance of a new start: in return, the White House had to accept her criticism of Guantánamo. Not only that, Merkel had a fascinating life story. Bush particularly liked the idea of freedom being championed by a woman from Eastern Europe – it fitted in with his personal agenda to be seen as an agent of freedom and democracy in the Arab world, however improbable that might seem. And finally, it was enough for Merkel not to be Schröder.

Her predecessor had veered off course with his foreign policy. Schröder had been too close to France, showed little interest in the European Union, insisted that Turkey should become a member, cultivated a pally relationship with Vladimir Putin – and had thus backed himself so far into a corner that he had nowhere left to go. Merkel was seen as representing a new departure from this. She could even impose conditions or express criticism – and, almost without effort, completely new options in foreign policy opened up. The SPD wanted to leave Gerhard Schröder behind and followed her in this – the Grand Coalition was hungry for success. "Emancipation without defiance clearly makes you free," wrote *Die Zeit*, mocking what it called Schröder's "strained silence" on the subject of the new direction in foreign affairs. Merkel had seized the moment – proving that her instincts were correct.

It was also very helpful that Angela Merkel and George W. Bush got on well. One needs to know Bush personally in order to be aware that behind the image of an ignorant, warmongering and deeply religious ultra-conservative there is also a private, entertaining and friendly man. Bush is essentially affable, with a stock of good stories and jokes, a man who enjoys life. Merkel's colleagues describe him as pleasant, not arrogant, a willing collaborator who never told a lie to the Chancellor.

He shares this open, cheerful nature with Merkel who, for all the reserve she likes to display in public, can be good company. Bush obviously made it clear to her from the outset that, despite the pressures of high office there can be informal moments. Experience shows that once two heads of government have left protocol and their advisers behind a sense of friendly companionship quickly develops – after all, on those dizzying heights, they only have one another. Whatever the case, the personal chemistry between them was evident. Bush would occasionally put his arm round Merkel's shoulder – something that she doesn't accept from many people. He famously attempted to massage the back of her neck during the G8 summit in Heiligendamm: she fended him off coquettishly, pretending to be shocked.

Even when they were at loggerheads at a critical stage in foreign affairs – Ukraine and Georgia's request to join NATO – Bush brushed any differences of opinion aside with professional aplomb.

During the 2008 NATO summit in Ceaușescu's sumptuous former palace in Bucharest, Merkel had been Bush's main opponent. Before he left office, the President wanted to give Georgia and Ukraine, as aspiring members of NATO, the prospect of full membership, the so-called Membership Action Plan, a preliminary stage to acceptance into the organization. Merkel objected. Although the Chancellor always let her reservations be known during preparatory meetings, Bush didn't think she would stand by them, and included the subject in the day's agenda.

Government delegations seldom clash in such a disorderly fashion. The wording of plans and documents is generally agreed before the beginning of any summit. The finishing touches may need to be decided, but there are not meant to be any surprises. This time, however, there was a potentially explosive difference of opinion: was NATO to reach out to two states who were in open confrontation with Russia, when neither of them could be regarded as stable? Russia's President Putin had voiced his disapproval, but Bush still wanted to see it through. Merkel stood firm, and when NATO tried to reach a unanimous agreement it was forced to adjourn. In the corridors of the conference centre, heads of government stood around looking at a loss, small groups gathered to try and come up with a final statement that would cast a veil over the fiasco. Afterwards Bush expressed his respect for Merkel – she was upright and honest, he said, that was why he thought so highly of her. And in a rare moment of gratitude, Putin told the Chancellor that he would never forget what she had done.

Merkel and Bush twice met in circumstances that protocol described as "private". Merkel took the first step in 2006, when she invited him to her constituency. At a meeting in Washington,

Bush had shown great interest in her GDR past. So the Chancellor invited him to Trinwillershagen, a municipality of about seven hundred people, on which the international political circus descended like a horde of locusts. A barbecue meal in the country, as rustic as possible (wild boar, venison and duck – the symbols of normality, of living close to nature), prepared by Olaf Micheel, the landlord of the village inn. Around thirty personal guests gathered, not far from the old "Red Banner" sign of the collective farm from GDR times, to have a taste of Arcadia in Mecklenburg-Western Pomerania.

Because of his passion for working the land and his love of his ranch, Bush has been nicknamed Shrub. He always said that he was happiest on his property, clearing the undergrowth with a chainsaw. So it made sense for the President to invite the Chancellor to his private ranch in Texas. It was a singular honour that Bush bestowed on seventeen foreign dignitaries: two kings, one prince and various presidents, premiers and chancellors. Such gestures are out of character for Merkel. Her private apartment opposite the Pergamon Museum on Museum Island in Berlin is out of bounds to visitors – a place of absolute privacy. So is her weekend cottage in the Uckermark: not even her closest colleagues have been inside it. Nicolas Sarkozy may have invited her to the Paris townhouse belonging to him and his wife, Carla Bruni; Gordon Brown to the British Prime Minister's weekend retreat at Chequers; Wen Jiabao into the heart of the governmental district – but to Merkel, private means private.

So in November 2007 she set off for Texas with certain reservations. For all her natural friendliness, Merkel likes to control whom she meets, and an invitation to the Presidential ranch was a very private occasion. Nonetheless, hardly any other foreign trip still makes so many eyes light up and evokes so many happy memories among the Chancellor's immediate circle. Bush loves his ranch, a complex of several buildings, with a swimming pool, a pond, a garage and a helicopter hangar on six square kilometres of prairie. The property once belonged to a German emigrant called Heinrich Engelbrecht. As President, Bush was often criticized for spending too much time at his ranch, which came to be known – even officially – as the Western White House. Bush feels most at ease there. He proudly gives his visitors a guided tour, takes them off on long mountain-biking tours, or goes fishing with them. Once he said (and he may have meant it seriously) that the finest moment of his presidency was when he caught a 7½-pound widemouth bass in his fishpond.

Merkel and her husband stayed in the main family house, while the Chancellor's chosen companions – her spokesman Uli Wilhelm and her foreign-affairs adviser Christoph Heusgen – slept in the guesthouse, in bedrooms used by Bush's daughters or his parents, George H.W. and Barbara Bush, when they came to stay. Bush handled the unusual intimacy of the occasion with great warmth. Merkel was somewhat reserved and wooden in conversation – she obviously didn't want to commit herself to an unreserved show of friendship. Early in the morning the Chancellor and the President went for a brisk walk in the grounds, but she did not feel like joining the mountain-biking expedition.

Half a year later Bush finally came to Germany for a farewell visit, staying at Schloss Meseberg, just outside the Berlin city gates – a small, almost private gesture, out of the public eye. The next US President was already on his way. Merkel, and particularly her advisers, were convinced that relations with the United States had never been better, and professional contacts between the German and American staff closer, than during the Bush presidency.

Senator Barack Obama, the rising star in the political firmament of the USA, had a problem: he couldn't lay claim to much expertise in foreign policy. For four years he had been chairman of the Senate's subcommittee on European Affairs, but in that time he had come to London only once – stopping off on his way from the Middle East to Washington – and no occasion had ever brought him to Berlin. Now, however, he wanted to make up for his lack of experience and, in preparation for his election campaign he planned an extended trip that would take him to the trouble spots of Afghanistan and Iraq, as well as to Europe: to the Brandenburg Gate, formerly the border between East and West, the monument that symbolized the Cold War and the United States' victory over the Soviet Union.

Obama had already played many character roles in his election campaign: Abraham Lincoln, Martin Luther King, John F. Kennedy. Now he clearly wanted to borrow Ronald Reagan's iconic status and show himself to be truly international. Although his campaign team never officially confirmed that the candidate would have liked to speak at the Brandenburg Gate, his possible appearance in front of Germany's best-known national symbol had people talking for days and divided the coalition, as has been mentioned previously. In the end, Obama backed down and made his speech at the Victory Column – but the episode gave Merkel a foretaste of what she might expect from the young senator if he were to be elected.

As we have already seen, Merkel doesn't like men who make a lot of noise, and despises the exaggerated masculinity of Vladimir Putin, someone who likes to show off his muscles and hunting prowess. And she does not care at all for the machismo of Silvio Berlusconi. She was speechless when the Italian premier left her standing on the red carpet at the NATO summit in Baden-Baden after driving up, only to finish his phone call walking up and down on the bank of the Rhine. Nor did Merkel care for the skittish vanity of Nicolas Sarkozy. Whenever a new example of this self-important type of character appears on her radar, she tells her staff: let's wait and see what he can actually do.

She was similarly sceptical, at first, about Barack Obama, whose talent for rhetoric she observed with reservations. Perhaps she also felt a certain envy. Merkel has never been a gifted orator. Her words convey trustworthiness and level-headedness – but she can never really cast a spell over an audience. Today people like to say that the Brandenburg Gate episode spoilt the relationship between Merkel and Obama, and neither of them has really recovered from it. By way of proof, they point out that Obama didn't come to Berlin during his first term of office.

That interpretation is wide of the mark. It would be more correct to say that human factors can even influence relationships between heads of government, and that Merkel and Obama may be more similar than they care to admit. With their analytical coolness they are unable to put on a show of informality and warm friendship. Merkel and Obama speak on the phone regularly and hold a video conference about once a week. It is true that Obama's immediate entourage doesn't keep in such close touch with Merkel's advisers as Bush's did. And it is also true that Obama has difficulty in transferring the charisma that he uses to such brilliant effect in his speeches to personal relationships.

There were times, such as on the margins of European summits, when Gordon Brown, Nicolas Sarkozy and Merkel wondered aloud among themselves whether the American President is only so awkward, cold and unapproachable towards them. Those who attend government consultations at the White House are always surprised by the President's passive approach at the conference table; Obama's staff say the President is forever asking how many hands he has to shake that day. That is not the Obama we are used to seeing in public.

Despite the passion in his speeches, Obama is not naturally outgoing; he tends to be introverted, focused on his family and above all his wife Michelle. Yet he is sensitive enough to know when unreasonable demands are being made. During the G20 summit in Cannes, Merkel was under enormous pressure from all the other heads of government to use the Bundesbank gold reserves during the Eurozone crisis. Obama sensed that the balance of power was moving in the wrong direction, and stepped in when Merkel was about to face humiliation. He called a halt: things had gone far enough, Angela Merkel should not have to undergo political execution.

A fair amount of psychology is involved in the relationship between Merkel and Obama, but there is also a hefty dose of realism. During his first term, Obama was a prisoner of domestic politics. He was operating in a deeply hostile climate in Washington, met great resistance to his healthcare reform, while at the same time having to deal with the complex legacy of his predecessor simply in order to regain room for manoeuvre for the United States in the balance of power. As a result, Germany and Europe were not at the top of his agenda. On her part, the Chancellor was mainly concerned with the euro crisis. If she made a telephone call to Obama it was usually to do with that problem.

Merkel and Obama did once manage to bring something like personal proximity into their relationship. They were comparing their rise to the leadership of their respective countries. Both are classic political outsiders: the young black man from Hawaii and the woman from the former GDR. Both made their way in the face of strong resistance. Their career paths are not typical – indeed they verge on the incredible. Both are ruled by their heads, are highly analytical and objective. Like Merkel, Obama always tries to think problems through. Like her, he hesitates over making decisions when he can see the possible consequences.

Merkel sometimes gets annoyed at the continual questions about her relationship with the President. She does not want to go to Washington like a schoolgirl, she does not want to be awarded marks for how much affection the American President shows her in public. Her self-respect forbids it and demands equal rights. We have interests, she says, we have values in common. Merkel cannot be accused of vanity. She is also upset by stereotypes: Bush the bad guy, Obama the angel of peace.

When she was in Washington in the early summer of 2011, she joked with Obama that the press would immediately be asking how close their relationship was now, since the President hadn't come to Berlin during his first term of office. For in fact Obama visited Germany only twice in those first four years, going first to a summit at Baden-Baden, then to Dresden and Buchenwald. He declined an invitation to the celebration of the twentieth anniversary of the fall of the Berlin Wall, saying he was too busy – something of an affront.

Sure enough, during the press conference in the East Room of the White House, the question of why the President hadn't yet been to Berlin was duly asked. Merkel gave a girlish grin, Obama grinned back, and she then assured him that Berlin was ready for a visit from him at any time and, as far as anyone could tell, the Brandenburg Gate would be standing for quite a while yet. The ice was broken, and the stumbling block of the Brandenburg Gate elegantly swept aside. With her light-hearted tone Merkel had let the President know that she hoped he wouldn't think of visiting Berlin as a tourist, in the same way as he had visited Paris during the summer after his election. That would seriously upset her. In fact, months before the American presidential election in November 2012, Merkel and Obama agreed that if the President were re-elected he would visit Berlin during his second period in office and before Merkel's rendezvous with the electorate. So before the German general elections, the delicate matter of the Brandenburg Gate incident was finally cleared up and Obama finally gave his speech in front of the landmark.

Merkel has high hopes for Obama's second term, but she is also anxious. Anxious for America itself: a great power racked by self-doubt, with high unemployment, an enormous debt burden, a growing gulf between rich and poor and extreme ideological tensions between left and right.

America is facing huge demographic change. Soon the white population will no longer be the majority, and the USA will increasingly lose its European character. At the same time the country is so inward-looking that it no longer understands or even sees the seismic shifts going on in the world. Merkel sometimes speaks of hegemonic diplomacy when she wants to express her uneasiness with the attitude to power of a nation like the United States. She experienced it in 1995 at the climate-change conference in Berlin, when the USA made compromise particularly difficult, and in the end refused to sign the Kyoto Agreement.

Today there is a no lack of important global issues, but the United States rarely undertakes to lead the way, and globalization tends not to fit in with the American schedule. Has the USA failed to understand the melting-pot process by which the world is changing? Those who study the country today, tracing the course taken by the old industrial regions, the impoverished south and all the isolationist undercurrents, may feel uneasy. Will the USA be the loser in the globalization process? Are we looking at the least globalized nation in the world?

The America of Merkel's nostalgic longings and the current political America are increasingly less in tune. The country has failed to bring two wars to a successful conclusion, and there is no meaningful strategy to help America stand tall again. Wars gnaw away at a society. Two wars in the wake of the terrorist attacks have brought about profound changes in the United States. Even an enthusiastic admirer of the country like Merkel can sense that. She doesn't like to see a weak America. She wants to offer the USA something, she wants to make Europe an attractive prospect for renewed cooperation. Since the beginning of her chancellorship she has been inspired by the idea of a transatlantic free-trade zone – something similar to the internal European market, but of vast dimensions. Free trade, however, is not a term to arouse enthusiasm in French socialists like François Hollande or American protectionists.

America's influence in the world is weaker now. That is not good news for those who, like Merkel, consider the weight of the United States an essential factor in European efforts to achieve equilibrium. There has been too much bad news for the country: this has drained it of its ability to get things done and has tarnished its aura. Merkel, who was more fascinated by that aura than anything else in the first thirty-five years of her life, is bound to feel concerned. She thinks in terms of strength and superiority, and would rather see a strong America than an over-powerful China.

However, on Tuesday 7th June 2011, under a clear blue sky, Angela Merkel experienced all the splendour, the glorious magnificence, the infinite generosity of the United States, the country of her dreams. On that Tuesday the President and the Washington political elite lavished on her all the honour that America has to bestow. Barack Obama was awarding Angela Merkel, the girl from the GDR who went on to achieve great things, the Presidential Medal of Freedom. This is the highest civil decoration in the United States, and it was given to Angela Merkel in a ceremony as splendid as any that Washington can provide.

The Chancellor had flown to Washington the day before, her official plane packed with members of the Cabinet, Prime Ministers of the different German regions, Members of Parliament and advisers. In the Chancellor's cabin at the front of the aircraft, the political elite sat with Merkel: the Foreign Minister, the Minister for Economic Affairs, the Finance Minister, the Defence Minister.

Her personal official guests sat farther back. In Washington they were joined by football coach Jürgen Klinsmann and by Merkel's husband Joachim Sauer. On this special day he obviously had to be there, even if – coming straight from a conference – he only joined them in time for the dinner.

Whenever she travels abroad, Merkel is accompanied by a large retinue: two doctors, interpreters, protocol experts and civil servants, members of the security services for internal and external protection, baggage handlers and a large flight crew, from the captain to telecommunications technicians to flight attendants. On every journey, whether for just a day or an overnight stay, Merkel's stylist is there to look after her hair and make-up.

The state visit to America was a rare occasion: no one in the delegation had been on one before. Helmut Kohl and Richard von Weizsäcker were the last Germans to have been accorded this honour. Merkel had a day of fanfares and flag-waving, guards of honour, political meetings, quiet moments with the President and lunch at the State Department with many distinguished guests. The high point, however, was the state dinner given by the President in the Rose Garden of the White House.

The apartments on the ground floor are generally used for state dinners, but the Obamas resurrected an old tradition and had the Rose Garden between the main house and the Oval Office covered with a wooden floor and carpets. The President's head of protocol chose a light, silvery decorative scheme reminiscent of the Bauhaus style – candles, crystal, simple lines, regular shapes. Later, the Washington tabloids gossiped about this new minimalist approach – not only in the style, but also in the guest list. "The event looked and felt like a sophisticated outdoor wedding reception, minus the drunken bridesmaids," wrote the *Washington Post*.

Before dinner, Merkel was joined by her personal guests at her residence. Obama had put the Chancellor up in Blair House, the President's guest house, directly opposite the White House on Pennsylvania Avenue and made up of several buildings. A small buffet had been laid out on the ground floor, where the Chancellor and her official guests could enjoy champagne, coffee, tea, small sandwiches and pastries. Merkel had chosen a black, short-sleeved evening gown, worn over one shoulder and falling in diagonal folds. The men were in dinner jackets, and only German talk-show host Thomas Gottschalk had allowed himself a pair of heavily embroidered black jeans and cowboy boots under his more formal top half. Germans might forgive him for that – they are familiar with Gottschalk's sartorial tastes – but it took American guests a moment or two to adjust. Later, the newspapers and Internet forums discussed the guest list, the ladies' wardrobes (too much blue, too little risk taken in the choice of dress, etc.) and the seating plan, which gave important clues about the internal ranking of Washington's political and social elite.

Merkel and her husband entered the White House through the main entrance and were taken by Obama and his wife up to the first floor – the private apartments of the President and his family – where they had some time for private conversation. Meanwhile, on the floor below, guests mingled in the East Room. Drinks were served by female soldiers from the Marine Corps, wearing dress uniforms and full-length wrap-over skirts. Then the President, the Chancellor and their spouses came down the wide staircase. 208 guests filed past, hands were shaken 208 times while an aide read out the names of the guests, 208 photographs of the event received 208 Presidential signatures, which were later sent to each guest – important trophies in status-conscious Washington.

Merkel surveyed the gathered dignitaries lined up in front of her with amusement, and even Joachim Sauer, who is usually publicity-shy, seemed to enjoy all the splendour. At dinner he sat between Michelle Obama and Eric Schmidt of Google and Bob McDonald of Procter & Gamble. The Chancellor sat between Obama and the architect Helmut Jahn, who was wearing the Federal Cross of Merit pinned to his lapel. Opposite was America's most senior judge, Chief Justice John Roberts. The conductor Christoph Eschenbach was also at their table, although he had to earn his supper by conducting a performance by the National Symphony Orchestra.

The finale to such occasions is traditionally provided by a big name from American show business or pop music. For a visit by the Chinese President Hu Jintao, Jackie Chan, Yo Yo Ma, Herbie Hancock and Barbra Streisand provided the glamour, while Beyoncé entertained the guests at the Mexican State Dinner. By the standards of the American gossip columns, and in line with her down-to-earth nature, Merkel was positively boring: James Taylor, the most American of American singer-songwriters, performed for her. Taylor later declared that the White House had specifically requested his song 'You've got a friend'. "When you're down and troubled," it begins on a melancholy note, "and you need a helping hand – and nothing, whoa, nothing is going right – close your eyes and think of me – and soon I will be there." It wasn't clear which of them the song was aimed at, Merkel or Obama. But one thing was for sure: "All you have to do is call and I'll be there – you've got a friend."

For Angela Merkel, who had first set foot on American soil twenty-two years earlier, this was a very special return. She had made freedom the leitmotiv of her political world view, and had now been awarded the Medal of Freedom in the heart of the free world. To Obama and the Americans it was simple: as the first East German to serve as Chancellor of a reunified German Republic, said a note in the menu, Dr Angela Merkel symbolized the triumph of freedom.

Her reply was brief. "History has often shown how strong the longing for freedom can be. It has inspired people to overcome their fears and oppose dictatorships." And she went on to say: "In the end, there is no chain of dictatorship, no fetter of oppression that can withstand the strength of freedom. That is my firm belief, and it will continue to guide me."

But Angela Merkel wouldn't be Angela Merkel if she had let it rest at that brief moment of emotion. So the state dinner in Washington ended with a heartfelt handshake. And while previous Presidents had rounded off the pomp and ceremony of state visits with an after-dinner party, she was driven straight to the airport from the south lawn of the White House and flew back to Berlin that same evening. She and her party changed out of their evening gowns and dinner jackets on the plane.

On the Defensive

Angela Merkel and War

Angela Merkel has rarely been as close to war as she was on 4th November 2007. She had been in office for two years, and had returned to Berlin from India the previous evening. That didn't prevent her from boarding another plane only a few hours later, and flying back in almost the same direction – this time to Uzbekistan, where an army Transall aircraft was waiting for her. She was flying on to Kabul. The journey had been kept strictly secret, like her three later visits to the Hindu Kush.

There were less than two dozen other passengers on board the government Airbus, and the few journalists accompanying them had been sworn to secrecy. The security guards from the Federal Criminal Investigation Agency carried an arsenal of weapons. Even the Chancellor had to wear a bullet-proof vest. The atmosphere became tense when the pilots of the military aircraft had to switch twice to an emergency flight path. The sensitive electronics of the helicopter and the Transall had picked up light reflections – an alarm signal. The flash from a rifle barrel? Anti-aircraft guns armed with infrared warheads? Or just sunlight reflecting?

The on-board electronic warning system reacted immediately and set off flares. Pyrotechnics were deployed on the tail of the aircraft. Magnesium flames were used to confuse incoming rockets, whose heat sensors navigate straight for the engines. Merkel's pilots took evasive action, smoke from the defensive missiles blew through the open gun hatches, the noise made the plane shake. At such moments, even experienced soldiers don't know whether or not the aircraft has taken a hit.

Angela Merkel took the incident with relative calm, and asked her military escort if they were planning to provide any more such entertainment. If you spend your life in aeroplanes, helicopters and cars, you presumably need to develop a fatalistic relationship with your protectors and their technology. On the same day, in Kabul, a would-be suicide bomber had been intercepted on his way to the airport, and two days earlier a bomb had been found in the street.

A year and a half later, during the Chancellor's second visit to Afghanistan, insurgents fired home-made rockets at the German base in Kunduz shortly after Merkel had taken off in a helicopter. They didn't hit it, but the message was clear: Afghanistan is at war, the Chancellor is a highly symbolic and valuable target, travelling to that part of the world is enormously dangerous – both for the visitor and for all the troops who are serving there.

It was two years before Chancellor Merkel managed to visit the troops in Afghanistan. Even as Leader of the Opposition, she had never once been to see the soldiers stationed there, and her image suffered as a result. When he was Foreign Minister, Steinmeier was still needling the Chancellor at the 2007 SPD party conference, saying that she was wriggling out of it. The last head of government to visit the ISAF (International Security Force) troops had been Gerhard Schröder – but that was four years earlier. Nothing better illustrates the German political establishment's discomfort about sending troops abroad than the question of how often senior politicians visit them.

Around the time of the general election in 2005, it was noticeable how the main political parties were skirting round this delicate issue. Merkel had learnt her lesson: just before the United States invaded Iraq in 2002, Gerhard Schröder had shown how to win a general election on the issues of war and peace. And although Merkel has a pragmatic attitude to the use of military power ("there are times when military intervention is unavoidable"), and visits the troops regularly, she handles the subject with great caution in public. Perhaps she learnt from her experience in the 2002 election that when it comes to military matters, she will get furthest by using quiet pragmatism.

Until the fatal bombing of two tanker trucks near the German base in Kunduz in September 2009, Merkel had mostly left Afghanistan to those ministers who were experts in the field. By taking this approach, the Chancellor was in good company both nationally and internationally. In 2003, American troops had marched into Baghdad and driven out Saddam Hussein, and as early as 2004 the number of violent incidents in both theatres of war – Iraq and Afghanistan – was rising. By the time of the 2005 elections, it was clear that the Taliban had reorganized in Pakistan and Afghanistan, and that the pressure on foreign troops was increasing. In Germany, however, neither the outgoing nor the incoming government wanted to admit that what had been described as a mission of reconstruction and stabilization was actually a war about the new world order: a military confrontation between insurgents and conventional forces. Afghanistan was a war to be ignored, a war that mustn't be talked about, just forgotten in the shadow of Iraq.

It was the American general David Petraeus who restructured the US forces in Afghanistan at this point, introducing great changes to the army's operational procedures and tactics while the conflict was still going on. But the United States' efforts to ensure that the risks were shared more equitably within NATO had no effect on Germany. The Schröder government and the first Merkel government agreed that German troops were doing fine where they were, in the relatively secure north. While the British, Canadian, Dutch and American forces suffered heavy losses in the south of Afghanistan, particularly in the provinces of Helmand and Kandahar, the Germans ignored the fact that the war was escalating.

When NATO called for an increase in troops on the ground early in 2007, Germany resorted to a ruse. Tornado reconnaissance planes were sent to take photographs of positions, enemy troops or suspect vehicles by using high-resolution cameras mounted in the fuselage. However, Tornadoes require a great deal of manpower. They need maintenance, repair and a ground crew – so suddenly the German army had 500 more soldiers on deployment, and could claim to have met its international obligations. The German rules of engagement were also more concerned about the threat posed by domestic politics than reducing the dangers faced by troops on the ground. Soldiers weren't allowed to use preventive measures, and only returned fire if the enemy engaged first. Nor could the Tornadoes attack from the air using the weaponry they carried. It needed the hapless Colonel Klein to order an air strike on tanker trucks that had got stuck in a river bed before the real nature of the operation was understood back home in Germany – there was a war on.

The semantic equivocation about the word "war" was justified on the one hand by long-established agreements under international law, and on the other by concern for domestic politics. From a legal point of view, any operation under the rules of war is subject to international law: war must be formally declared and then concluded by a peace treaty. Anyone waging war must have an opponent, and must treat prisoners according to the Geneva Convention. But no one wanted to recognize the Taliban as the enemy in a war which would have enhanced its status and given it legitimacy under international law.

The word "war" also caused unforeseen problems for every soldier who took part in the operation. For instance, life insurance doesn't cover death in the course of wartime operations. Insurance cover and care of the wounded, as well as the bereaved families of the dead, have kept experts busy for years. Eventually it was the up-and-coming Defence Minister Karl-Theodor zu Guttenberg who broke the taboo, first speaking of "warlike circumstances" and then suggesting that "in colloquial terms" it could be called a war. It was a few months before Angela Merkel, during her third visit to Afghanistan on 17th December 2010, would also admit to soldiers: "You are engaged in combat of the kind found in war."

Politicians, and in particular Merkel's first Defence Minister, Franz Josef Jung, were not just worried about legal ambiguities. More than anything else they were concerned with public opinion, which didn't appreciate the finely calculated security policy that underpinned the operation. The last SPD Defence Minister, Peter Struck, was greeted with laughter when he pronounced the phrase: "The security of Germany is also being defended in the Hindu Kush." Although defence experts agreed with Struck's analysis, the deep-rooted pacifism of modern Germany and the lack of any culture of strategic discussion clashed once again with sober Realpolitik and the constraints of international alliances. At first Merkel did little to resolve the conflict. Like every other member of the coalition government, she no doubt realized that political careers could be decided by this operation. And in any case, as there was no public consensus on what the German army was doing, it was unlikely to win many votes.

For this reason, what had happened to Franz Josef Jung acted as a warning. After the Kunduz bombing on 4th September 2009, Afghanistan was suddenly at the centre of German domestic politics. Everyone now realized the true nature of the operation. The debate about stability and helping the local people to look after themselves was over. Germany was discussing a war – just a few days before the general election. Immediately after the bombing, Merkel took the lead and delivered a formal statement in the Bundestag – her first on the subject of Afghanistan. She uttered one memorable phrase after another. "The presence of the army in Afghanistan, together with that of our partners in the North Atlantic alliance, is necessary. It contributes to international security, world peace and the protection of life here in Germany from the evil of international terrorism." And: "Germany is pledged to the service of world peace; it says so in the preamble to our Constitution. In this world, Germany has strong alliances and partnerships; Germany's special needs are not an alternative to German foreign policy." And she reminded her audience – as if issuing a warning to any doubters in the Bundestag – of its responsibility: "This military operation was and remains of vital importance to the safety of this country. It is based on the resolutions of the Security Council of the United Nations. Since the beginning of 2002, it has been the responsibility of every federal government to send troops."

Due to the inner workings of the Grand Coalition, the full weight of the confrontation was felt only after the election at the beginning of October. Until the votes were cast, the CDU and the SPD found themselves jointly responsible for the military operation. Only with the bombing in Kunduz did Merkel realize that she must make more of an effort and become personally involved. The increasing number of conferences on Afghanistan – London in 2010, Bonn in 2011 – and the importance the subject was accorded at NATO summit meetings made it clear that the Chancellor now meant to lead the movement for withdrawal, in order to extract Germany from the operation with as little damage as possible. In her official statement on the day after Kunduz, she held out hope of such a withdrawal.

Since her first visit in 2007, Merkel has not been back to Kabul, but has been to northern Afghanistan three times. Her second trip was a few months before the bombing of the tanker trucks, and took her to the town of Mazar-i-Safif, where she met Governor Atta Muhammad Nur and some local dignitaries. Nur organized a lavish reception for the Chancellor; he sat enthroned on a gilded chair decorated with Medusa heads. In the middle of the room a table groaned under the weight of pastries and sweetmeats. The governor's court sat in a circle. Several specially selected Afghan women talked about the progress being made in women's rights, and Nur graciously called on his people to speak.

When a loud bang was heard outside, the regional security chief assured everyone that it was probably just a burst tyre. However, the German security staff felt uneasy. When she went outside, Merkel was delighted at the building work that was going on around the governor's residence, and at all the workmen on the scaffolding. She hadn't been told that these "workmen" were actually German Army snipers. Her bodyguards urged her to go back to the comparative security of the base camp – the explosion in the street had alarmed everyone. But Merkel wasn't going to show signs of weakness. She sent most of the delegation back to the camp, while she was driven to her next official engagement and visited a hospital, although she didn't stay long.

Visits by a German Chancellor are always theatrical productions, and in Afghanistan they are particularly stage-managed. Delighted as she was to hear the soldiers expressing their honest opinions at a barbecue that evening, this fact couldn't have been entirely lost on Merkel – even if the only thing the men wanted urgently was a new flag. The visit essentially served to recognize the troops' achievements, to flatter them – and help safeguard her political position. If the Chancellor didn't lead from the front she made herself vulnerable to attack and would be accused of lacking interest. But if she became too closely involved she might ultimately be held responsible for the transporter trucks not having the right sort of armour.

Nowhere can the dilemma that confronts the head of government be better illustrated than in the microcosm of a German army base far from home. On one hand, she can't avoid being part of the whole show – for instance, when a representative of the German Investment and Development Corporation tells her about the "Womens' Peace Caravan" project in the city of Kunduz. On the other, she is also representing a major political security operation that has to be coordinated on many different levels: with those who exercise power in Afghanistan (the government, the tribes, the local rulers); with the inner workings of military alliances that operate according to concepts such as solidarity and mutual support; and finally with the expectation of voters at home who don't really understand this distant war and don't want to hear bad news.

Yet the bad news came thick and fast in the spring of 2010, when seven German soldiers were killed in action within the space of a few weeks. Three men from Schleswig-Holstein died on Good Friday: their unit had been involved in a skirmish near Kunduz. Merkel was told as she was flying off for her Easter break. She cut short her holiday and went to the funeral in the town of Selsingen, where she talked to the victims' relatives – a moving experience. The families wanted to hear one thing above all from the Chancellor: that their sons' deaths had not been in vain, that the soldiers' mission was of importance to the country. Many family members also wrote to her after the funeral. One case affected her personally: Jörg Ringel, a police officer who for many years was a member of her close-protection team, was killed on a trip to Kabul. Merkel is still in touch with his family.

The day after the funeral in Selsingen she made a point of visiting the Bundeswehr Operational Command in Potsdam, from where the German forces in Afghanistan were controlled. General Rainer Glatz and his officers described the combat in detail, telling her about the large quantities of ammunition used. Soldiers from Afghanistan had their own say in a video conference, and demanded more moral support from Germany. Merkel was visibly moved by their accounts, and asked a simple question: how many Taliban had been shot in those ten hours? Embarrassed, the generals looked at the floor. No one knew the answer.

A week later, just after Merkel arrived in San Francisco on the last stage of a visit to the USA, her personal private secretary Beate Baumann was woken in the middle of the night by a call from Berlin: more fighting, more dead, this time four men had lost their lives. Merkel always takes black clothes with her on foreign trips so that she can be suitably dressed on such occasions, and the Federal press office always brings a folding blue screen to provide a neutral background for the cameras when she is giving interviews and making statements. Merkel gave a press conference early that morning, and set off for home in the evening.

On 22nd April 2010 she made what was probably her most forceful statement on Afghanistan, publicly acknowledging the troops and their mission. She spoke of their bravery, the fighting, the war, the alleged cowardice of politicians. "We cannot ask our soldiers to be brave if we ourselves lack the courage to stand up for our decisions," she warned MPs. Never before had Merkel spoken about the business of war with such feeling. She did so using the words of Staff Sergeant Daniel Seibert, who had been involved in a skirmish nine months earlier and was asked by an interviewer whether he had killed anyone. His reply, quoted by Merkel in the Bundestag, was this: "Yes, I shot my opponent. It was either him or me."

This, the primitive aspect of war, is not something that seems alien to Merkel. She can identify with the idea of a duel. The

Chancellor has reflected deeply on the act of killing as a last resort. She gave people an insight into her views on the morning of 2nd May 2011, when the news of Osama bin Laden's death was the focus of the world's attention. Merkel appeared in front of the cameras, made a statement, then answered three questions. One of them was this: "Chancellor, the successful operation that you describe was obviously a deliberate killing – there's plenty of evidence of that. Should German security forces be in a position to act in such a way against terrorists?" Merkel replied, "I am here today, first and foremost, to say that I am glad to hear that the plan to kill bin Laden succeeded... As a result I have sent a message to the American President expressing my respect for this successful operation; it was something I felt a need to do." She could not have conveyed her need to do so more clearly.

War and peace, the basis of present-day Germany's reservations about all that is military, the high expectations of the Federal Republic's partners in the alliance, the difficulty of getting a clear overview of the modern world, the speed with which moral indignation flares up over injustice, violence and tyranny – perhaps it was only logical that Merkel's foreign-policy decision that had the most serious consequences so far had to do with these difficult issues. It was 17th March 2011, a Thursday, and her closest colleagues had gathered in Beate Baumann's office to drink a toast to Merkel's foreign-policy adviser, Christoph Heusgen, on his birthday. But no one felt like celebrating. Baumann's office is not luxuriously furnished. Its only decoration is a geopolitical map of the world hanging on the wall and looking a little lost. That political world had taken another surprising turn.

The night before there had been a sudden change of mood at the United Nations in New York. The French President had got his way in the UN Security Council. A no-fly zone was to be declared over Libya, there would be war. The German government had to decide on a course of action. The Security Council was due to vote that evening, and as a non-permanent member Germany would have to take part in that vote. Did the Federal Government agree with a no-fly zone? And was it prepared to send German soldiers to get involved in a civil war in Libya?

March 2011 turned out to be a terrible month for Merkel. Everywhere, events seemed to be accelerating, one crisis came after another. In February the chairman of the Bundesbank, Axel Weber, had announced that he was retiring – he obviously distrusted the European Central Bank over the Eurozone crisis, although he never fully explained his reasons. On 1st March the country held its breath when Defence Minister Karl-Theodor zu Guttenberg accepted the consequences of a plagiarism scandal and announced his retirement from politics. At the end of February the Hamburg elections provided a foretaste of the problems the CDU, and particularly the FDP, were likely to face at the polls. The next regional elections – which included the CDU strongholds of Hesse and Baden-Württemberg – were on 20th and 27th March. There was also growing dissatisfaction with Merkel's coalition partner, Guido Westerwelle, leader of the FDP and Foreign Minister.

Then, further blows came in swift succession: at 14.47 on 11th March there was the Japanese tsunami, followed by the Fukushima nuclear disaster. During a summit in Brussels,

Merkel watched the spectacular hydrogen explosions on her iPad. As a believer in the power of images, she knew that this was another moment of reckoning: this tragedy turned everything upside down. "Until recently," she said in an interview, "I thought the dangers were beyond anything I was likely to see in my lifetime." Three days after the catastrophe she cancelled the extension of operational life for German nuclear plants and spectacularly reversed her energy policy – an act of defiance in the eyes of the industry and the coalition government.

Meanwhile the crisis in Libya was escalating. Since mid-February, the rebel forces had been taking over more and more of the country. At the beginning of March the regime began a counter-offensive, gradually winning back some of the territory. The city of Misrata and the suburbs of the rebel stronghold of Benghazi in eastern Libya were soon being shelled by government troops. Gaddafi announced that he would fight "from house to house" and that "no mercy would be shown".

The French President had been canvassing support for a Western intervention in Libya for a long time. Nicolas Sarkozy was under pressure: he had cut a poor figure in the first weeks of the Arab Spring. His proximity to the former Tunisian ruler was a problem. He had received Gaddafi in Paris. The eccentric potentate had come to France with his whole court, camping opposite the Élysée Palace in a Bedouin tent with his private Amazonian Guard. At the time, Sarkozy assured his countrymen that the dictator was a guarantee of stability and prosperous economic relations. Libyan oil was tempting too.

Now his favourite Mediterranean neighbour was butchering his own people.

Merkel was unenthusiastic about Sarkozy's eagerness to intervene in Libya, seeing it as a diversion. This was the most important reason for her abstaining to vote on it. She didn't want to be drawn into a war that, in her opinion, the Frenchman only wanted for reasons of domestic politics. Sarkozy was attempting to rewrite history – that was her damning verdict. Unlike him, she had always avoided Gaddafi, and had never met him except on the margins of large international gatherings. She also viewed the rebel movement in Libya and the rest of the Arab world with scepticism. She rejected any comparison with the Eastern European freedom movement in 1989 – although Guido Westerwelle had made use of the parallel. She thought that the political currents in these countries gave no clear indication of their likely future character as states.

Yet the Chancellor had another concern about military intervention. The Iraq experience had made a profound impression on her. She had pinned her hopes on the USA's ability to direct the course of events and bring peace. So her disappointment was all the greater when resistance in Iraq increased. The United States had essentially failed, and soon had to withdraw. Merkel was worried about America's ability to achieve its goals, and feared that Washington's influence would suffer, thus weakening the West as a whole in the rivalry between different systems. Exporting democracy is no easy matter, but Merkel's experience had given her confidence in the USA's ability to bring their values and their system to other countries. She was afraid it wouldn't work in Libya. And Washington couldn't afford another Iraq – a war that had had disastrous consequences. The next intervention had to work and lead to a better situation than the one that had existed before, or the credibility of the West as a whole would be in danger.

Finally, Merkel also had a reason based on domestic politics. If Germany voted for military intervention, then in her view Germany would have to take part. She told her colleagues that it would be disingenuous to agree to an operation and then not send any troops. In the days before the vote, this was discussed over and over again. Merkel was told that the country could take part symbolically – perhaps with German crew in AWACS reconnaissance planes. Or Germany could support a sea blockade, or provide financial assistance. Merkel and the Defence Minister, Thomas de Maizière, were not keen on this half-hearted option. From her analysis of the situation, a full-scale intervention would be too much for the Bundeswehr. Operations in Afghanistan, the Balkans, off the coast of Lebanon and in Somalia were stretching the German military to the limit.

However, the government was taken by surprise on the morning of Thursday 17th March 2011, because it had believed that the American President would refuse to go to war, and neither France nor Great Britain could do so without the United States. On the Wednesday morning, de Maizière returned from his inaugural visit to Washington as Foreign Minister – bringing with him a simple message from the Pentagon: the United States did not want war either. Particularly since all the American generals were clearly against it. In the course of that Wednesday, however, the situation of the rebels in Benghazi became increasingly desperate, and in

Washington the interventionist lobby around Secretary of State Hillary Clinton and UN Ambassador Susan Rice persuaded the President to change his mind. Barack Obama didn't call Merkel to let her know, which was an affront. But neither did the Chancellor call Washington. There was radio silence between their respective staffs. It wasn't until three months later that Merkel and Obama were able to have a conversation about it. On the evening before her state visit to Washington the Chancellor had dinner with the President in a small restaurant and told him, probably in fairly blunt terms, that there must never be such a breach of trust between them again.

So Merkel learnt of this change of heart indirectly, through the German Ambassador to the United Nations, Peter Wittig. Wittig, one of the most experienced German diplomats, had used Germany's non-permanent seat in the Security Council, set for a two-year period, to improve its image at the UN. On the Thursday he asked for instructions: should he vote for the no-fly zone that evening, vote against it or abstain? The advice of diplomats, including those from the Foreign Ministry and the Chancellery, was to vote in favour. A humanitarian disaster was looming – world reaction to a German abstention or a vote the other way didn't bear thinking about.

Besides, Germany could not oppose its most important allies. Adopting a different position to that of France and the USA would break two rules that to Merkel were particularly sacred: never act against the United States and never contribute to a split in Europe. If Germany were to abstain or vote against, then it would find itself on the same side as the Chinese and Russians, questionable bedfellows on the matter of human rights and domestic freedoms. Both countries rejected the intervention-ist policy of the West, but for a different reason: they feared that it would set a precedent. Interfering in another country's domestic affairs on humanitarian grounds – it could happen to them as well.

The decision about the German vote was made in the Chancellor's office. It involved the Chancellor, the Foreign Minister and the Defence Minister. Their civil-service advisers – Christoph Heusgen on Merkel's side, Minister of State Emily Haber for Westerwelle – had argued for a "yes" vote. Now Westerwelle, de Maizière and Merkel were on the same side. In a telephone conversation with his British counterpart, Westerwelle had made it clear that they ought to leave room for negotiations with the Arab League, and plans were made to persuade Gaddafi to leave Libya and go into exile abroad.

Westerwelle is always reluctant to support military intervention. In the early days of the coalition both parties had to argue for a long time over the continuation of the United Nations man-date in Lebanon. The Foreign Minister sees himself as having a "traditionally reserved" position regarding the military, and likes to quote the well-known foreign-policy father figure of the FDP, Hans-Dietrich Genscher: "I will be happy to give anyone in search of adventure the telephone number of the French Foreign Legion."

After the meeting between the three Ministers, instructions were sent to New York for the German Ambassador to abstain. Merkel had weighed up her options. What worried her most was the possibility of an unsuccessful operation with unpredictable consequences. The prospect of the likely domestic consequences of a decision in favour of war was not appealing, particularly in the run-up to regional elections. The situation was clearly heading towards a major conflict with the CDU's coalition partner, the FDP, and in his role as chairman, Guido Westerwelle was already severely tarnished and pleaded particularly strongly against sending German soldiers.

Yet to its partners in the alliance, the media and even the opposition, the government appeared in a very different light: while Gaddafi's troops were storming towards Benghazi, Germany refused to vote for humanitarian intervention – aligning itself with China and Russia.

No one among the coalition leadership had expected what would come next. Reaction to the German vote was devastating. Internationally and at home, Merkel and Westerwelle were chastised: a tidal wave of anger broke over the government. At home, there was great turmoil: the Greens and elements of the SPD led the chorus of criticism. Germany was accused of lack of solidarity and isolationism. Merkel, once Schröder's greatest critic, was now repeating what he had done in 2003. There was uproar at the NATO council meeting when, after remarks made by the General Secretary, Anders Fogh Rasmussen, the German envoy stormed out. The alliance was in crisis. Germany was isolated, and felt the bitterness that came from every side. Western strategists almost tore themselves apart trying to analyse the significance and likely consequences of the abstention. Where did this government think it was going? Had Merkel and Westerwelle acted out of fear of the regional elections, in other words was it nothing but a calculated move based on domestic politics? Had Merkel even been blackmailed with the threat of a split in the coalition?

With his pacifist slogans, Westerwelle had always been accused of populism. The rumour mill went into overdrive.

On the Friday, after the Bundestag had discussed the situation following an official statement by the Foreign Minister, speculation was heightened by a rumour. It was suggested that Westerwelle had wanted to vote "no", but the Chancellor had persuaded him to content himself with abstention – a form of compromise. The Foreign Office blamed the Chancellery for the rumour, the Chancellery strenuously denied it. But the Foreign Minister was seething. He felt that Merkel had gone behind his back and made him look foolish. In his view, the Chancellor had shied away from the vote and now wanted to escape the consequences at his expense, leaving him to defend the decision in public. In the event Westerwelle did defend it – first by making a statement to the Bundestag, and then in a series of interviews and newspaper articles that only made matters worse.

It was Westerwelle's statement that set the tone for a line of argument in which the Minister whipped himself into a frenzy of self-justification. He constantly pressed the point that Germany hadn't been alone in abstaining. Brazil and India – as well as China and Russia – were also sceptical. Westerwelle even spoke of "strategic partners". Among Germany's allies this was met with astonishment. Was Westerwelle trying to rewrite alliance policy? Was the Foreign Minister currying favour with the emerging economies? Westerwelle proceeded to distance himself further and further by repeating at every available opportunity that military action would have been over-hasty and counter-productive. In contrast, Merkel said little. She gave only two press conferences, in which she tried to strike a conciliatory note, wishing Germany's allies success, emphasizing the solidarity of the alliance.

Libya left deep, painful scars. Even now, the rift between Westerwelle and Merkel has still not been mended. Westerwelle is at ease with himself and his decision, and unlike the Chancellor now makes his distaste for military intervention almost an article of faith. Merkel blows hot and cold. Depending on her mood, friends say, she either justifies Germany's abstention or broods on it. She paid a high price for her decision. She would prefer not to have to go through it all again. In the end, was the price too high? She would never admit as much in public, but it might have been the worst decision she has made on foreign policy during her time as Chancellor.

The Light of Zion

The Fascination of Israel

Angela Merkel's foreign policy is above all carefully controlled, measured and flexible. If it is likely to contribute to a positive outcome, then she will always leave room for compromise. But there is one exception: Israel. Merkel's relationship with Israel is a wholly emotional one. The Chancellor is rarely as passionate and single-minded than when it comes to the State of Israel and the Jews. Israel forms the basis of her foreign-policy axis – comparable in significance to the European Union and the USA. It is Merkel's deeply held conviction that Israel is part of Germany's raison d'être as a state. This has been the subject of much intense debate, and yet such discussions leave Merkel unmoved. She has developed a profound connection with Israel and the Jews. Her understanding of German history, and thus the historical context of the direction taken by her policies as Chancellor, is inextricably bound up with the Shoah, the annihilation of the Jews by Germans. Consequently, her policy towards Israel, her respect and support for the Jewish way of life and the interpretation of its history are a major priority. Merkel is unequivocal on the subject: she loves the country, and in Germany's historical involvement with Israel she sees a national duty that goes beyond anything envisaged by her predecessors.

It is not quite clear where this deeply felt proximity to Israel originated. Even those who are closest to her and have witnessed her at decisive moments in matters of foreign policy cannot really provide an answer. Merkel has established close connections with many representatives of Jewish life in Germany, and keeps in touch with the more important factions in Israeli politics. She has a particularly good relationship with the former Prime Minister of Israel, Ehud Olmert.

Her inner circle of advisers serves as a sounding board when it comes to Israel: Beate Baumann has a particular interest in the history of relationships with Israel and the significance of the Holocaust. Christoph Heusgen maintains strategic contact, especially when Merkel acts as mediator in the peace process; the former minister of state in the Chancellery, Hildegard Müller, and her successor Eckart von Klaeden, are responsible for social contact with the Jewish community. For years – at Merkel's request – Müller was chairman of the German-Israeli group of MPs, and has an excellent network of contacts in Israel. Finally, there is Shimon Stein, the Israeli Ambassador to Germany from 2001 to 2007. Merkel developed a personal friendship with him that continued after his time as ambassador – Stein has a level of access to her that only two or three other ambassadors enjoy. He has characteristics that allow such relationships to work: he is passionate and hot-headed, enjoys a debate, knows how to be discreet and likes opera – always an advantage in getting to know Merkel and especially her husband.

The reason for Merkel's strong feelings for Israel and the Jews do not lie only in her personal history. In interviews she has said that when she was at school, she and her class used to go to the former concentration camp at Ravensbrück, thirty kilometres from Templin. These visits were part of the history curriculum in schools in the GDR. Ravensbrück was originally built as a concentration camp for women; later, a camp for men and young people was added. The Nazis kept 150,000 prisoners there, using them as forced labour before sending them to death camps. It isn't known how many people died in total at Ravensbrück. Towards the end of the war, a gas chamber was built in the camp, and about 6,000 inmates were murdered there.

Merkel remembers that under the East German educational system emphasis was placed on any Communist and Social Democrat victims in the camp. According to the GDR's version of history, East Germany had played only a minor role in the persecution of the Jews. In fact the state's very legitimacy was based on distancing itself from the National Socialists. "I spent the first thirty-five years of my life in a part of Germany – the German Democratic Republic – that regarded National Socialism as solely a West German problem," she explained in her historic speech to the Israeli Parliament. The GDR considered itself the antithesis of Fascist Germany; it based its historical image on Communist and Socialist – and perhaps also Social Democrat – resistance. To acknowledge the Holocaust would have meant sharing responsibility for it. Then the GDR would have had its own historical burden to bear.

Merkel remembers that if any of the pupils at her school ever asked what happened to the Jews at Ravensbrück, then they were told. But only if they asked. At home, however, the

Kasners talked a lot about National Socialism and the murder of the Jews. So it can be assumed that Merkel's understanding of history is based on discussions with her parents and articles in the Western media. The West German President Richard von Weizsäcker's speech on 8th May 1985, which marked the fortieth anniversary of the end of the war, made a strong impression on her. Through her father's Church contacts she managed to get a copy, and took it to work with her at the Academy of Sciences, where it circulated and was discussed. "It was an impressive speech," she said later – although not because von Weizsäcker presented the 8th of May to West Germans as the Day of Liberation. People were already familiar with that term in the GDR, where the Soviet designation of 8th May as the Day of Liberation and 9th May as the Day of Victory of the Great Fatherland had long been adopted. The main reason why Weizsäcker made such a deep impression on the East Germans was because he spoke of the history of Germany as indivisible. "We Germans are one people and one nation. We feel that we belong together, because we have lived through the same history" – these were the comments that stuck in Merkel's mind. But having the same history meant sharing responsibility for what the National Socialists had done.

The East German attitude to its history and to the state of Israel used to make Merkel furious. She was always saying that, as a scientist, she wasn't able to quote Israeli sources in her subject area; the GDR didn't recognize it as a state, and there was no official contact with the country. Yet important research papers were being produced at the Weizmann Institute near Tel Aviv. Merkel said that she wrote to scientists in the United States to try and get hold of Israeli material by a roundabout route. Yet that alone is not enough to account for her feelings for Israel. So is she attempting to overcompensate for what she felt was GDR guilt about the Jews? This could be one of the factors, although not the deciding one. Merkel didn't develop any connections with Israel as a girl, didn't have any conversations with Israelis of her own age during exchange visits, and never thought about herself or her own role in the way every post-war West German politician had in his or her youth when taking part in German-Israeli meetings. Merkel had no such experiences until she became a government minister. So we must assume that other factors played a part: religion, and particularly her understanding of history.

In 1991, when Merkel had just become Minister for Women and Youth, one of her first foreign trips was to Israel. The story of her arrival has often been repeated with much satisfaction. Merkel flew to Tel Aviv with the Minister for Research, Heinz Riesenhuber. Riesenhuber was a heavyweight in Helmut Kohl's Cabinet, and was given an adequately warm reception by his Israeli counterpart and the media – while the young minister from the East suddenly found herself shunted into the background. The German ambassador, Otto von der Gablentz, who had been Chancellor Helmut Schmidt's foreign-policy adviser and was an outstanding diplomat, devoted all his attention to Riesenhuber. He didn't even notice that the young minister from the East was shedding tears of rage – a weakness that Merkel quite often displayed early on in her political career. With great effort she managed to control herself. Journalists present were sympathetic towards this young woman from former East Germany, tolerated as a kind of mouse figure in the great game of politics. But when on her own initiative Merkel managed to engineer a meeting with the Israeli Foreign Minister, David Levy, her stock rose rapidly in the Ambassador's eyes – suddenly he was anxious to be seen in her company.

Merkel later recalled another episode on that visit. In the Monastery of Tabgha on the Sea of Galilee, she visited German monks at a priory that was connected to the Benedictine Abbey of Dormitio on Mount Zion in Jerusalem. At the 1995 Hamburg Church Congress she spoke openly about her faith, and among other things mentioned her visit to Tabgha. A monk took her round the monastery and pointed out the alleged site of the parable of the miraculous loaves and fishes. "So we stood in that hilly landscape and looked at the fertile plain in which the Sea of Galilee lies, and the monk told us: 'This is where Jesus came down from the mountain, and then he was here, beside the lake; and if you go along to the next bay, that is where he met Peter the fisherman, and if you go a little farther you are at the scene of the feeding of the five thousand, and then he crossed from here, and then came the storm on the lake.'"

Merkel was clearly impressed by the man's profound faith. "That monk had a source of strength which was evident from his words. I envied him a little." Merkel knows her Bible, as she has repeatedly shown when working on texts at Church congresses, and can distinguish between Luther's translation and the modern "Unified Translation". A woman who grew up so close to the Old and New Testaments in her father's parsonage was bound to be awestruck when she saw the scenes of the Biblical tales of her childhood with her own eyes.

Unlike her predecessor Helmut Kohl, Angela Merkel is not a politician who indulges in history lessons. When Kohl spoke of the significance of Europe it was a matter of war and peace. At the heart of Merkel's Europe lies globalization and the dangers of the future. Merkel is the first Chancellor of Germany to have been born after the end of the Second World War – in 1954, ten years after Gerhard Schröder, who was a war baby. If she embodies German history in any way, it is for the period of the GDR and reunification; she was an eyewitness to the divided Germany. She gladly accepts invitations to events that further historical under-standing of the GDR and help people to come to terms with its past. Apart from that she is sparing in her use of historical refer-ences and memories. But there is one exception: the systematic annihilation of European Jews by National Socialist Germany.

Merkel prefers not to use the word Holocaust. She speaks of the Shoah, as they do in Israel, and the term is becoming increasingly accepted in Germany. The choice of word is not insignificant. Historical studies tend to concentrate on the Jews' image of themselves as victims, and the distinction between those who were murdered and those who were born later. Holocaust research has always been faced with the problem of finding adequate words to describe the unique nature of what happened without being judgemental. "Holocaust", an ancient term for the burnt offering of an animal, complete destruction by fire, is a divisive word. It is frequently associated – particularly in English-speaking countries and Germany – with the American television series shown in 1978, and the debate about the museum built in Washington at the time, in memory of the murdered Jews. But it is precisely because of this reference to burnt offerings that the word is rejected in Israel. European Jews were not killed as sacrifices to God, and their annihilation was not a religious act. It was the act of a godless, bloodthirsty dictatorship. As a result, and particularly in Israel, the term that has come to be accepted is Shoah – the Hebrew word for "great catastrophe" or "disaster". Merkel has adopted Hebrew terminology, which shows how close she is to the Jewish understanding of this uniquely horrifying act.

Merkel went to Israel four times in her first seven years as Chancellor, has made important policy speeches before the Knesset and has received an honorary doctorate from the Hebrew University. In Germany, the Jewish community has bestowed many awards on her, including the famous Leo Baeck Prize. In 2009, at the height of the financial crisis, she gave the memorial speech on the seventieth anniversary of Kristallnacht. She takes such speeches very seriously, writing them in close collaboration with colleagues, who supply her with the initial drafts. She often writes them herself, or makes many changes to the text. And her speeches never fail to mention that, because of the Shoah, Germany bears responsibility for Israel. "In a very particular sense, Germany and Israel are and will remain for ever linked by the memory of the Shoah," she said in the Israeli parliament.

Whenever Merkel speaks of the Shoah, two lines of argument appear: "Never again" and "What is to be done?" In her view, the lesson we have to learn is that xenophobia, racism and anti-Semitism must never be allowed to happen again. Merkel often uses these three terms, and it is worth noting that, depending on the occasion, she mentions xenophobia or racism ahead of anti-Semitism. Only in the Israeli parliament did she deliberately put anti-Semitism first. Today, she probably sees racism in general as a greater danger than hatred of the Jews in particular. For Merkel, "never again" implies the task of promoting the relationship between Germans and the Jewish community, and taking responsibility for "the security of the State of Israel and our common values". Values play a key role in Merkel's view of Israel. It was during the Arab Spring that she came to see that only Israel, as a constitutional democracy, upholds a European value system in the region. So she is all the more upset when Israel doesn't respect these values – especially in the building of settlements.

But she also takes concrete steps to convey the lessons of history. For instance, she asked in the Knesset, "How do we keep the memory of the Shoah alive when there are no more contemporary witnesses, when those who experienced that time have all gone?" On another occasion she said that it always disconcerts her to think how quickly those living witnesses, and the terrible things they saw, can pass into oblivion. "That brings me to a crucial question: how are we to understand our historical responsibility when the generation who experienced and survived the Shoah is no longer with us?"

Merkel has twice been faced very directly with the question of how to deal with responsibility, given the modern tendency to see everything in relative terms and to rewrite history. On both occasions she clashed with the conservative and Christian wing of her own party. On both occasions she paid a price: on the first because she did too little, on the second because she made too forceful a stand. The first of these challenges to her authority concerns a certain Martin Hohmann. An MP from Fulda, he made a speech on 3rd October 2003 – when Merkel was Chairman of the CDU and its parliamentary party. Hohmann claimed that the view of the German people as murderers was only relative, and said that "the godless, with their godless ideologies" were to blame. "They were the perpetrators of the bloodshed in the last century." Going even further, Hohmann asked a rhetorical question: whether there was not also "a dark side" to the Jewish people. Later, in the context of the Russian Revolution, he said that there was "a certain justification" for describing the Jews themselves as perpetrators.

As Party Chairman Merkel reprimanded Hohmann, and made him apologize. However, when the ultra-conservative MP repeated his theories in an interview, Merkel felt she should suspend him from the party. There was resistance from all sides of the CDU. The main problem was that Merkel couldn't provide any good reasons for expelling Hohmann from the parliamentary party but not from the party itself. But then she changed her mind and demanded his expulsion from the entire party. She was to pay a high price for her indecision.

By contrast, in February 2009, at the end of her first term as Chancellor, Merkel showed great decisiveness when she took on no less a man than the Pope, Benedict XVI. At the end of January, the Pope had received four bishops of the traditionalist Society of St Pius X back into the Roman Catholic Church. A few days earlier, Bishop Richard Williamson, one of the four, had denied that any Jews were murdered during the Nazi period. The incident put great pressure on Pope Benedict, who was strongly criticized within the Church. Merkel waited for a few days, and then used a press conference with the President of Kazakhstan to answer an obviously planted question about her opinion of Williamson and the Pope. Significantly, Merkel began by speaking of a "matter of principle", and then went on to say: "It must be so unambiguously clarified by the Pope and the Vatican that there can be no denial of what happened [...]. As I see it, those clarifications have not yet been adequately made."

The Catholic areas of Germany – and the Christian Democratic Union – all shuddered. Could Merkel criticize the Pope in such an aggressive manner? Could she really issue him with a warning and demand clarification? Could she imply that he had an ambiguous attitude to the Holocaust? The Vatican reacted immediately by publishing a clarification. Nonetheless, the atmosphere had been soured. The diplomatic repercussions went on for weeks. Bishops discussed the case, many German Catholics praised Merkel's comments, while others thought her criticism disrespectful. But the main problem was that Merkel had created friction within her own party. Once again, she was accused of neglecting the Christian aspect of the Christian Democratic Union and betraying its Catholic roots – an allegation that, as a Protestant from East Germany, had dogged her from her first day as Party Leader. The CDU was submerged with criticism from the media. Catholic voters wondered where they stood in the party; this was about values, political ideas, security, traditions. With a single sentence, Merkel had exposed a hotbed of mistrust within her party.

Yet Merkel believed that she was only being true to herself. Anyone who had heard or read her speech to the Knesset or the one she gave when she received the Leo Baeck Prize – anyone who was familiar with the background to the Chancellor's personal ties with Israel – knew that this was a matter of principle, not political manoeuvring.

But is that strictly true? Is everything concerning Israel perfectly clear? In Merkel's complex tapestry of relationships there is always a political dimension. In this respect, too, the Chancellor differs from her predecessors. She has raised German-Israeli relations to a new level, because questions of war, peace and security have suddenly become an issue again. Yet in order to examine this dimension, one must start from the conclusion: for Merkel, Germany's existence as a united country and a democracy is inseparably bound up with a correct understanding of the history of Israel. As early as 2009, during the Hohmann debate within the CDU, she made this remarkable comment: "It is because we have recognized the Holocaust as a singular event that we can say today: we are free, we are united. That recognition has made us what we are today." Or, to put it the other way round: if Germany had not accepted its history and had been forced to come to terms with its past, the country would have been excluded from the unity and sovereignty of its neighbours, from the community of nations. A close friend of the Chancellor sums it up quite simply: without the USA and the Holocaust, Germany would not exist.

For Merkel, an urgent political duty arises from that historical recognition: the Shoah has not only bound Germany and Israel inextricably together, it has also given Germany a leading role in the construction of Israel's security and the protection of the country's right to exist. Merkel describes this operational and political task as a "reason of state".

Merkel's speeches tend to be more significant than the public generally realizes. She puts more thought, intellectual effort and subtext into a speech than is read into it later. It is unfortunate that, as a politician who is acknowledged not to be an eloquent speaker, she can seldom make this second level of her thought process accessible to a wider public. It is also unfortunate that Merkel always makes her most important statements in front of the democratically elected representatives of the people. She sees parliament as the centre of democracy – and so, for her, that is where her major speeches should be made. Anyone wanting to know what Merkel has to say on important matters – Europe, the transatlantic alliance, the state of the nation – will always be told the same thing: read the official statement, the Chancellor said it all there. It is a shame that the public usually fails to grasp the true meaning of those statements – they are drowned out in the hubbub of Berlin politics.

On occasion, Merkel has successfully avoided the trap of her own self-effacement and managed to attract attention, once at the United Nations in New York, and another time when speaking to the Knesset. She had been in office for just under two years when, in September 2007, she spoke to the UN assembly, that forum of the world community, outlining her personal beliefs on what holds the world together. Among the things she mentioned were growth and social justice, the importance of the rule of international law, embodied by the United Nations, and her inevitable profession of faith – Merkel spoke passionately, and concealed within her speech was a political gem. In the passage about the UN's authority and ability to assert itself, particularly with regard to Iran, readers will find these remarks, which are laden with meaning:

"Every Chancellor before me was committed to Germany's special responsibility for the existence of Israel. I too pledge myself to that historical responsibility. It is part of my country's reason of state. Which is to say that to me, as Chancellor of Germany, the security of Israel is never negotiable." The press sat up and took notice, the message had been delivered – although it hadn't quite sunk in yet.

Six months later Merkel was awarded an unexpected honour. The state of Israel was sixty years old, and the German Chancellor, who had a particularly close relationship with the Olmert government, was invited to speak in the Knesset. Up till then, only heads of state had been allowed to speak in the Israeli parliament. Merkel was the first head of government to do so; not only that, she made her speech in German, a language likely to attract hostility.

This was probably the most emotionally charged foreign trip she had ever made – Merkel felt the weight of history and expectation. As so often, her visit began at Yad Vashem, the impressive monument to the Shoah outside the gates of Jerusalem. There are two places there that move Merkel particularly: as you leave the museum tunnel and climb towards the light, as if walking up a ramp, the sky and the landscape suddenly opens out before you in a vast sweep. The second is the memorial to the murdered children. This is where the tour of Yad Vashem officially ends, at the place where the children are remembered. Visitors are taken up a spiral passage like the inside of a snail shell into a dark cave, where the eyes become accustomed to the half-light only slowly. You make your way through the darkness step by step, and the light of three candles is reflected to infinity around the room. The effect of so many reflections induces a sense of vertigo. A quiet voice reads out the names of the children and young people murdered in the Shoah, with their age and the place where they lived – a million and a half of them lost their lives. A million and a half names, every name a human being. As you come out you are dazzled by the sun reflecting on the surrounding rocks.

For official visitors, there is a guestbook to sign as they leave. It is an unforgiving moment: at the very point when their emotions are in turmoil, all cameras are focused on them as they attempt to sum up their feelings in a single sentence which they then have to read out. In Merkel's case, of course, provision had been made, and she wrote her carefully prepared words in the book: "In acknowledgement of Germany's responsibility for the Shoah, the Federal Government wishes to emphasize its determination, after the first German-Israeli consultations, to shape a joint future."

It is images such as these that bear witness to the emotional effect that the Shoah has on Merkel. With every visit to Yad Vashem she understands less and less how the Germans could kill so many people – simply for belonging to a different ethnic group.

The last day of Merkel's visit to Israel took her to the Knesset. In 2000, President Johannes Rau had been invited to speak to the parliament – at the time the first and only German to do so. Now the Chancellor stood in front of the stone wall, and several MPs left the hall in protest. For the most part, Merkel repeated passages that she had used in speeches on other occasions – such as when she was given an honorary degree by the Hebrew University the year before. In the Knesset, she had to outline her view of the German-Israeli relationship, and her words resembled a legacy.

Once again, Merkel began by saying that Germany and Israel were linked for ever by the memory of the Shoah; again she mentioned the break with civilization that the event represented and the responsibility laid upon Germany by history. But then she spelt out what she understood by a modern German-Israeli partnership. Only the day before, the first German-Israeli governmental consultations had taken place. The Merkel government established this diplomatic practice with various states in order to emphasize the particular depth of their relationship. It involves a delegation of ministers meeting their counterparts in the other state – almost like a bilateral cabinet session. It had been Ambassador Shimon Stein who, three years earlier, had regretted the absence of any formal symbol for the relationship between their countries to Merkel over a glass of red wine in the King David Hotel in Jerusalem, and so the idea of intergovernmental dialogue was born.

Now Merkel was standing in front of the Israeli parliament and reading out the small print. "What exactly do unique relationships mean? Is my country actually aware of what those words mean – not just in speeches and on official occasions, but when it really matters?" asked the Chancellor. She went through the list of issues that lay ahead: continuing to preserve the memory of the past, driven by the concern that the Shoah might one day be forgotten; the massive shift in public attitudes to Israel as a result of the unresolved problems of the Middle East; and finally, threats to Israel from outside, particularly from Iran, its President Mahmoud Ahmadinejad and its nuclear programme. The moment had come, as it had six months earlier at the United Nations, for a key statement that would bind Merkel to Israel for ever: "Every German government and every German Chancellor before me was pledged to Germany's particular historical responsibility for the security of Israel. That historical responsibility of Germany is one of my country's reasons of state. This means that for me as German Chancellor, Israel's security is non-negotiable – and if that is the case, then when those words are put to the test they must not be found to be empty."

What exactly does Merkel mean, then, by "reasons of state", in practical terms? Does she contemplate sending in troops in the event of an attack on Israel? Would Germany take part in a military strike on Iranian nuclear plants? Merkel would not have been acting in character if she had given clear answers to these crucial questions. For all her loyalty in principle to Israel, she has left the details somewhat unclear in order to leave her room for manoeuvre. In the Knesset she gave only vague answers to the many questions about Iran. "Germany and its partners are hoping for a diplomatic solution. If Iran does not make concessions, the Federal Government will continue in its firm support for sanctions." Sanctions? Merkel doesn't even address the genuine danger of an escalation. She doesn't seem to have heeded her own warning that "when those words [on the non-negotiability of Israel's security] are put to the test they must not be found to be empty". It was in 2011, at the beginning of the Arab Spring, that Merkel last used reasons of state as an argument. "Supporting the security of the state of Israel as a democratic Jewish state is part of Germany's reasons of state." Full stop. No more words. No more decisions to be carried out.

Merkel has been much criticized for this vagueness. Frank-Walter Steinmeier, the then Foreign Minister, and later SPD Leader of the Opposition, said there was a "responsibility to keep promises" that had been made in such a significant place as the Knesset, which had raised expectations. But what are these expectations? In Israel itself, the "reason of state" has not produced any importunate demands. None of its politicians has insisted that Merkel should explain the meaning of the phrase. The country looks after its own security, and the last thing it expects is guarantees of solidarity from Germany or even NATO. If they want anything at all, the Israelis would wish to use German anti-aircraft systems such as the Patriot as a fall-back option, as they did during the Iraq war. Nor will Merkel's words intimidate Iran. It is certainly a matter of making a clear political statement, such as the one Germany has made many times regarding the Iranian nuclear programme: Iran must disclose its plans and be subject to controls. In practice, however, sanctions and export controls have attracted severe criticism from countries such as the USA, which called for more determined action from Germany in isolating Iran.

And then there is Merkel herself: she has not said anything to clarify the question. Even among her inner circle there are different shades of interpretation. Some speak of symbolism, a political statement. The fact is that Germany cannot be neutral on the subject of Israel, and in a war against Iran that could be demonstrated in many ways: financial assistance, no-fly zones, weapons. Yet it is unrealistic for Germany to contemplate sending troops. True, Merkel has always pointed out that after a peaceful solution to the problems between the Israelis and the

Palestinians, Germany could make a contribution on the ground – such as providing soldiers to man a buffer zone in the Jordan valley. But Israel would not take kindly to that, nor would it be easy to get a majority in the Bundestag to approve a German military presence anywhere near Israel. As for the possibility of German soldiers having to open fire on Israelis in a conflict – that is unthinkable.

Merkel realizes that when it comes to the military protection of Israel, she has raised expectations that no one will be able to meet. The reason-of-state argument will probably fade away eventually, when she is no longer Chancellor. Nonetheless, her unequivocal declaration of faith follows the logic of her Middle East policy, which has been working in very practical ways towards a peace settlement between Israel and the Palestinians. When Merkel first became Chancellor, she seized the moment in the key areas of her policy towards Israel. Her predecessor, Gerhard Schröder, had left Israel and the two-state solution to his Foreign Minister, while he concentrated on economic relations with the Gulf states and Saudi Arabia. In the immediate aftermath of the Iraq war, the United States and President George W. Bush were weakened as guarantors of order. Later, Secretary of State Condoleezza Rice, after intensive preliminary work with Germany, invested much political capital in setting up a peace process, although the negotiations at Annapolis failed at the eleventh hour.

Merkel acquired much political capital for herself from the Israelis, not only for speaking out so convincingly on German responsibility and guilt, but also for meeting a key demand of the Israeli government by recognizing the "Jewish character of the State of Israel". This phrase implies a number of political consequences: first there is the idea that in order to retain its present character, Israel must be a religious state. However, this concession to the religious lobby ignores the question of what will happen to the Arab minority in the country and what rights they will have. Second, the phrase gives voice to the expectation that there must be a two-state solution. The demographic reality in the area occupied by the Israelis and Palestinians could not be clearer. A single state with a Jewish character cannot expect to hold its own, because the Jews are clearly in a minority. If Israel were to refuse to allow the Palestinians to have their own state, and thus under international law remain an occupying power in Palestine, then a Jewish minority would dominate an Arab majority, and the democratic character of Israel and its unique characteristic in the region would be destroyed, and it would become an apartheid state.

Before she became Chancellor, Merkel made sure that the phrase concerning the "Jewish character of the state" was in the CDU party manifesto. The majority of MPs had not noticed the fine distinction, but experts on foreign policy such as Wolfgang Schäuble had heated arguments with Merkel. Schäuble's warnings now seem justified. Under the Netanyahu government the possibility of a two-state solution has retreated into the distance, and a number of people now believe that it cannot be achieved because of the policy over the settlements – in which case Merkel ought to change the wording. But she not only enshrined the mention of "Jewish character" in the party manifesto, but also in the coalition agreement with the SPD and later the FDP. To Israel this is evidence of good faith, a sign that Germany and Israel are coming together.

The confidence that she inspired came in useful to Merkel in the war in Lebanon in 2006. At the request of the governments of both countries, Berlin sent inspectors to Beirut airport, while ships from the German navy lay off the Lebanese coast to intercept illegal supplies of armaments to Hezbollah. This operation provoked fierce arguments in the Bundestag – it was the first dispatch of German soldiers to the immediate vicinity of Israel. In the end Merkel got her way, and in the process established her reputation in the Arab camp as a credible mediator. Israel's Prime Minister Olmert described her as "a real friend", and said that Europe was lucky to have her.

Enthusiasm continued to grow over the course of the next few months, when prisoners, both alive and dead, were exchanged by Israel and Hezbollah, an operation facilitated by Germany. Later, German secret-service contacts proved useful when, after being imprisoned in the Gaza Strip for five years, the Israeli soldier, Gilad Shalit, a symbol of Israeli self-determination, was exchanged in 2011 for over a thousand Palestinian prisoners. Merkel presided over this important phase of European mediation in the Middle East, telephoning and travelling constantly to the region, maintaining equilibrium in the uncertain atmosphere of the European Union and doing important preliminary work for the USA's peace conference in Annapolis. Overall, as the Foundation for Science and Politics put it, the Chancellor made efforts to bring balance to the process. In particular she developed a close relationship with the Egyptian President Hosni Mubarak, the Lebanese Prime Minister Fuad Siniora and the Palestinian President Mahmud Abbas. But Merkel soon realized the limits of her influence when she came down openly on Israel's side after the 2009 war in Gaza. After a change of government in Israel in the spring of 2009, when Benjamin Netanyahu took over, her mediation efforts collapsed. Netanyahu gradually destroyed all hope of breathing new life into the peace process. UN reports of war crimes and human-rights violations during the Gaza conflict put the relationship under enormous strain, as did Israel's unusually violent reaction to the Gaza flotilla and their policy on settlements.

The final break with Netanyahu came in the autumn of 2011. For months, the Palestinians had been skilfully building up diplomatic pressure, and during the United Nations General Assembly they tried to force a reassessment of their status. It was clear that any attempt to be recognized as a state would fail in the Security Council. But their demand for reassessment enjoyed a great deal of support around the world. Merkel and the EU High Representative, Catherine Ashton, tried to broker a deal, forcing the Middle East Quartet to make a statement – but just before the breakthrough came, Jerusalem issued a rebuff: Netanyahu had agreed to the building of new settlements in the eastern part of the city.

Merkel was furious. She felt that Netanyahu had betrayed her. So when the Israeli Prime Minister tried her patience several more times in the late spring of 2012 – among other things, the content of confidential telephone calls was published in the Israeli press – Merkel drew her own conclusions. To phrase it in diplomatic language, "relations cooled". A year later, in November 2012, the Palestinians finally succeeded in getting their status upgraded by the United Nations: they would now be described as a "non-member observer state". This time Germany did not stand by Israel; like many other European countries they abstained from the vote, making it clear that in essence they supported the Palestinian policy of becoming a member state. In the difficult political situation between Germany and Israel, Merkel had come full circle. But it seems that the real test is yet to come.

Russia and Putin: Parallel Lives

A Much Loved Country, a Difficult President

Vladimir Putin must have known exactly what he was doing in the case of the dog. The Russian President loves dogs, but Angela Merkel does not. In fact she is afraid of them, especially after being attacked by a dog called Bessi in August 1995. Merkel was out cycling near her weekend cottage in the Uckermark, when her neighbour's gun dog went for her and bit her knee. After that Merkel gave up cycling and still tends to give dogs a wide berth. A man like Putin knows that kind of thing. He has an instinct for it.

So when Angela Merkel, who had just been sworn in as Chancellor, went on an official visit to Moscow in January 2006, the overtly muscular Putin presented her with a cuddly toy dog. It sat on the arm of her chair until her foreign-affairs adviser, Christoph Heusgen, had a chance to pick it up and whisked it out of the Kremlin as unobtrusively as possible. This was the first part of the malicious little act. The second came a year later. This time Putin received Merkel at his official residence on the Black Sea. The door suddenly burst open and his black Labrador, Koni, came bounding into the room, sniffed at Merkel and then lay down at her feet. Cameras recorded the scene: Merkel with lips pursed, legs tightly crossed, Putin with his legs apart, leant back in his chair, eyelids patronizingly lowered – what might be described as a sadistic pose. Obviously, Merkel doesn't like that kind of thing. Ever since then, her meetings with Putin have stuck strictly to the official programme and observed the correct protocol, so dogs are kept well away.

As with the United States, in her heart Merkel knows two Russias – her private Russia, and what might be referred to as her "business" Russia. As we have seen, Angela Kasner came to know this private Russia through language competitions at school, trips to the country, and reading its literature – Tolstoy and Dostoevsky are among her favourite authors. Contrary to rumours, she never studied in Russia, but she did visit Moscow, as well as the south of the country and the Caucasus. This aspect of Russia has positive associations for the Chancellor, who loves the Russian language and is fluent in it. But political Russia is inseparable from Vladimir Putin.

Putin had been President for five years when she became Chancellor. Later he swapped roles and spent some time as Prime Minister before returning as head of state in 2012. Ever since Merkel became Chairman of the CDU, Putin has been the leader of Russia. Not only that, they are almost the same age – Putin is two years older than her – and have followed similar paths in life, almost as if they were mirror images. Putin spent five years in Dresden, where he witnessed the collapse of the GDR and the Warsaw Pact and became fluent in German. Merkel grew up in the Soviet garrison town of Templin, showed her gift for languages by learning Russian, and like Putin experienced the fall of the Wall at first hand. While Merkel had always glorified the West, and demonstrated her love of freedom by following Western politics, 1989, the great year of change, certainly didn't transform Putin into an ardent democrat. Whenever Merkel and Putin meet, two world views collide. For Merkel, the fall of the Berlin Wall was a liberating experience, whereas for Putin, a lieutenant colonel in the KGB, it was a deeply traumatic event. He sees the collapse of the Soviet Union as a historic defeat.

So it is hardly surprising that their personal relationship has an enormous influence on German-Russian relations in general. In this instance foreign policy definitely has a personal dimension. Nor is it surprising that meetings between the two leaders are still sometimes marked by biting sarcasm. While a considerable amount of respect has also grown between them over the years, the rivalry has never quite disappeared, and the slightest cooling in their relationship is keenly felt. When Merkel received Putin in Berlin just after he had been reinstated as President, she chided him in stern, maternal tones that he was late as usual – possibly an allusion to Mikhail Gorbachev, who once said that "life punishes those who come too late".

Putin retorted that that was the Russian character – surely she knew that by now. The two of them have had some heated arguments. Merkel and her advisers will never forget a visit to the Black Sea in 2007. The year before she had won respect at home because she had used her first visit to Moscow after her election to meet Russian opposition politicians. Putin, who doesn't have many women in his entourage, had to learn that he wasn't dealing with someone to whom he could suggest a fashion show as evidence of German-Russian cooperation.

But the first real test of strength took place in Sochi. On the agenda were the oil and gas industries, matters of security,

Ukraine – all the usual topics. Putin played the KGB officer. Sometimes he shouted, then he would lower his voice and speak softly and insistently, using obscenities, scribbling on documents, pointing at figures, waving his arms about – the whole gamut of communication methods taught by the secret service. Not surprisingly, this behaviour reminded Merkel of the Stasi. She stood up to him; her old reflexes were suddenly aroused. Those who were there said later that he squeezed her arm at one point.

This sparring atmosphere still remains between Merkel and Putin. Yet the Russian President has learnt a lot by it, and now tries to beat Merkel at her own game. For example, if the Chancellor criticizes the way the Russian authorities deal with foreign dona- tions to political parties, Putin counters by referring to the German law on charities and societies and the conditions imposed on political activity. His message is: so what's the difference? In these clashes it is sometimes difficult not to get the impression that the Chancellor and the President are like an old married couple who have long got used to each other's ploys. As Merkel would say, you have to be on the qui vive with him. And Putin is always on his guard as well.

This fundamental mistrust hasn't prevented Merkel from pursuing policies beneficial to Russia when they coincide with her own convictions. In April 2008, for instance, as we have seen, she resisted fierce pressure from the United States when they wanted to smooth the way for Georgia and Ukraine to join NATO. At the NATO summit in Bucharest it was Merkel who refused to implement what was called the Membership Action Plan for these two unstable nations. The USA wanted to strengthen Georgia in particular, and use it as a bulwark and outpost on Russia's southern borders, as well as a gateway to Central Asia, which is rich in raw materials. Merkel baulked – there were too many unresolved conflicts, a constant danger of war, an unstable democracy and an odd choice of President in Saakashvili, whose only claim to fame so far was paying court to Washington.

President George W. Bush reacted angrily, whereas Putin showed his gratitude. As Merkel saw it, her decision was entirely objective – after all, she had every reason to snub Putin. The Russian President had offended her the year before at the Munich conference on security, when he delivered a violent polemic against the West, as if they were on the verge of war. Merkel had sat stony-faced and said nothing – as did the entire Western security establishment.

Merkel had great hopes for Putin's interim President, Dmitri Medvedev, who took office in the spring of 2008. Although the handover of power was carefully controlled and the new President was the protégé of the old one, the Chancellor hoped that it would now be easier to do business with Russia. She had long been among those who thought that the two men might represent two extremes, and that one day Medvedev would break free of Putin and develop a style of his own. She refused to accept the theory that as the representative of an authoritarian and bureaucratic Russia, Putin had Medvedev, who supported the oligarchs, on a leash. In the end the mystery was solved by Medvedev's presidency itself, when the outgoing head of state revealed the real plan for the handover of power at a press conference: their exchange of roles had been planned months before. Merkel was deeply disappointed – she had been duped.

The worst crisis involving Russia came in Medvedev's time in office when, at the beginning of August 2008, the President of Georgia, Mikheil Saakashvili, attacked the breakaway province of South Ossetia after a series of provocations and counter-provocations. Long, detailed studies were written about the out-break, causes and course of those hostilities: today they can be summed up in a few words. Saakashvili overestimated his own power and wanted conflict. Expecting support from abroad, he provoked people and reacted to taunts; he attacked and promptly fell into a Russian trap. Russia responded with a counter-attack and occupied South Ossetia, which has since declared independ-ence but has been recognized by only four states – naturally including Russia.

Merkel followed the crisis in the shadow of French President Nicolas Sarkozy, who had just taken over the presidency of the EU, and was whirling back and forth between the warring par-ties like a dervish. Her main concern was for the United States, in case they were forced to show more than political solidarity with Saakashvili. Her anger, however, was directed at Russia, which was flexing its muscles by parading columns of tanks in the heart of Georgia, far from South Ossetia. The Chancellor stood with Sarkozy and had to weather a fair amount of criti-cism, particularly from the USA: if Saakashvili had been allowed to join NATO three months earlier, there would have been no war. Merkel was indirectly accused of giving the green light to Russia, because her decision meant that this might be the last opportunity to consolidate the borders in the southern Caucasus.

Wrong, replied Merkel: Saakashvili started the war, and it would not have been good for NATO if he had done so under its auspices.

In any case, during the conflict she had flown to see Medvedev, and then to meet Saakashvili in Tbilisi. She made it clear on the flight back that she had made up her mind. Weighing the foolishness of Saakashvili against the disproportionate Russian reaction, she said, "Georgia is a free and independent country, and every free and independent country can decide, together with the members of NATO, how and when it will be accepted into that organiza-tion. There will be a preliminary report in December, and then the way will be clear to apply for membership of NATO." It was trademark Merkel: "together with the members of NATO" – in other words Germany also had to agree. Even four years later, the way had not cleared up. But Merkel wanted to stress to Russia that she would not tolerate occupations of the kind seen during the Cold War.

After seven years as Chancellor, Merkel is pragmatic to the point of bafflement over Russia. At the beginning of her Chancellorship she made use of her predecessor's close relationship with Putin – as the direct opposite of Schröder it was easy for her to keep her distance and take advantage of the recognition she gained as a result. A meeting with opposition politicians, a glass of wine with the Democrats – and an appropriate distance from the political oligarchy was restored. The ostentatious machismo of men like Gerhard Schröder and Helmut Kohl's love of saunas were not to her liking. She is also at odds with the romantic view that many Germans have of Russia, who see a spiritual bond between the two countries. Merkel certainly loves Russia as a country, but in her own way. She has difficulty with the wing of the CDU that glorifies it, having formed its impression of Russia in the time of Gorbachev and Yeltsin, and which now accuses her of failing to make strategic capital of that legacy. She replies that the days of Gorbachev are long gone – and that the old Russia no longer exists.

The Russian initiatives taken by her first Foreign Minister, Frank-Walter Steinmeier – the joint modernization initiative and the Central Asian strategy – are now on the back burner, perhaps because the world has again turned and Russia has embarked on a policy of obstructionism, and not only over problems such as Iraq or Syria, which affect the international community as a whole. Russia now rarely accepts any foreign-policy initiatives taken by Germany or the EU. The country no longer seeks rapprochement: it wants distance, and is busy building a Eurasian Union, a new sphere of influence. A somewhat more pragmatic attitude to Russia has been adopted by Merkel herself. The country resists all attempts to come closer; after many years as both President and Prime Minister, Putin has hardened rather than softened; the country's opposition is stronger and is currently reinventing itself. In the midst of the euro crisis Merkel has been evading the subject – but as a European neighbour, Russia is not about to disappear from the map.

Business or Conviction

A Conflict of Systems with China

Sometimes all it takes to see how quickly the world is changing is to look out of the car window. Angela Merkel has often had little choice but to do so, especially when she goes to China. The Chancellor has often been there, almost once a year. And, before he had to give up his post after the change of power in the Central Committee of the Communist Party, China's Premier Wen Jiabao used to come to Germany once a year. Presidents and heads of government come and go, which is why her relationship to Wen Jiabao was one of the constants in Merkel's Chancellorship.

And that view out of the car window is also a constant on Merkel's visits to China: it shows her whether there are more bicycles or cars on the roads, what makes of car are stuck in traffic jams, how the various districts of cities are rapidly evolving. Since Merkel became Chancellor there have been far fewer bicycles on Chinese roads and many more German cars. In Beijing you sometimes take your life in your hands by riding a bike. And beside the unchanging, honeycomb-like houses, new ones have been built in the style of old colonial villas or those in the historic areas of the city. A touch of Disney, Chinese-style – but also a sign of increasing prosperity that goes hand in hand with a sense of what is beautiful and valuable.

Angela Merkel cannot simply walk down the street when she is in China. It would offend her hosts if, as a guest of the state, she were to slip out of her hotel like a tourist and go for a walk. Security, protocol and political good manners all forbid it. Visits to the People's Republic – she always goes to Beijing and then visits one of the regions – are planned to the very last detail. China's leadership leaves nothing to chance. Once the German delegation tried to outwit their hosts and told them – on the spur of the moment – that the Chancellor would like to visit a street market. It didn't work: Chinese visitors to the market were carefully selected men and women from State Security. Only the stallholders couldn't be substituted in a hurry, as a brief conversation with the interpreter revealed.

Merkel adores this kind of experience, especially in China. Like any tourist she loves anything exotic, such as looking out of her hotel window and seeing a group of pensioners doing early-morning exercises. She likes to describe her visit to the Terracotta Army – a present to herself on her 56th birthday, which she celebrated in China. She was also impressed by the deputy governors whom she met over dinner at the German Embassy in Beijing. They were from regions that had hosted a travelling exhibition arranged by the Foreign Office and the Goethe Institute. Now they had come to Beijing, and had been invited to dinner by the German Ambassador, Michael Schäfer, who entertains regularly in his house on the Dongzhimenwai Dajie. During the meal there was simultaneous interpreting, which livened up the occasion. A simple question from Merkel elicited a torrent of responses from the guests: what did the governors think about when they went to bed at night, and what was the first thing they thought about when they woke up?

The reaction was completely uncensored: the governors told her about the enormous number of jobs that had to be created every year, the problem of migrant workers, social tensions in their regions, environmental problems and the high number of students. Merkel gulped. She had seldom been given such an unvarnished view of the host of problems in China. That evening she realized how vast the country really is.

Merkel's view of China has changed greatly during her two terms as Chancellor. Much of that is due to Wen Jiabao, the first Chinese politician she got to know. Over the years she built up a confident relationship with him. Wen Jiabao kept his promises, and in the same way Merkel was regarded in Beijing as reliable. The Chinese are masters at maintaining a distance in relationships. No one can truly penetrate their façade. It is quite possible that Merkel was deeply disappointed in her view of Wen Jiabao, whom she saw as honest and close to the people; one sometimes got the impression that she felt sorry for the man, who is very short, wears a permanently melancholy expression and has a heavy workload. Yet as she was unable to go any deeper, she has no real idea of the labyrinth of relationships and loyalties that surrounds a senior Chinese politician. Wen Jiabao's clan is regarded as very wealthy, and it is possible to pick up gossip about the combination of family interests and state power on every street corner in Beijing. Merkel has never said anything about that – but her respect for the achievements of the government of the diverse country of China, shaken by the explosion in its growth, has certainly increased with every visit.

Her closeness to Wen Jiabao was obvious even physically – the Premier became more and more relaxed with her. On her second visit, in 2007, he received the Chancellor in what, by Chinese standards, was a private atmosphere, wearing an open-necked shirt, in the hermetically sealed quarter of Zhongnanhai, reserved for VIPs, where the Party leadership lives and works. Behind tall walls and gates, there is an extensive area of parkland with residences, guesthouses, meeting rooms and pavilions, all attractively located on the banks of a lake. Few foreigners are invited there. In 2012 it was decided that the interpreting of the delegates' conversations should be simultaneous instead of consecutive, in order to save time. That was a considerable concession on the part of the cautious Chinese politicians, because spontaneity gives more time for conversation and less to thinking about the correct response. The art of dealing with these highly formal meetings consists, in any case, in getting through the worn-out subjects as quickly as possible, so as to leave that hackneyed conversation behind. Not an easy task, because the prearranged set of rules is inhibiting. Anyone who talks to a Chinese person and causes him or her embarrassment will get nowhere. Visits to China are also cultural case studies in openness and communication.

As a child of the GDR, Angela Merkel's experience of China is full of contradictions. On one hand she was bound to feel a deep dislike for the one-party system, its authoritarian leadership and suppression of dissidents. On the other she is obviously fascinated by China's dynamism and resilience. As banal as it may sound, in

German-Chinese relationships, imports, exports, money and commerce play a prominent role. Idealism versus realism – as Merkel's predecessors, Gerhard Schröder and Helmut Kohl, found out: the shrewdest approach was to strike a balance, avoid currying favour and insist on one's own values and the power of the law within certain limits. But what exactly are these limits?

For Merkel, China is a learning process. In 2007, the second year of the CDU-SPD coalition, she received the Dalai Lama in the Chancellery, causing the first government disagreement over foreign policy as well as upsetting Beijing. One of the major concerns of the Chinese leadership is the disintegration of the People's Republic. Few subjects preoccupy the leaders of the Communist Party as much as the collapse of the Warsaw Pact and the Soviet Union at the end of the Cold War. A vast amount of research has been commissioned in an attempt to understand the reasons for their downfall. The Chinese want to avoid suffering the same fate.

China is an enormously diverse nation, with seventy officially recognized nationalities, as well as twenty ethnic groups that are not recognized. The strongest independence movement is found in Tibet, and to Beijing the Dalai Lama symbolizes the Tibetan separatist movement. In the eyes of the Chinese Communist Party, anyone who receives him is encouraging the disintegration of the People's Republic of China. Does Merkel support Tibetan autonomy, or does she simply want to strengthen the rights of minorities and protest against oppression? She has never answered that question, but she did receive the Dalai Lama. The Foreign Minister, Frank-Walter Steinmeier, and his ministry advised her strongly against it. There were two particularly awkward areas: one was the location, the Chancellor's office, which gave the visit high political status and an official character. The other was the circumstances in which the visit became public knowledge: Merkel had not mentioned it during an informal meeting with Wen Jiabao only a few weeks earlier. The Chinese felt that she had been duplicitous. Diplomats were beside themselves.

The Chinese reacted angrily and fast: meetings were cancelled, discussions about the rule of law came to a halt. Germany felt the full weight of Chinese indignation. Steinmeier had to soothe hurt feelings in a complex attempt at rapprochement, and produced a letter of apology in which Germany acknowledged China's territorial integrity – a kowtowing that is still regarded as excessive in the Chancellor's office, who were of the opinion that China had exploited an internal coalition disagreement over the incident. Of course that was not how it was viewed by Steinmeier's Foreign Office, where it was described as maladroitness on the Chancellor's part. Whichever way the pendulum between ethics and Realpolitik swings, the episode shows that Germany must calibrate its use of power towards China very carefully. From then on the Chancellor has always borne this practical insight into her relationship with China in mind. So far there hasn't been another Dalai Lama incident. But that may simply be because there has been no request for another meeting, although the Chancellor's office remains in contact with the representatives of the spiritual leader of the Tibetans.

Whenever Merkel travels abroad, her information comes from two sources. Experts from the Federal Intelligence Agency present their findings to the advisers on those areas in the Chancellor's office. Briefing documents are then passed on to the Chancellor. This procedure is repeated by experts from the Institute for

International and Security Affairs, the main foreign-policy think tank in Berlin, which is financed by the government. These two processes of information-gathering operate separately, both agencies requesting confidentiality. The Intelligence Agency in particular prefers to keep its cards close to its chest. Whenever there is to be a visit to China, the question of human rights is always raised, lists are drawn up of particularly delicate cases involving dissidents who have been imprisoned or who are facing the death penalty. Working on the margins of the discussions, Merkel's adviser on foreign policy, Christoph Heusgen, always produces a list of cases of human-rights abuse, and the member of the government who deals with such cases is asked to make further inquiries about the fate of the dissidents in question.

Criticism of China and its human-rights abuses has become a bit of a show – and is treated as such by Beijing, although there are small signs of improvement. For example, just before he left office, Wen Jiabao wanted to have one last German-Chinese dialogue – he clearly liked the ministerial meetings that had been set up under Merkel and that became increasingly popular as an instrument of foreign policy. Wen Jiabao obviously wanted to establish this means of communication permanently before his successor took over. So he asked for the meeting to be brought forward to the summer of 2012. The Chancellor's office agreed on one condition: the discussions on human rights, which had been discontinued after a protest by the Chinese, had to be resumed.

So the talks on human rights and freedom resumed, but what was the result? Were they still only a show? The Chinese Communist Party chooses those who take part and closely monitors the meetings. Even conversations involving less important political delegations from Germany are subject to strict checks. Christoph Heusgen has repeatedly failed in his attempts to maintain personal contact with his main counterparts in Chinese foreign policy. It is true that mobile phone numbers were exchanged, that there were mutual reassurances of close and straightforward cooperation, but then contact was suddenly broken off. Language barriers and other cultural differences are major obstacles, and the Chinese leadership doesn't like special relationships to be set up without due monitoring, still less if these are confidential. So now no one bothers to answer if they get a call from a mobile.

It is all the more surprising that over the course of time Merkel has made a conscious decision to cooperate rather than confront. German-Chinese relations take place mainly at the level of the balance sheet. A volume of trade of 144 billion euros, exports increased by twenty per cent in 2011 alone, to what is now 65 billion euros, 5,000 German businesses operating in China: China is fast becoming Germany's most important trading partner outside the EU; no other EU country enjoys such an economic relationship with China as does Germany. The European Council on Foreign Relations has warned about German-Chinese "special relationships". Economic dependency creates political pressure. Berlin is seen as being in a separate category from other European and Western countries. Germany is China's biggest supporter in transforming its industrial society from being purely one of mass production to that of a high-tech country, and the rapid rise of China could not succeed without German engineering expertise. But at some point the pendulum will swing the other way – even now the majority of Europe is of no interest to the Chinese market.

Merkel is unmoved by the criticism. She is guided by the conviction that China will develop rapidly even without Germany – Europe has to measure up to Chinese standards if it wants to withstand the pressure of globalization.

She sees China itself as an exciting experiment: how long will the country remain under authoritarian rule, when the desire for prosperity and freedom is constantly growing? In a speech to the Party University in Beijing in 2010, she said that there comes a time when every country ceases to see difference as a threat, but rather as part of the human condition. Two years later she observed: "The struggle for freedom is gaining ground in China. It makes people want to be free. When more people are better educated, when more people have enough to eat and can develop, the louder and more insistently that question will be asked."

There it is again, Merkel's leitmotiv of the competition between systems, the ability of the West and its values to prevail. Us or them – the freedom of the West or the authoritarianism of China. For Merkel, that is the real message behind all the visits, balance sheets and gestures of friendship.

But there is one great risk: China's foreign policy is offensive rather than defensive, especially when it comes to its nearest neighbours. China is rearming: nationalist and aggressive notes set alarm bells ringing in other Asian countries – as well as among investors. Germany is too weak to challenge China in the game of geopolitics – the United States has taken on that role with the Obama administration's Pacific offensive, as well as a strategy of military equilibrium intended to give China's neighbours room to breathe, especially in the South China Sea. Merkel welcomes this policy, and sees it as Germany's duty to make Europe stronger in order to provide an economic counterweight. The time may come when she is forced to decide between US interests and Germany's economic interests in China. As yet she has not been faced with that choice – but there is little doubt which side she would ultimately take.

The Great Crisis

Angela Merkel's Battle for Europe

The College of Europe in picturesque Bruges could be called a centre for idealism. Those who believe in Europe and the spirit that unites the continent come here to study. The new College building on Verversdijk looks like an enormous oxygen pump, a concrete cube reminiscent of a honeycomb with a glazed pitched roof, constantly supplying the European organism with fresh air. The spirit of the Union breathes more easily here than anywhere else, and it was here that Angela Merkel wanted to offer a few words of wisdom to young Europeans who were just starting out on their way. Or perhaps she simply wanted to cheer herself up.

It was on Tuesday 2nd November 2010. A few days earlier, EU heads of government had decided that the hastily assembled safety net for member states in economic difficulty had to be dismantled and reconstructed. Something permanent was needed. In order to do this, European treaties had to be altered – a nightmare to anyone who remembered the tedious process of drawing them up, and the resistance that was encountered in national referendums. But something had to be done: Europe was in a pitiful state. For about a year the financial crisis had been ravaging all the European countries, and their budgets were in turmoil as a result of bailing out the banks. The problem was particularly acute in Greece, and in November Ireland and then Portugal would ask for help from the EU. Germany and France were at odds over the way out of this impasse, and in any case it was difficult to understand the nature of the disease, for which there was no tried-and-tested cure and which seemed to be fatal.

That morning Angela Merkel had received something through the post. A small package had arrived: the Chancellery noticed it, and security immediately withdrew it from circulation. It was a parcel bomb, sent from Greece and addressed to the Chancellor. Such things rarely happen, and when they do the public doesn't usually hear about them. Angela Merkel a target of Greek extremists? After the first few heated months of the crisis, that would be no great surprise. But the Chancellor's mind was focused on another message that day. The public was due to hear an anecdote about Albert Einstein, and Merkel told it to the best of her ability at the beginning of her speech in Bruges. The Chancellor had gone to Belgium to inaugurate the College's 61st academic year. Every new intake of students was given the name of a patron, and this year the patron was that master of theoretical physics, Albert Einstein, a choice that particularly pleased Angela Merkel, who had herself studied physics.

Merkel asked the students to think back to the late nineteenth century. She reminded them of Marie Curie, of Niels Bohr and Albert Einstein. Then she said that even a great scientist like Einstein had always had difficulty understanding "another great world, the world of quantum mechanics – even though many of the significant aspects of the two fields are closely connected". The students probably smiled to themselves: that was why they had chosen to study social sciences rather than physics, sensing that they would never grasp its connection to quantum mechanics. Merkel knew something about the subject, but she was trying to make a different point: the case of Einstein, she said, showed how difficult it is to move away from a familiar concept of the world and accept a new one, acquired through scientific findings. "It demonstrates our limitations – the limitations of our own understanding and of a given period in time."

Merkel is not prepared to accept limitations to her understanding. She wants to understand, to test her limitations, in the Eurozone crisis as in everything else. This event had confronted her with her own limitations, so on 2nd November Merkel was playing for time. Time is always helpful when you sense that you have gone as far as you can. And as she was speaking at the College of Europe, Merkel expressed her confidence that at some point the barriers would come down, destroyed by "great minds". "If you think, act and explore in that new space, everything suddenly seems simple, you can't understand why it was a closed book to earlier generations."

That was Merkel the natural scientist speaking, wanting to get to the point where she could solve the problem she faced by way of "scientific findings". She hoped to enter a new space, where matters could be seen clearly and simply. The crisis didn't feel like that yet. It was – as she said on another occasion – like being in a dark room, so dark that you couldn't see your hand in front of your face, and having to grope your way forward. One false step and you would never find the way out.

The Way to Europe

At the beginning of her political career, Angela Merkel's path towards Europe was cautious: she felt her way forward. In the last days of the GDR, as spokeswoman for the de Maizière government, she discovered how brutal the workings of the European Economic Community can be. When the West German Deutschmark was introduced into the former East Germany at an exchange rate of 2:1, not all the money in the West could save the ramshackle agriculture of the ailing former state. Overnight, goods became unsellable, farmers burnt their crops in the fields; it was as if an entire sector had been cast aside. An avalanche of foodstuffs from the West came pouring through the East, all of them products of a highly subsidized market. At the time, subsidies were one of the specialities of the European Economic Community.

Merkel was not born a child of the European Union. At almost every opportunity she stressed that for thirty-five years she had seen Europe from the outside. Like many Central Europeans, her view of the West was shaped by English-speaking countries. This might have been the influence of her mother, who taught English, as well as the fascination that America held for her. The classic European influence on south-west German CDU politicians such as Helmut Kohl and Wolfgang Schäuble was denied to her. They were students of Adenauer, who saw German-French reconciliation as the basis of European unity. Helmut Kohl was forever talking about how, as students, they had torn down the barriers on the border between the Palatinate and Lorraine. From the top of the town of Gengenbach at home in Baden-Württemberg, Wolfgang Schäuble can see all the way to France. Angela Merkel is a stranger to this barrier-obsessed mindset. She has learnt the European repertory partly from long conversations with colleagues who had to explain this kind of West German conditioning to her.

France struck her as a particularly foreign European country. She had learnt French for a short time at school in the GDR, but her teacher married a Canadian, applied for an exit visa and didn't come back. Merkel didn't visit France or explore the country until the first few years after German reunification. She travelled in Provence, and through Kohl got to know Joseph Rovan, the French journalist and historian of German-Jewish descent who was one of the founding fathers of Franco-German reconciliation. She made friends with the political scientist Henri Ménudier, who showed her and her partner Joachim Sauer round Normandy. As a young Minister for Women and Youth, she had her first experiences of the arrogance that can be shown by an *énarque*, a graduate of the elite French university, the École Nationale d'Administration. Her counterpart in the French Cabinet was one such graduate, and he made his lack of interest in the German minister quite plain by letting his staff talk to her while he read files. So Merkel too studied files, and got her own civil servants to do the talking.

As Environment Minister, she lived through the heyday of the informal ministerial study groups who went to the most beautiful places on the Continent for a few days – an unimaginable luxury today. An Irish colleague took a group of them to the pubs of Dublin to hear banjo music, and the next day they ate lobster by the sea. In the Camargue the ministers rode horses, while in Spain they drank sherry from large casks – all in the cause of European folklore.

Nonetheless, when Merkel first went to Brussels for a Council meeting as the German head of government, she was seen as a blank canvas – although as Chairman of the CDU she had been instrumental in appointing the Portuguese conservative Barroso to the post of President of the Commission. Apart from that she had a reputation as an Anglophile with little experience in European politics. This reputation underwent something of a change at about 3 a.m. on the morning of 20th December 2005. In her first overnight summit Merkel negotiated the new EU budget (or the financial forecast as it is known in EU terminology) up to the year 2013. She was the most prepared among all the government leaders present, spoke to everyone individually, and was the only one absolutely determined to broker a deal. In the end the Merkel method prevailed over the methods of Blair, Chirac and Kaczyński: she walled her opponents in with facts, demolished one argument after another with better arguments, thus forcing everyone to come to an agreement – there were no loopholes left. She earned great respect that night.

Her second coup came two years later, when Germany had both the presidency of the Council and that of the G8. By that time Merkel was recognized as a stateswoman: she had given Germany more of a presence on the world stage, and had shown in the Middle East that she could hold her own in the most difficult diplomatic chess games. But the presidency of the Council was a harder task. Europe was going nowhere. The Constitutional Treaty, signed by government leaders in a solemn ceremony in front of a kitsch colonnaded backdrop in Rome in 2004, was a resounding failure. Vetoed by the citizens of France and the Netherlands, it had no legal standing, so something new was needed, and quickly. The EU, which had just been enlarged by ten states from Central and Eastern Europe, was incapable of action. All hopes were pinned on Merkel, who took over the presidency of the Council on 1st January 2007.

In the months leading up to this, the Chancellor's office had been hard at work. Merkel's Europe team – Thomas de Maizière, then head of the Chancellery, her personal private secretary Beate Baumann, her spokesman Uli Wilhelm, Uwe Corsepius, then head of the European Department, and her foreign-policy adviser Christoph Heusgen – had produced a comprehensive analysis of the problems with the Treaty, a draft of the constitutional document and, most importantly, of the main players involved. Merkel enjoyed discovering where her colleagues on the European Council stood in terms of domestic politics. She drew up a programme for the six months of negotiations, although she was well aware that a solution might not be found before the end of the German presidency. Such issues are not usually resolved until the last moment.

When Merkel began work in January, she followed a detailed schedule of whom she had to visit, work with and when. One of her advisers said later that the Chancellor laid out the problem like the plot of a novel "with seventeen subplots that had to be gradually worked out". Working things out is Merkel's idea of a political process. She identifies a theme, locates it in her world of ideas, divides it into sub-problems, and then solves them. So a list was made of the key countries and personalities involved in the constitutional question, a matrix showing the most important political actors and advisers. Merkel wanted to know what it would mean if Adviser X to the French President reacted negatively on a given subject, and whether going over it with the help of an adviser from a third country would work. The programme envisaged individual discussions, and then meetings of small groups of people at weekend conferences at Schloss Meseberg, the German government's guest residence. She went from room to room like the manager of a youth hostel, and as the date of the summit in Brussels approached she was the only one who knew exactly how much pain each European leader could take.

But she hadn't reckoned with the resistance of the Polish President, Lech Kaczyński, who – along with his Prime Minister, his twin brother Jarosław, in the background – kept making fresh demands about the different number of votes allocated to individual countries. Poland wanted the voting weight for majority decisions to be fixed by means of a "square-root formula", at which the other heads of government rolled their eyes in annoyance. Lech Kaczyński kept leaving the room to get instructions from his brother in Warsaw. The Poles claimed that the negotiations were a matter of life and death – making everyone else groan at such a melodramatic statement. Merkel was kept busy moderating, steering conversations towards the result that she had planned. And when Poland still refused to vote in favour, she pointedly walked out of that round of the negotiations. She wasn't taking much of a risk – she knew she could rely on the others. Even before the outcome – later to be known as the Lisbon Treaty – was settled, *Die Zeit* was praising Merkel's negotiating skills: "The Chancellor has grasped the mechanics of post-modern politics and with it the nature of Europe, for in the EU progress can only be made by means of ongoing dialogue." Merkel and the nature of Europe – two things that had never been seen as a single entity – had suddenly come together.

Merkel had to work hard for her idea of Europe. As so often it depended on reason: it was a rational construct. And as so often Merkel communicated the result of her intellectual efforts in speeches, preferably to a parliament, sometimes at a celebratory event. Twice in her European coronation year of 2007 she conveyed it to the EU in writing. Once she timed the speech to coincide with the fiftieth anniversary of the signing of the Treaty of Rome. The calendar meant that the occasion would come within the German presidency of the EU, so Merkel organized a celebration in Berlin in March 2007. On that occasion, too, she repeated her leitmotiv of the power of freedom. "If we pin our hopes on the power of freedom, then we are pinning them on humanity. Humanity is at the centre," she added. "Stagnation means retreat. Building up confidence takes decades, but hopes can be dashed overnight" – as would happen a few years later.

In Berlin, the political world was still in order. Merkel was the new star in the firmament of foreign policy. The media hailed her as the most influential woman in the world. She had wrested an ambitious promise on climate change from EU leaders, and shortly afterwards from the US President as well. And now, on the fiftieth anniversary of the founding of the EU, she produced a theme that was to appear again and again in her speeches, to the approval or disapproval of the continent. "We are fortunate to be citizens of a united European Union." This is a highly charged statement: it has something inevitable and almost fateful about it, as if a higher power were forcing Europe to unite. Not only that, she was playing with the double meaning of the word *Glück* in German – which can mean good fortune or something that happens by chance – and Merkel knew that this would make an impression. The Chancellor's office had chosen the phrase in an allusion to the rights enshrined in the American Declaration of Independence – life, liberty and the pursuit of happiness (*Glück*).

Her other speech from that period conveying a statement of principle didn't attract so much attention. Merkel delivered it on 17th January 2007 in Strasbourg, a dull winter day that seemed to be a harbinger of misfortune. The rain was lashing down, the wind howled, the weather forecast spoke of the kind of storm that comes once a century: the terrible area of low pressure known in Europe as Kyrill was on its way. It would reach Germany the next day, bringing death and destruction. Perhaps that was why no one paid much attention to the Chancellor when she told the European Parliament what she was expecting.

It is usual for the incumbent head of government to visit the Strasbourg seat of the European Parliament at the beginning of their EU presidency – a tiresome duty for most heads of government. The Parliament is the weakest link in the European power structure. Nicolas Sarkozy showed his lack of respect for it by having – albeit slight – alterations made to the hall used for plenary sessions. The officiating President of the Council usually sits on a chair in the main auditorium before being summoned to the speaker's lectern. Like all the other seats in the plenary hall, this chair is numbered: it is Number 2. No French President could be expected to settle for that. In Sarkozy's opinion, the President of France doesn't take second place to anyone. So he had the 2 removed before he came to the hall.

In Angela Merkel's world, seat numbers are of no significance. For her, parliaments have greater relevance, and the Bundestag has always been at the centre of her democratic blueprint. She also felt a duty to the European Parliament when she was preparing to make her European declaration of faith in Strasbourg. It was a powerful speech, undoubtedly the most important that she gave on the EU before the crisis. The Chancellery had devoted a great deal of time to it. Several weeks before the presidency began there had been discussions on the fundamental message that it would send. Merkel assembled her inner circle and two external advisers over dinner in the small Chancellor's suite on the eighth floor of the Chancellery. Those who had the most to say were Wilhelm and Corsepius, the adviser on Europe: how could they really grip European hearts and minds? There had to be a message going beyond the usual "bread and butter", as those in her office refer to the constant stream of talk in the political programme. So the discussion centred on classic themes: diversity, respect, war and peace – until someone mentioned tolerance. They still speak of the "tolerance speech" in the Chancellor's office today, as if everyone should know which one they are talking about. Merkel tried to find an answer to the question about the meaning of Europe, the very heart of the matter. What holds Europe together? What is the use of it? How can one actually feel Europe?

Her answer was a triad of values: diversity, freedom, tolerance. "The creator of Europe made it small and even divided it into tiny pieces, so our hearts would delight not in size but in diversity," she said, quoting the Czech writer Karel Čapek. Yet in Merkel's view, pleasure in diversity is not enough, because diversity has an important requirement without which it cannot exist. Merkel spins the thread further: diversity will not last long if it doesn't go hand in hand with freedom. "Freedom in all its forms: freedom to express your opinions publicly, freedom to believe or not believe, freedom to trade and do business, the artist's freedom to shape his work according to his own ideas."

Here again was Merkel's freedom, the freedom "that Europe needs in the same way as it needs air to breathe". Because "where it is restricted we wither away". But she goes even further, asking the crucial question: What allows human beings to see profit in diversity, and deal responsibly with their freedom in all that diversity? The answer: tolerance. "The heart and soul of Europe is tolerance. Europe is the continent of tolerance."

Is a German Chancellor allowed to say such things? Is she allowed to speak of tolerance when German intolerance has brought Europe to its knees over and over again? Following her reasoning, the Chancellor had no choice: she had to say it. "It has taken us centuries to understand this. On the road to tolerance we have had to live through many disasters. We have persecuted and annihilated one another. We have laid our own country waste. [...] The worst period of hatred, devastation and destruction happened not even a generation ago. It was done in the name of my people." If this is the case, said Merkel, in a warning about showing arrogance towards others, to all those who have difficulty with the idea of tolerance, then Europe has a duty to exercise tolerance and encourage it wherever it is found. "We must be thankful that everything we Europeans have ever achieved is due to our contradictory nature," said Merkel, quoting the writer Peter Prange, "to the eternal conflict within ourselves, the constant exchange of opinion and counter-opinion, idea and counter-idea, thesis and antithesis." So why should Europe not succeed? Merkel's answer is now well known: because Europe has learnt the value of tolerance. But shortly after her speech, that tolerance was to be put to a severe test.

To understand Merkel as a politician dealing with crises, we must spend a moment in the pre-crisis phase, the time of policy speeches and professions of faith. Europe requires its political figures to produce a constant stream of such statements. It seems to have a definite thirst for them. In Brussels, think tanks offer an environment for all manner of deep reflection. In Berlin there is a well-established series of speeches delivered at the Humboldt University, the "Humboldt Speeches", in which guest speakers bare their political soul. Berlin's "Europe Speech", a theoretical rather than topical address on "the state of the Union", is made every year. And then there is the prestigious Charlemagne Prize.

Merkel has spoken widely on principles. She has won the Charlemagne Prize and given the Europe Speech. But like other leading European politicians she failed to foresee the existential crisis that seized hold of Europe in the autumn of 2009. Not once did she analyse the budget deficits that might be caused by a currency union without a common European economic policy. She never drew up a plan for repairing Europe's greatest weak spots. The first sign of any action plan for dealing with the crisis came in her Humboldt Speech in May 2009, six months before Greece's disclosure of its deficit. Here, with remarkable foresight, she pointed out that European policy was the same as domestic policy – a year later the Bundestag would be dealing with precious little else.

Merkel's reference to the Constitution is also important in this context: the Federal Republic states that its aim is "to serve the cause of world peace as a member of a united Europe with equal rights" – these words are from the preamble to the German Constitution, and were crucial in evaluating the crisis three years later, when the Constitutional Court had to decide on the legitimacy of transfers of sovereignty, because for all those who support Europe, the reference in the preamble is evidence that there is no contradiction between the Constitution and the European Union. Merkel made that clear in a major political statement: "Germany has always understood European unity as part of its reasons of state." Once again she refers to reasons of state, something that she usually mentions only when speaking about transatlantic relations or Israel. But nowhere is it more important than in Europe. Without Europe, Germany is nothing.

Merkel could be said to see Europe as the most important German interest. So she dislikes Germany being referred to as the "paymaster" of Europe, because Germany profits a great deal from the internal market, and derives a huge political advantage from its integration in the EU. In her Humboldt speech, Merkel also argued that Europe could not go on accepting an unlimited number of new member states. Consolidation, the improvement of existing structures, comes before expansion. Nor can consolidation mean that Brussels acquires more and more power by the back door. "The nation states are masters of the treaties" has been a favourite saying of Merkel's during the crisis. Those who measure the EU by "the standards of constitutional law", giving the European Parliament the right to make new laws or shift even more power to Brussels, will only help "overtax the system and set off alarm bells".

Merkel had got her own European house in order before Europe itself put her to the test. She struggled with the system, which she felt wanted to extend its powers, and struggled with the impatience of individual nations, who preferred to be in a Europe that moved at different speeds. At that point, Merkel was reluctant to admit such a system was plausible, because, as she said, "Are we to throw out the MPs from the countries that don't work with us? Then who will make the decisions? That would destroy the whole structure of the European Union." In fact the Chancellor became quite heated over this question. "So I would ask those who propose such ideas to think again." Three years later – in the very depths of the crisis – her principles no longer sound quite so set in stone. Merkel had thought again, and accepted that it was possible to go at different speeds. She had prudently given herself a way out in 2009, when she said: "I may have overlooked something, but I don't think so."

There was something else that she had been wise enough to make clear in advance to her domestic audience: she would not produce any financial blueprints – at least, not publicly. In his Humboldt Speech many years earlier, Joschka Fischer had set the standard when he spoke about finality. She was not going to contribute to the finality debate, or answer the all-important question of what the EU might be like when its structure was complete. "I shall have to disappoint you, because I think that long-term aims […] sometimes make it difficult to take the next necessary political step." Her message was that anyone speaking of finality robs himself or herself of flexibility. As a tactician, Merkel was not going to fall into that trap. She would rather study individual trees than praise the beauty of the whole forest. You never know: one day you might get lost in the forest.

Greece's Disclosure

The crisis really began on 15th September 2008, with the bankruptcy of Lehman Brothers. In its final year, the CDU-SPD coalition was struggling to prevent a spectacular collapse of the economy, and had only a few weeks to make decisions about guaranteeing huge funds, saving the banks and providing a stimulus to the economy. By October 2009 the crisis had only shifted – into the budgets of the European states. Everywhere, national debt was growing, governments had come to the aid of failing banks, thereby exposing themselves to risk. When the Papandreou government, elected only that month, took advantage of this new beginning to revise its estimate of Greece's budget deficit, there was no immediate outcry. People had been expecting bad news from Athens: the budget deficit amounted to twelve instead of six per cent of the gross domestic product.

It was a few weeks before the significance of this announcement sank in. Twelve per cent of GDP far overstepped the debt limit set by the EU, but there was no indication as to how it might be adjusted. Not only that, but the total amount of debt was phenomenally high. This had immediate effects on the financing of debt: creditors in the international financial markets put enormous surcharges on Greek state borrowing. As early as December, the ratings agency Fitch was the first to downgrade the country's credit rating. Borrowing money became prohibitively expensive for Greece.

A vicious circle set in, and no one could break out of it in a hurry. High debts, a high demand for credit; high surcharges with even more expensive loans – a chain that could be broken only if the state reduced its debts. But then the economy had to grow. For that to happen, income from taxation had to increase sharply, and for *that* to happen high-interest loans had to be lowered and spending cuts made. Social-security, pensions and healthcare costs

had to be significantly reduced. And for that to happen, civil servants would have to be made redundant and taxes raised. Every
economist understood the task that faced Greece in theory. But in
practice it was extremely difficult, and Greece and its politicians
are notoriously incapable of taking decisive action.

Nor could Greece be put into quarantine, although its problems
were infectious. Everyone realized that this vicious circle might end
in the state declaring itself insolvent. Greece would go bankrupt
and be unable to pay its debts. States in this unfortunate position
usually reset the counter to zero and either issue a new currency
or devalue the old one. But for Greece that was impossible,
because all transactions were in euros – as they were in sixteen
other countries of the European Union. If Greece were allowed
to go bankrupt in an uncontrolled way it would take some other
European states with it.

The second problem was that Greek banks are closely linked
to other banks in Europe, and foreign banks were holding vast
amounts of worthless Greek loans. A sudden bankruptcy would
not just mean the collapse of one single bank in Greece: it would
set off a domino effect with unforeseeable consequences, perhaps
affecting the Deutsche Bank or the Commerzbank in Germany.
Financial failure would cut Greece off from the economic area,
Greek reserves of euros would exceed the limits – and the country
would no longer be able to pay for vital goods and services from
abroad. All manner of dark, gloomy scenarios were envisaged,
with mass emigration and unrest in various trouble spots. Things
couldn't be allowed to get to that stage.

But was a controlled exit an option? Could a deal be reached
on Greece's departure, cushioned by agreements and plenty of

cash? Greece would have to leave the Eurozone and introduce a new currency – with all the risks that were involved for the banks and the economy. The Papandreou government soon made it clear that it was not interested in this option. And it had the law on its side: a nation cannot be thrown out of the European Union: the treaties do not provide for such an eventuality. A parting of the ways could be quite ugly, and the euro itself would be irreparably damaged. It wasn't a question of states who were solvent being able to threaten Greece: it was the crisis states, which would later include Spain and Italy, that made the club of richer states tremble.

The essence of the crisis has not changed. The dilemma became even clearer when Ireland and Portugal asked to be included in the rescue plan, and then Spain and Italy found themselves in stormy waters. At this point it became evident that the problem was not only one of debt, but that the Eurozone had a major flaw in its construction that couldn't be remedied by pouring in money or by throwing out Greece. Europe was not simply undergoing a currency crisis; the community, and particularly the countries of the Eurozone, was under fire from three directions: there were clearly states that had too much debt; there were huge disparities in competitiveness between the economically dynamic and stagnant countries; and no political mechanism had yet been created that could help avert a disaster such as the one that was threatening Greece.

It was the markets that mercilessly revealed this triple crisis. Everywhere in Europe there was loud condemnation of "the markets", of anonymous hedge-fund managers and investment sharks who made a living at the expense of indebted countries, drove up interest rates and lined their pockets by betting on future developments. It would be several years before the furore died down. It wasn't until 2012 that people realized that the markets were acting in a perfectly logical way. And that the markets also included the pension funds of firms such as Siemens and Volkswagen, savings funds and ordinary people with one thousand euros placed in rock-solid investment funds. Should these investors be blamed for preferring to lend their customers' money to countries whose economies had better balance sheets, that were competitive and had modern, productive industries?

No, Europe was on the wrong track, a fact that the markets had exposed in the wake of the debt crises; the Eurozone may be a currency area, but it is also an area of very different competitive forces. If this diverse bloc enjoys the advantage of having the same monetary policy, if all the countries are able to borrow money under the same conditions despite their different abilities, then there is a problem. It simply couldn't work like that.

After 2010, one advantage of the crisis was that not only did every Member of Parliament get a free crash course in economics and monetary policy, but so did every intelligent member of the public. And yet for a long time the crisis seemed to be an abstract concept in Germany: while the fifty per cent of young people who were unemployed in Spain and property owners in Ireland soon had personal experience of the effects of a currency crisis, the Germans had either to take the Chancellor's word or ride the emotional rollercoaster of the evening news, in which sometimes the Greeks were thrown off the tracks, or furious MPs roared "Enough!" and demanded the return of the Deutschmark.

It was clear that there was no simple solution, as the Chancellor realized on 23rd April 2010, when the Greek government applied for aid from the European Union and the International Monetary Fund. From that moment on, nothing in Europe would ever be the same: all European feel-good rhetoric came to a halt, and the Union turned to political infighting. Anyone who still believed that they were living in the United States of Europe was soon disillusioned: every state suddenly became a nation state, a phase of hardline self-centred politics had begun – and interests were defined by national borders. Europe was now in a state of political emergency, and its leaders were at times plunged into existential crises. The continent saw a resurrection of prejudices long thought dead and buried, and realized that its community was built on sand. For even if no politician – and certainly not Angela Merkel – dared to speak the plain truth, the crisis had the potential to destroy the European Union. If a single country left the Eurozone, it would prove that Europe was unable to keep up in the globalization race, that it was reverting to being a number of small states with many minor currencies, old-fashioned and with no power to innovate. The biggest experiment of the century, an attempt to reconcile and pacify a notoriously unstable continent, was in danger. Anyone with a sense of history might well have felt uneasy during those months of crisis.

At first, Angela Merkel herself didn't understand the full extent of the crisis. No one did. Even as she was addressing the new intake of students in the Einstein year in Bruges in November 2010, she was praying for inspiration. Only in the middle of 2011 did she begin to speak with any certainty about the causes and effects of the crisis. Yet even then it was clear that the crisis fed off the surprise factor, that unforeseen problems were constantly emerging. "Driving blind" was a much used metaphor in the Chancellor's office. It must have been depressing for Merkel, who likes to work systematically, to find that the crisis refused to reveal its inner workings. European politicians worked their way through the problems, continually surprised by new developments and new incidents, terrible new figures and frustratingly endless discussions. In a highly complex mechanism, cogs began turning in the form of monetary and economic policies, immediate reactions to crises and long-term plans for security, domestic politics and constitutional law. Election dates, resignations, parliaments, discussions – all these things took time, and time was the most valuable commodity of all, one that Merkel sorely missed in her search for stability.

If there was one thing the Chancellor felt certain about far too soon, it was her mistrust of the quick solutions that were being brought to her attention, and which were provided by the many external advisers. It was the reason why she increasingly cut herself off from them. The 2008 banking crisis had taken her by surprise; the government had been ill prepared for the full extent of the problem. There was perhaps a handful of experts among its ranks who could explain short-selling, derivatives and collateral debt obligations. One evening has stuck in the memory of Merkel's advisers: Josef Ackermann, then CEO of Deutsche Bank, explained the system of value adjustments to Merkel using bottles of expensive red wine. If you have 500 bottles, each worth 500 euros, in your cellar, and you sell one of those bottles for only 100 euros, then the value of the other bottles has to be reduced accordingly.

Merkel and her team learnt their lesson from the wine-bottle example. The Chief Economic Adviser in the Chancellor's office, Jens Weidmann, set up a special unit to save the banks, recruiting people who were specialists in the capital markets. He himself was the leading expert on European monetary policy, having written his PhD on the subject. Anyone who wishes to understand Merkel's crisis-management policy must first understand this economist, born in 1968, who is the Chancellor's typical colleague of choice: discreet, workaholic, highly intelligent. Thomas de Maizière, the Minister in the Chancellor's office, has called him a bright spark.

Merkel and Weidmann are very similar: both are analytical, cautious, mistrustful. So it was not surprising that Weidmann's hackles were raised early in May 2010, when a fund was created virtually in the space of a weekend, because the Council of Europe wanted to fill it with money, simply to give a clear signal to the Greek request for aid. On 2nd May, finance ministers had approved a rescue package of 110 billion euros, but that had left the markets unimpressed. Speculation on Greece continued, so the Eurozone decided to set up the EFSF, the European Financial Stability Facility, as a form of safety net.

Merkel objected, saying that she needed time to think about it, and on 8th May went to Moscow for the celebration of the fifty-fifth anniversary of the end of the Second World War. Even on the dais during the veterans' parade she was bombarded with questions by the Russians and Chinese. At the end of the weekend she agreed to the creation of the fund, but on two conditions: the money was conditional on results and the International Monetary Fund had be involved as a form of safeguard, because IMF rules could not be broken, even by Europe's debtor states. Germany felt protected by the involvement of the IMF. When the safety net was set up, it provided a breathing space, bought time – time to understand the crisis, to try and counter it and calm things down.

In this first phase, Merkel had many opponents. The President of France, for instance, was convinced that if only enough money were to be made available then the markets would settle down. In fact that was the opinion of most international economists: they couldn't make sense of Merkel's demands for budget cuts. Merkel and Sarkozy had a difficult relationship: this was obvious at first sight. When Sarkozy came to Berlin for the first time as President – he was elected a year and a half after she became Chancellor, and so according to protocol had to pay a courtesy visit – there was quite a long delay before he got out of his car at the entrance to the Chancellery. Merkel was waiting at the other end of the red carpet, but the President had no intention of making the first move. As far as he was concerned, Merkel had to come to him, but she didn't. After an awkward moment, the guest finally obliged.

Merkel and Sarkozy were like chalk and cheese. So the relationship they managed to develop over five years is all the more remarkable. Merkel would claim that she wasn't the one who changed – so it must have been Sarkozy who was suddenly ready for compromise, more understanding, less erratic. One of his first visits to Merkel's office was memorable for the fact that the

President suddenly leapt up in the middle of a conversation and began making a phone call. Or there was the lecture he gave over lunch in the Paris apartment belonging to his wife Carla Bruni: at a sensitive stage of the financial crisis he told the public that Germany was still busy thinking while France was taking action. Merkel and Sarkozy walked on beaches together, argued in their respective offices, quarrelled publicly, but Merkel noted with amusement that her counterpart seemed to become less and less combative towards her over the years, as if she had had a calming influence on him. In the first months of the crisis, Sarkozy used his ministers to attack Merkel and branded Germany's economic power as one of the main causes of the crisis, but by October 2011 he had started using Merkel's manual on crisis management, and even began preparing his compatriots to start making cuts.

A Race against Collapse

The European Union reacted to the crisis like a body in the grip of fever. At that stage it hadn't built up any immunity to the virus, and it is impossible to predict how many more bouts of fever there will be in future. But at least the doctors have learnt how to recognize the symptoms. So far it has been possible to define three phases of the crisis. The first phase began with the Greek request for aid in April 2010, and the hastily agreed rescue plan that initially prevented the country's bankruptcy. Greece was at the centre of this phase, although Ireland had to be moved into intensive care in November 2010, followed by Portugal in May 2011. Yet the liquidity crisis seemed to be a national problem, a phenomenon that had geographic limits, and defined by the distinctive economic features of the three individual countries. It was at this point that Europeans became acquainted with the main US rating agencies, who, like Cassandra, were always bearers of bad news – or were themselves the cause of it. Whatever the case, intense anger was directed at these agencies, and there were loud demands for the problem to be solved once and for all by means of a vast injection of cash.

This demand was made of Merkel, who as Chancellor of the largest economy in the Eurozone led the way for other, less prosperous countries. She was always faced with the same requests: Eurobonds could help the three countries out of trouble. A single, identical state loan for everyone – it would make life a little more expensive for the Germans and a little more bearable for the Greeks, but at least the supply of money from the financial markets would be taken care of. The logical argument was that those who share a currency need the same financial instruments. Merkel's counter-argument was that the currency might be the same, but the economic policy was not. Eurobonds only make sense if all governments stake their money, borrowed at the same, reasonable rate, and are monitored in the same way. Even more important was the treaties argument: such bonds or liability for debts are not only impossible, but expressly forbidden by European treaties. States cannot finance each other. And even if they wanted to, then German public opinion would have something to say about it.

At an early stage two important institutions supported Merkel's position: the Federal Constitutional Court and the German parliament, the Bundestag. Merkel could feel her own party breathing down her neck, a party in which enemies of the euro could form an angry mob in the space of a few moments. Not only that, the very existence of the coalition was in danger, because the FDP was also split over its policy towards the crisis. The party even had to take a straw poll of its members on whether it would continue with the rescue attempt. And then there was the Supreme Court in Karlsruhe, keeping its beady eye on national sovereignty, which would be undermined if the government removed authority over the budget from the Bundestag.

Merkel soon made it clear that she would give up her resistance to the rescue plan and the support of Greece only on the following conditions. Her first requirement was that debtor states must implement the full package of reforms: they had to get their economies moving and become competitive. It was the only way out of the debt trap. Her second was that she could only politically justify German aid if a repetition of this regrettable situation were to be precluded once and for all – preferably by binding treaties.

Merkel looked for an ally of suitable stature for her plan, and found one in the French President. In October 2010, she and Sarkozy walked along the beach in Deauville at sunset and agreed on the next steps to take. The rescue plan is not enough, they said, there must be a lasting structure, one that is backed by a great deal of money and has equally great credibility. Secondly, this protection can be provided only if the stability pact – what could be described as a constitution that lays down the correct way for Europe to deal with its own money – is improved and embedded in the treaties. Yet Merkel failed in one important demand: she wanted draconian penalties contained in the list of sanctions that would be applied to any state that broke the treaties, the most effective being the withdrawal of voting rights. In Deauville, Sarkozy agreed with her, but soon afterwards the summit of heads of government refused to approve it. Withdrawal of democratic rights was probably a step too far.

This, along with what was generally seen as the Chancellor's diffidence, earned her an almost demonic reputation. Merkel the European Thatcher; Merkel the new Bismarck; Merkel the disciplinarian of Europe. On that year's Forbes List of the most powerful people on earth she slipped to fourth place, and even had to share it with the Pope. In the women's list she was ousted from the podium by Michelle Obama. By the time the Finance Ministers finally agreed to the reform of the stability pact and the creation of the permanent rescue plan of the ESM (the European Stability Mechanism) had got under way, Merkel could consider herself one of the most hated and least understood politicians in the world. But there was worse to come.

The second phase of the crisis began in the summer of 2011, when there was little time left for strolling along the beach. The house was now ablaze, Greece was again on the brink of defaulting on its debts, demands were raining down on Merkel from all sides. Germany and France organized a special summit in Brussels for 21st July. First the various advisers met in Paris, and then President Sarkozy flew to Berlin on the evening before the summit. At the last minute the head of the European Central Bank had been asked to come as well. A government plane brought Jean-Claude Trichet from Frankfurt, and all night long there was heated argument in the Chancellor's office – centred above all on the question of whether private creditors should be asked to make a contribution to the rescue. Sarkozy had many doubts.

Once again the decision required the rescue package of April 2010 to be extended by another 109 billion euros. Private creditors were asked, or rather forced, to exchange their government bonds for securities of inferior value. This dramatic moment, the first time that private investors had been involved in the rescue of Greece, had a price: mistrust grew – and then suddenly spiralled out of control. In July, the interest rate on Italian and Spanish government loans went up, while in August the European Central Bank was forced to buy up the loans of these two countries in order to ease the pressure on the markets. But within only a few days this measure ran out of steam. It was no longer a question of individual countries: a discussion was now in progress about the Eurozone as a whole, and the rationale behind its currency. The experts' message was clear: the euro can't go on like this. A common currency needs a common economic policy. The debt crisis had become a crisis of the system itself.

Three months later there was another crisis. Again it was Greece, the danger of yet another imminent meltdown, endless negotiations on conditions for reform and the extension of credit. Amid all the criticism Merkel stuck firmly to her basic principle: money only in return for results. But it was increasingly obvious that not all the money in Greece would be enough to keep the country's debt mountain from crashing down. So, after three rounds of discussion about savings and reforms, Merkel was willing to allow Greek debt to be cut from 160 to 120 per cent of its gross domestic product – a show of strength that required a double summit in Brussels, with a few days in between, because the Bundestag had to be consulted. Among all this turmoil, President Sarkozy missed the birth of his daughter, because he was busy in a crucial meeting in the Frankfurt Opera House.

Merkel was plagued by very different problems. She could no longer rely on the support of the Bundestag. In addition, and with obvious annoyance, the Constitutional Court had made aid for Greece contingent on strict conditions. Merkel was isolated. To an increasing majority she seemed to be the only obstacle to the resolution of the Greek debt problem, because she refused to admit that making aid conditional on cuts was choking the life out of the country. The problem was that no one had a better solution, no one could counter her logic with a credible plan. Everyone acknowledged that injecting all this money might buy time, but it wouldn't solve the basic problems of reform and Greek competitiveness.

German reaction to the catastrophe was self-contradictory: two thirds of the population thought that the conditions were too harsh, and felt sorry for the Greeks. But at the same time a majority would have been happy to see Athens shown the door immediately. Merkel bore the brunt of German anger – never before had the approval ratings for her rescue policy, measured by the research group Wahlen, been as bad as in the autumn of 2011. Merkel responded with an emotional outburst. "If the euro fails, Europe will fail," she said in a statement to the Bundestag on 26th October. With these words she immediately caught the attention of the German people, who were not necessarily feeling the pain themselves, alerting them to the fact that this was the most severe test that the European Union had faced since its foundation. A heated debate broke out: could Europe really fail, was the Chancellor exaggerating the situation? Surely Europe could function perfectly well without the euro? Among all the turmoil, no one remembered that Merkel had been here before – a year and a half earlier, when the vote was taken on the first rescue package for Greece in May 2010.

At this point Merkel felt deeply disappointed with "her" Europe – a mood that was to continue well into 2012. She hadn't expected to encounter such resentment over her rational approach to the crisis. It made her seethe inwardly when she had to keep explaining to other heads of government why Eurobonds would not put an end to the crisis, but were more likely to make it worse – because they wouldn't make every country equally competitive, which meant that the lifestyle of southern Europe would be financed by the productivity of Germany and the rest of northern Europe. No society would accept that. Merkel always took charts with her to support her argument, brightly coloured curves illustrating the unit labour costs or debts of individual European countries. From the curves it was remarkable to see how stable the euro had been for the last ten years, although Eurozone countries differed enormously in their levels of debt and economic strength.

Merkel often viewed the crisis through East German eyes. She had witnessed the collapse of a system at first hand, and wanted to spare Europe such an experience. She increasingly found allies in the heads of government from Central Europe and the Baltic states, who knew what it was like to fall into the abyss, and were becoming more and more annoyed with the southern Europeans who – as the Poles saw it, for instance – were complaining about what was actually still a high standard of living. By 2011, Europe had become a group of states fighting for national interests, while only idealists were concerned about the functioning of the community.

Merkel felt particularly isolated at the G20 summit in Cannes at the beginning of November. The EU summit in October had agreed the haircut to the Greek debt, the EFSF had been increased again and heads of government were discussing the fiscal compact that they wanted to adopt by December at the latest – a significant political signal, because a legally binding brake on debt would finally become part of the constitutions of all the Eurozone countries. Merkel fended off a request by the French President, who wanted to give the rescue plan a banking licence – another ploy to circumvent control by national parliaments. But then the Greek Prime Minister took everyone, including his colleagues, by surprise, by refusing to accept the haircut that was conditional on more stringent economic action. He announced that the Greek people had to decide. The likely outcome was obvious: rejection.

Merkel fumed, as did France's President Sarkozy. Papandreou was about to ruin all their efforts and throw the single currency overboard. It was at this moment that the group of twenty industrial and newly industrialized states met, and Merkel was shocked to find that a new plan to raise even more money to support the states in crisis was being discussed: the International Monetary Fund would do this by what amounted to mortgaging the gold reserves of the various national banks. Germany froze in horror: gold reserves are sacred, in fact it was illegal to go anywhere near them. Merkel was exposed to a barrage of criticism from all sides but, as tempting as it was to give way, she had to stand her ground. There could be no exceptional levies on the Bundesbank. The other heads of government were furious, statements were drafted, considered and rejected. Eventually, President Obama saw reason and called off the attack. On the flight back from Cannes, Merkel impassively told journalists that yet more work had been done to promote one's own views in the crisis.

This autumn of discontent, however, produced two victories: first, Sarkozy came out in support of the German rescue plan. German-French cooperation worked so well that other members of the EU had to endorse it. The second victory was that the December summit gave the go-ahead to develop the latest product from the House of Merkel. This was the fiscal compact – a comprehensive commitment to keep national budgets under control.

Merkel could also enjoy two quiet triumphs. In Italy, Silvio Berlusconi resigned: the pressure had simply become too much, and the Prime Minister could not get his coalition government to agree to any more reforms. Merkel must have been delighted, as Berlusconi belonged to the group of self-serving politicians whom she tried to avoid. He had always been deaf to the reasoning behind her rescue plan: his newspapers mounted attack after attack on "Merkel's Third Reich", and records of bugged phone calls emerged in which he poured unprintable scorn on the German Chancellor. With the consent of all the political parties, the technocrat Mario Monti took over, and within four weeks had managed to change the markets' attitude in favour of his country. In the meantime Spain was holding elections, and ejected the Zapatero government, which was unwilling to introduce reforms. The new Prime Minister was a conservative, Mariano Rajoy, of whom Merkel initially had high hopes. In all, seven European governments succumbed to the crisis – almost half the Eurozone had had to change its leaders.

But Merkel had made two bad mistakes, the consequences of which were to be felt within the next six months. Along with Sarkozy, she prevented the Greek people from voting against the rescue package by indirectly threatening the despairing Prime Minister, Papandreou, that Greece would be kicked out of the Eurozone. Never before had Merkel expressed herself so clearly about the Greek problem, and she would never do so again. Papandreou gave way, withdrew his plans and resigned. As a result Merkel landed herself with a huge domestic problem in the form of Greece. For six months, work in Athens came to a standstill, with transitional governments and two elections.

The second mistake was more serious, because it caused the crisis virus to spread round the entire Eurozone even more rapidly: Merkel assured the community that private creditors would have to play their part in writing off Greek debt. The message to investors was a stark one: trust your money with us and you might not get it back. The financial markets obviously understand risk, and generally take it into account. Yet up till now there had been virtually no risk involved in lending to governments. Government bonds had to be secure in the Eurozone, even more so than anywhere else. So the decision to involve private creditors had an immediate effect on the behaviour of investors. Suddenly, no one wanted Italian and Spanish government bonds.

Finally, there was a third piece of news that gave cause for concern: Great Britain and the Czech Republic didn't want to be part of the fiscal compact. Prime Minister David Cameron had got carried away with his demands. The Tory MPs in the House of Commons was unwilling to agree to any new European treaty. This refusal had consequences: the fiscal compact could not be included in the existing European treaties – this would only work if all the EU member states agreed. So the compact had to be negotiated separately, and concluded directly between the states concerned. When it comes to international law, this was no trivial matter; the very logic behind the European treaties was being twisted – and many people didn't even notice. In the Chancellor's office there were no doubt some who rubbed their hands with glee. Merkel herself preferred Brussels not to have any new rights of supervision, and thus more power.

Merkel can be ruthless when she is implementing her step-by-step strategy. And the next step was the summit on 31st January 2012, at which the fiscal compact received the final blessing of heads of government. Three weeks later, the long-planned second rescue package for Greece was concluded, for the sum of 130 billion euros, and linked to a Greek debt haircut.

So was that the end of it? Did Greece finally have enough money and breathing space to resurrect itself? There were great hopes, as is usual after such enormous efforts. But the second phase of the crisis was not over yet. The Greek election debacle created constant problems: the country was unable to form a stable government, and so there was little chance of calm. And now the genie of mistrust had been let out of the bottle, things became far more serious: there was still a great deal of anxiety, especially in Spain. The governments in Rome and Madrid were making efforts to introduce reforms, but these efforts were not acknowledged by the markets. In Spain, something had to be done about banks with bad loans of over sixty billion euros on their books, while in Italy the resolute Monti's courage failed him when it came to reforming the labour market.

By now Merkel herself had become the problem. The people of the countries worst affected by the crisis saw her as the main reason for their misery. Her picture featured on swastika flags; she was depicted as a witch, a dominatrix or a wicked stepmother; there were references to the Third and sometimes a Fourth Reich, and she was accused of planning to subjugate the entire continent. Merkel was the subject of the wildest conspiracy theories, and any part played by the indebted countries themselves was ignored. European's national prejudices suddenly reappeared, proving the truth of the saying that it takes decades to dismantle resentments but only a few weeks to revive them.

When Merkel went to Rome in the summer of 2012 for government talks, it was intended as a gesture of goodwill and support for Mario Monti. But the Italian people had quite a different opinion of their powerful visitor. A female journalist addressed her as the Empress of Europe. Merkel ignored the remark. Later in the year, when she was planning visits to crisis-hit Spain, Greece and Portugal, the centre of Athens had to be cordoned off by an army of police officers, as if it were the US President who was coming. An adviser who had accompanied her to many European Council meetings once commented with a note of resignation: "They just don't understand globalization."

Probably the most powerful image of the crisis at the end of its second phase was Merkel herself, at about five o'clock in the morning on 29th June. Another summit in Brussels, another two days in the Belgian capital. Merkel doesn't like sleeping in hotels: she prefers to be at home in Berlin, and arranges her schedule so that she is away for as few nights as possible. Evening engagements outside Berlin usually end early so the Chancellor can fly back to

Tegel airport late at night. But when the engagement is a summit, that is rarely possible: summits are for night owls, and it is part of the ritual that negotiations have to last all night.

The summit of 28th June was such an occasion. This time it was about Spanish bank debts, and Italian fears that they too might need to ask for funds from the rescue package at some point, although they didn't want to be subjected to the strict regime of reforms. As it turned out, the Italian Prime Minister did most of the talking, saying that he was going to break the "mental block" – meaning the strict rules laid down by Germany for giving money from the rescue fund to countries such as Ireland, Portugal and Greece. Monti threatened to bring the summit to a halt if he were unable to get an agreement about easier access to the rescue fund. His plan was for Italy to refuse to agree to the growth pact, an agreement to support countries in need that was of little long-term significance, but which at this point was symbolic. The summit would then have ended without any result, causing problems for Merkel, because she would return from the summit the next day to a very nervous Bundestag; firstly, MPs were waiting to go off on their summer recess, and secondly there was to be a vote on the momentous laws concerning the permanent rescue plan, the European Stability Mechanism, and the fiscal compact – Merkel's personal contribution in the battle against disaster. The SPD supported her in principle, but it wanted the growth pact that Monti was now threatening to boycott. Without it, the Social Democrats would have refused to vote in favour of the other laws. So Monti was taking advantage of the trap that Merkel had built into her own schedule.

Negotiations went on until 4.20 a.m., the official communiqué ran to only two pages, and at five in the morning Monti produced his own version of events. Merkel had already gone back to her hotel to snatch a few hours' sleep. At that moment Monti faced the cameras and expressed his pleasure, first at Italy's victory over Germany in the World Cup the evening before, and secondly at his defeat of Merkel. Germany had given way, he said: the banks would now receive direct aid, and Italy would have easier access to the rescue fund.

It caused a sensation; the Iron Chancellor had been defeated, and the press agencies sent off the breaking news. Of course, Monti's version didn't quite coincide with the communiqué, in which a few other things had been agreed: first, a unified instrument for bank supervision was to be created, so a check could be kept on financial institutions using common guidelines. Only then would banks be able to receive money from the rescue fund – under the usual strict conditions. To put it in plain language, the whole thing would take some time, because a supervisory authority of this kind isn't created overnight. The German version went further: even when there was such an authority, the Spanish banks would not be able to offload their problems quite so easily, as the agreement did not apply to old cases, only to future problems, and the liability would not apply retrospectively. As for the Italian wish to get quick money from the rescue pot, the communiqué was equally vague, saying only that, as before, aid was linked to certain conditions, and a memorandum had to be negotiated to establish the details.

When Merkel left her hotel at nine o'clock, a Reuters photographer was waiting for her. The next day, his picture became a symbol of what was apparently the Chancellor's defeat. Merkel was looking out of the back window of the car – a troubled, drained, exhausted figure with rings round her eyes after a long night. People saw a vanquished Chancellor, as Monti had said. It was only when she got up that Merkel grasped the extent of this communications disaster. Any delay might transform it into a political one. At home, the Bundestag was waiting. The majority vote for the ESM and the fiscal compact was now under threat. Merkel was angry. Monti had broken the rules and gone in front of the cameras, in spite of the agreement that no head of government would give their own interpretation of events. On the flight back to Berlin the atmosphere was tense, and meanwhile bizarre reports from Parliament were arriving in the Chancellor's office. MPs were searching the Internet to find out how the outcome of the summit was being interpreted. *Der Spiegel* wrote of "the night Merkel lost".

Merkel had great difficulty in explaining her own interpretation of the summit to the Bundestag. She spoke to each parliamentary party separately, made a rousing speech, but in the end she was short by twenty-six votes from her own coalition. The government could not reach a majority on its own, and the laws were only adopted thanks to votes from the SPD and the Green Party. Yet, a few days later, Monti himself was no longer sticking to his version. In an interview he played down what he had said; the reaction had obviously given him a fright. A conflict with the Bundestag – which had yet to release the aid funds – would not be good for him either. Nonetheless, the Italian Premier had brought matters to a head. The psychology of the crisis had changed; Merkel's supposed defeat had calmed the markets. They assumed that the pots of aid money would not be so well guarded, and felt reassured. In the battle for attention and opinions, facts are unimportant, at least initially. Perception is what matters. In the political fencing match, Monti's foil had struck a blow against Merkel, the great expert in facts.

A month later, Mario Draghi, the head of the European Central Bank, made the next move in this game of interpretation and perception. On 26th July, at the Global Investment Conference in London, he assured the assembled financial community that "the ECB will do all it takes to support the euro". And then he added: "Believe me, it will be enough." A murmur of relief ran through the ranks of financiers. "All it takes" – was this the longed-for miracle weapon that simply had to be big enough to frighten off any speculators? Not exactly, because this weapon had a safety catch. On 6th December, against the will of the president of the Bundesbank, the governing body of the ECB agreed unanimously on a programme to buy up government bonds from the countries in crisis – but on one condition: countries had to agree to make the cuts that had been laid down.

Crisis over? Everything fine? Christine Lagarde, the head of the IMF, had not been right in May that year when she gave the euro a life expectancy of three months. George Soros, the investor who predicted the collapse of the euro by 2nd September had been proved wrong. The high rates of risk for government bonds began to fall. Those who were supervising Greece could now afford to spend months arguing with Athens over the implementation of economic measures. The immediate danger of state bankruptcy seemed to have been averted. And the prospect of a European banking union managed to calm the markets and let Spain off the hook, at least for the moment. Yet Merkel's original dictum still stood: no Eurobonds and no pooling of debts, because that not only contravened the treaties, but it contradicted the logic of cause and effect. Those who wanted a solution also had to make sacrifices; those who wanted growth had to create the right conditions for it. Merkel's new Europe had to put the mistakes of the old Europe behind it once and for all. But for that to happen, drastic structural reform was required. What Europe needed was a special kind of reconstruction. It was a political task, and one that Merkel was determined to take up. And so began the third act in the European drama.

A Plan for Europe

When Merkel began her second term as Chancellor in 2009, an atmosphere of confidence reigned at the heart of government. The Lisbon Treaty was settled; Europe had a new framework for what was now a community of twenty-seven member states. In Brussels there was unconcealed euphoria: a new European age was dawning, opening up great opportunities. Berlin believed that a period of extensive law-making such as the previous one was unlikely to be repeated. That assumption proved to be wrong. The financial figures from Greece were published, and it immediately became apparent that Brussels alone was powerless to help. The institutions of the Union had neither the authority nor the money to intervene. The disease had spread to organs of state that were outside the community and which therefore couldn't be controlled from Brussels. Europe was witnessing the rebirth of nation states. Even if there was still much discussion in Germany about a United States of Europe and the new European superstate, the crisis was heading in the opposite direction.

José Manuel Barroso, the President of the Commission, wanted to set up a stimulus package in December 2009 to prove that the Commission was capable of action. But he had very little money to give away. In fact, over the next few years he would see his own importance drastically reduced. He owed his position to Merkel, but became a marginal figure in the debts drama, and if he did play a significant role it was only in a negative sense.

When the heads of government decided to increase the rescue package for Greece in the summer of 2011, for instance, and the financial markets accordingly calmed down, the President declared that the sum was insufficient. The markets reacted immediately. The good mood was completely destroyed. Merkel was furious. A year later, the heads of the four great European institutions – the President of the Commission, the President of the Council, the head of the Euro Group and the head of the Central Bank – were asked to put forward a comprehensive plan of reform for the EU. Everyone knew it was a suicide mission, and that they would only make themselves unpopular. Barroso promised to publish the results in the spring of 2014. His plan was blatantly obvious: his term of office was due to end in three months' time, and Barroso didn't want to be damaged politically. He is a prisoner of his own ambitions, and the presidency of his native Portugal might be beckoning. It was quite some time since the President of the Commission had given Merkel anything to smile about.

As the strongest member of the community, Germany became the centre of attention, and the Chancellor the key player. The country's economic figures and low rate of unemployment set her apart from all the other heads of government and strengthened her position. Someone in the Chancellor's office at the time remarked: "It came to the point where we didn't go to Brussels. They came to Berlin. You could actually feel it. Everyone came to us."

In 2010, when Merkel went to Bruges to address the new intake of students in the College of Europe, she brought with her a less than pleasant message for Brussels: the era of the European superstate is over, this is a time for nations. She remembered how difficult it had been to set up the Lisbon Treaty. As she noted rather bitterly: "Never again will any of us approach the making of treaties lightly. Another ten years to make one alteration to a treaty? Such a Europe will be regarded as incapable of acting, both by the international financial markets and the rest of the world."

Merkel aimed her blows carefully, but the message was clear. She regretted that the Commission and the Parliament had set themselves up as the protectors of the European order; she even detected a certain arrogance among the Brussels elite in their view of the nation states – an arrogance based on the "community method", a concept that Brussels guards jealously, like the eternal flame. It states that the Commission has the right to take the initiative in all its policies – a virtual sovereignty in the subjects to be discussed. This also suggests that the Council, the assembly of heads of government, represents a form of rival organization – but the true guardians of the European spirit are in Brussels.

Merkel finds this view deeply worrying, which is why she wrote in the students' yearbook: "The member states are constituent parts of the European Union, not its opponents." And for anyone who still hadn't understood, she had one last message about the power relationships. The question of authority, she said, was laid down quite clearly. "The Lisbon Treaty says that the member states are masters of the treaties," she reminded her audience, "and where there is no common authority, the community method cannot be applied." In other words: Brussels had lost nothing in the rescue of the euro. A head of government could not have pointed out the Commission's limits more clearly. She had also made it plain early on in the crisis that she had no wish to start the complicated and tedious process of creating treaties just so the Commission and its community method could get involved in the economic and fiscal crisis.

In November 2010, this clear rejection of Brussels was drowned out by the crisis. But Merkel always means what she says, and wants her own way, even if it takes years. Her Bruges speech also explains why she reacted so coldly to the image conjured up by the Minister of Labour and Social Affairs, Ursula von der Leyen, who in the midst of the crisis began talking about the "United States of Europe". Merkel had no desire to get involved in a debate about the transfer of yet more powers. She was keeping a watchful eye on the mood in Germany, and her instincts told her that you have to be careful when it comes to people's feelings. More Brussels would not be well received.

The eighty million Germans are remarkably patient with Europe. Germany was spared the worst of the crisis, and for a long time any anti-European populism was taboo. But that can change in an instant. Merkel knows how quickly a crisis can be felt at home, how quickly a downturn in the economy can affect pensioners and the unemployed. That would be the end of her popularity and the confidence that the German people have in her. In internal meetings she has always said that her main task is to create an atmosphere of trust. Positive thinking, a hopeful approach – that is what people want to see in her, however urgent the crisis is, however many sleepless nights or panic attacks it might cause. When Merkel flew back to Berlin for the Bundestag debate on the morning after the June summit, she didn't know whether the day would end in disaster or not. It was only a minor indication, but on that Friday her adviser on European politics, Nikolaus Meyer-Landrut, was sitting in the place reserved for civil servants behind the government bench. He is hardly ever seen there. At such moments, even Merkel seems to like having people she trusts nearby.

And yet in principle she could rely on the Bundestag during the crisis. All the parliamentary parties except the left-wing Linkspartei supported her rescue plans. Merkel can be extremely glad to have governed with the help of the SPD for four years. During the first financial crisis, a feeling of trust had built up among the various players, yet now – when it became a crisis that threatened the existence of the single currency – it was becoming a burden. Merkel set great store by keeping the opposition parties informed about the state of the latest negotiations. And the SPD showed a sense of national responsibility without which Merkel could never be secure in the Bundestag. At least not on days such as 29th June 2012.

Again and again, Merkel has been accused of not making major speeches and reminded that she must give a basic explanation of how Europe works, preferably on television, to make the dramatic situation clear to people. The Chancellor doesn't think much of this idea. In 2006, Matthias Platzeck, then Chairman of the SPD, showed her a study of how people react to too much information. A focus group was asked for its opinion on the Grand Coalition's major reforms, such as raising VAT, additional contributions towards medical insurance and retirement at sixty-seven. The results were mostly negative. The same group was then given large quantities of information, provided with facts and arguments and asked to vote again. The result was even less favourable towards the government. In view of the complexity of the reforms, people felt that nothing would come of them anyway.

Merkel digested this study, and has since preferred to say only why she is doing something, keeping quiet about the details of how she is doing it. In any case, major speeches are not in her nature. Firstly, she knows she is no great orator. Her sober, factual style does not arouse emotion. And secondly, the view of the Chancellor's office is that a speech of that kind wouldn't be consistent with the Merkel method. The Merkel method is the quiet battle involving herself and her closest and most loyal colleagues, methodically working through a problem, splitting it into its various parts and then working on a solution step by step, bit by bit. If it turns out well, Merkel is happy. If parts of it fail to work, no one will notice. If Merkel were to announce a great success, she would be judged by her words. And in any case, she doesn't believe in grandiloquence – experience has taught her that big words seldom lead to great deeds. A speech would not be the solution. "You won't get a new Merkel now, the brand isn't going to change at this point," said one of her collaborators who helps with the groundwork.

People are often amused by the fact that throughout her career, Merkel has surrounded herself with ambitious young men. The image is not entirely inaccurate. As Leader of the Opposition, she was followed around by a team of young MPs who were passionate about foreign policy – many of them ended up as ministers or secretaries of state. As Chancellor, Merkel has gathered together a boy group of a different kind: young, loyal, highly intelligent and hard-working civil servants, none of whom have any desire to show off, who avoid publicity and, like Merkel herself, think objectively. Grand strategic designs are not their style, and in any case that is not the way Merkel works. Like the Chancellor, they prefer going in small stages, using discussion groups to find a consensus, making compromises. And they know their files inside out.

Government spokesman Ulrich Wilhelm probably played the most prominent part in this group, which is conspicuous for its strong cohesion. For her first four and a half years, Wilhelm was Merkel's public face before leaving the Chancellor's orbit and becoming Director of Bavarian Radio. Yet, aside from his public role, he was one of her most important advisers on all political matters. As Wilhelm had great input into foreign policy and hardly left Merkel's side, his influence was enormous. Equally important was his function as a sparring partner, a perfect private tutor in the social history of the western half of the Republic and post-war West German history. In fact, for history in general, no one else in the Chancellor's office had such a grasp of the lessons of the past. Wilhelm is a quiet but forceful character, a workaholic with a tactical mind, who learnt his trade from Edmund Stoiber. It has also done him no harm to be compared with Robert Redford – for the journalists of Berlin he was an honest communicator who won sympathy for his boss.

Wilhelm's successor, Steffen Seibert, spends as much time as he did with the Chancellor, but his is the fate of the second child: Merkel is more independent now: she works at a higher speed, her circle of advisers is less important, access to her is more difficult, and it is now taken for granted that the spokesman will spend most of his time with her. Merkel's loyalty to Seibert showed after Monti's early-morning coup at the fateful Brussels summit. Seibert was not held responsible for the breakdown in communication, although Berlin was furious and wanted a scapegoat. The only lesson drawn from the incident was: always hold a press conference immediately, even at 5.20 in the morning.

It is with gestures such as this that Merkel reinforces the round-table ethos among those who work with her most closely. All heads of department in the Chancellor's office have the boss's mobile number – she herself will phone or send a text at the weekend if something comes up. Merkel is uncomplicated but demanding in her requirements, and will sometimes ask managers or experts from more junior levels to say what they think when she needs a well-informed opinion. She doesn't send emails; that would create problems in terms of security. Nor does the Chancellor use a computer – the only exception is her iPad, on which she follows the news and results on the financial markets, and watches news documentaries. She doesn't keep a diary – any reconstruction of her life in government could be obtained from the extremely detailed

diary of her engagements, the most important tool for steering the ship of state.

Merkel would not have got through the most difficult task
in her entire Chancellorship without her civil servants. In the
end it was only a very small circle, no more than a handful of
people, who masterminded her second period in office and gave
a direction to her Chancellorship. As if under siege, Merkel
could withdraw with these people to the innermost part of her
citadel, not listening to external advisers but trusting entirely her
instinct, her acumen and the advice of her faithful confidants.
The Chancellor's office functions like the Kasner parsonage
of her youth: impenetrable from outside, while on the inside
demanding and ambitious.

A key figure in this select group, besides her private secretary
and personal private secretary Beate Baumann, is the second
woman in Merkel's "girls' camp", Eva Christiansen. The stability and efficiency of this trio of women, Christiansen, Baumann
and Merkel is no longer questioned: in a sense the trio is integral
to the Chancellor's modus operandi. Born in 1970, Christiansen
has been with Merkel since 1998, first as a spokeswoman and
now, in a broader sense, as someone to whisper information to
the media. She surprised the small world of Berlin when she went
on maternity leave at the beginning of Merkel's Chancellorship
but came back in 2007 and carried on with her job as if it were
the most natural thing in the world – for in the Chancellor's
office even that is possible. And there is more: besides the post
of media adviser specially created for her, Christiansen now runs
the department of political planning, including the nitty-gritty
– speech-writing and, unofficially, looking after the image of the

Chancellery. Christiansen is one of Merkel's most trusted colleagues, part of the inner circle that knows everything and says little. If she didn't have sound political judgement and above all an infallible instinct for the public mood, allowing her to exert the right amount of restraint at the right moment, she would be unable to do her job. But very few people know that, because Christiansen, like all its really powerful members, belongs to Merkel's silent order.

In the first phase of the euro crisis and before he moved on to become head of the Bundesbank, economic adviser Jens Weidmann was the man for analysis and ideas. If he or any of the Europe advisers were summoned to the Chancellor's office on the seventh floor, it was about the most crucial points of the crisis: the ESM in the late summer of 2010, then the pact to encourage competitiveness, and later the fiscal compact. The secretary of state in the Finance Ministry, Jörg Asmussen, was also called upon to provide economic advice. Asmussen and Weidmann have known each other since university, and both studied under the former head of the Bundesbank, Axel Weber. Merkel showed her high opinion of Asmussen when she took him to the state dinner at the White House as a guest of the German government, which was not strictly necessary, since Finance Minister Wolfgang Schäuble was also there. At the beginning of 2012, Asmussen left Berlin for the European Central Bank, where he joined the board of directors. Like Weidmann, he still advises Merkel informally.

Her closest circle during the crisis naturally also includes Christoph Heusgen from the Department of Foreign Policy, and the head of the Europe Department, Uwe Corsepius, who was in charge of the

Europe team until the summer of 2011, and his successor, Nikolaus Meyer-Landrut. Corsepius was responsible for the German presidency of the Council of Europe in Merkel's first term. He played a prominent role in negotiations over the Lisbon Treaty and was responsible for the Berlin Declaration, which was unveiled at the end of the EU's Golden Jubilee celebrations. In the summer of 2011 his long-term deputy took over from him: Nikolaus Meyer-Landrut, a career diplomat from the Foreign Ministry, who has spent most of his professional life dealing with the EU and its treaty projects, particularly as a member of Valéry Giscard d'Estaing's entourage. Meyer-Landrut is not only a first cousin of the singer Lena, which brought him a certain amount of public attention, he is above all an expert on the structure and organizations of the EU, knows its treaties and loopholes better than anyone else and – like all of Merkel's advisers – is decidedly Francophile.

So it might have been a lucky coincidence that Meyer-Landrut took over as head of the Europe Department at the moment when the crisis was reaching its climax, causing the Chancellor to realize that she urgently needed to become a driver and not a passenger. Until the summer of 2011, the main players had been mostly preoccupied with coming to an agreement about the cause of the crisis. Only at that point did the voices that were claiming that the real problem was Germany's diktat about budget cuts begin to die down – the same voices that had suggested Eurobonds, or a common fund as a means of erasing debt. Europe had a deficit problem, a competitiveness problem and a structural problem – and also, according to some experts, a governance problem. Slowly, then, some sort of unanimity began to prevail.

At that point Merkel asked her colleagues to find ways in which the crisis could be tackled at its root. She wanted a political answer, because the problem was a political one. If policy simply chased the markets by using the markets' own methods, it would never catch up with them. Yet there was one decision that seemed to lead in the right direction: the fiscal compact, a treaty that would enforce improvements in budget discipline. But this wasn't enough. Merkel wanted to tackle the actual source of the infection. The various analyses strengthened her opinion that something fundamental had to be done. Something new was called for, because the largest crisis since the founding of the European Union could only be resolved with correspondingly large reforms.

In 2011, Meyer-Landrut used his summer holiday in France to put some distance between himself and the frenzied atmosphere of the crisis and make a few notes. The most important thing was to get inside the problem. In the end he reduced Europe's political deficit to a simple diagram, a few circles and lines on an A4 sheet of paper. It showed a system of coordinates: a vertical axis and a horizontal axis. The left-hand side of the diagram represented the individual member states, the right-hand side the European Union. All the political areas that were working smoothly were in the space above the horizontal axis. Below the line were the trouble spots.

It showed that there were no problems in the upper right-hand area, the European Union side. Justice, the single market, competition and the environment were all above the X-shaped axis and hence in the green. No constituent parts of the EU figured in the panopticon of the crisis. On the left-hand side of the diagram, however, in the half that contained the member states, the outlook was bleak. All the sources of trouble were here, all the problems that had triggered the currency crisis and caused disparities in competitiveness: labour laws, tax laws, budgets, social-security systems – they were all below the horizontal line. The message in the diagram was this: if the root causes of the crisis in the member states cannot be controlled, then neither will be the currency crisis. Europe needs a means of governing its economy, a common financial policy, a harmonized tax system and comparable levels of social security. The main political issues must be dealt with at a European level.

To anyone who studied the drawing there seemed to be only two options. This was where the real message lay for Merkel: the critical issues could be moved out of the bottom left-hand side and put in the top right-hand area – in other words, into the jurisdiction of the European Union and its institutions. Member states would thus give up sovereignty over taxes, the economy, budgets and social-security systems. That would mean a European superstate, a United States of Europe. Alternatively, these issues could be left on the side of the member states – but ensuring that they were moved to the upper area on that side of the axis. Merkel had a choice: she could opt firmly for European integration, shifting all power to Brussels. Or she could come up with something new, a union that worked in parallel with the EU, a new conglomerate of nations. International law describes such cases as intergovernmental solutions: states conclude treaties with each other and find ways of solving problems together.

In coming to a decision, Merkel asked herself a simple question: which of these will bring better results? The answer was:

it will be better if the individual states are simply coordinated and allowed to retain their sovereignty. There were several strong arguments in favour of this. Above all else, she was concerned about national sensitivities. The social models in the various European countries are too different to allow any quick consensus to be reached on social-security systems, pensions and taxation. Trying to integrate these into the community may cause social unrest. Not only that, Merkel foresaw huge legal obstacles and problems in domestic markets – and not just in Germany. Treaties would have to be reopened, altered and ratified. So she made a firm decision: member states should make their own arrangements: this would not require too much alteration to European treaties. Those who had read her Bruges speech already knew that the Chancellor would come to this conclusion.

So is this Merkel's great plan? Is that the Chancellor's idea of European finality? It would be out of character if she carried that diagram about with her like a Bible. She would never openly admit that she has a master plan to rescue the European Union. If she says anything at all, she takes things slowly, step by step, because it is a matter of the greatest importance, involving a change of paradigms, a form of revolution. In her own mind, Merkel has abandoned the community method: Europe's most urgent problems can no longer be dealt with by a Commissioner. The Chancellor wants a parallel organization, one that will coordinate individual nations' requests, with a supervisor who might work in the President of the Council's office and supervise the implementation of treaties concluded between individual states. The plan also specifies that, in the future, different countries would move at different speeds. Many countries would agree to coordination, others would not. The United Kingdom already took the first step in the second direction when it decided not to join the fiscal compact.

Merkel gathered her strength for the decisive attack. She wanted her idea of the new order to be adopted by the European Council in December. The basic principles for fighting the crisis had already been accepted: aid in exchange for reforms, competition rather than levelling-down. Now it was a matter of fitting the building blocks of reform into the European decision process as gently as possible. In that respect at least, the summit in June 2012 was a success. The heads of the various EU institutions were asked to come up with proposals for reform, so the ball was already rolling. It is true that the first working group on reform met with little enthusiasm at the autumn summit in October, but that made no difference. The crucial thing was that reform was now firmly on the agenda for all heads of government – because it would ultimately be up to them to decide what needed to be done.

Merkel launched her idea just before the October summit. Once again she chose to make a statement in the Bundestag to outline her vision of the future structure of the EU. Once again her speech was mostly drowned out by everyday business. But she had another string to her bow. Three weeks later she spoke to the European Parliament, where, for the sake of simplicity, she repeated her plan.

She began by giving this new Europe a name: a stability union, which would rest on four pillars. The first of these was that the new Europe would need a common policy for the financial markets, the second a common fiscal policy, the third a common economic policy and the fourth more democratic authority and control.

What Merkel was not quite so clear about was that behind this four-pillared structure lay her idea for a new division of powers in the EU – on one hand the community centred on Brussels, on the other the Europe of individual states.

In principle, heads of government had already agreed on pillar number one, although there was heated debate about the form that the supervision of the banks would take. A regulated financial market and joint supervision of the banks were part of a common financial policy, and with this came commonly agreed rules in the event that banks got into difficulty and needed to be protected by the rescue plan. Merkel's second pillar, a common fiscal policy, had also taken hold: the fiscal compact had been concluded, and the Eurozone countries had signed up to more budget discipline. Yet what it still lacked was the right to take drastic measures. What would happen if a member state broke the stability pact and incurred all the possible sanctions? Merkel wanted to give the currency supervisor full powers – but she had yet to find sufficient support for that.

The genuinely revolutionary development came with the third pillar, the common economic policy. Her adviser, Meyer-Landrut, produced a key witness in the shape of the former President of the Commission, Jacques Delors, who is highly respected, especially among French Socialists. In 1989 he wrote a report on the dangers of currency union, in which he noted drily and succinctly: "A common currency calls for a high degree of consensus on economic policy as well as in a number of other political areas, especially fiscal policy." Merkel hoped that the Socialist French President, François Hollande, would be unable to contradict that opinion. In her view, coordination of economic policy was necessary, particularly where it touches on questions of national sovereignty – in policies on the labour market and taxation. Because these, as the diagram drawn in September 2011 had illustrated, were the headaches.

Merkel immediately made it clear to her audience in the Bundestag that she was not keen to give more power to the European Commission. What had first to be taken into consideration was "the right of member states and their parliaments to self-determination and the scope to create their own structures". Nonetheless, there had to be guidelines: more unity, more control, the right of a "European power" to intervene. Merkel didn't specify which European power she meant – that would become clear later. It could only be the new system of supervision that member states would create for themselves, far away from the Commission and the European treaties. And as something was needed to provide a stimulus, Merkel promised money. A new "solidarity element" would be created, perhaps funded by a tax on financial transactions, which countries in difficulty could use to finance projects to improve their competitiveness.

When she came to pillar number four, MPs in Berlin would have swallowed hard – if they understood the implications. The Commission was going to set up a form of European government, controlled by a strong parliament – which could only be the European Parliament. But that wasn't enough for Merkel: "I am in favour of the Council becoming something like a second chamber," she said after her speech to the European Parliament. Almost a year before, in an interview with leading European newspapers, she had gone on record saying: "Beside the Commission, this second chamber will in a sense form the Council with the heads of government."

The December summit was nonetheless a disappointment for Merkel. The President of the Council, Herman Van Rompuy, proposed a completely different agenda for reform: once again Eurobonds featured on the wish list; once again it was a case of providing money without asking for anything in return. Merkel spent the weeks before the summit and the summit itself fighting a defensive battle; she lacked allies, and her counterparts clearly no longer saw any urgency for large-scale reform. Yet at least she managed to turn the counter back to zero. She still had her sights set on Europe, and Van Rompuy's plans ran aground. But six months had gone by, time had been wasted. Merkel began turning the matter over in her mind again.

All the same, a first step had been made – Merkel had spoken publicly about her idea for a new European economic order. Europe had a choice: either a middling solution, the classic model based on compromise that would be swept away by the tidal wave of globalization, or a difficult programme of reform that would allow the continent to compete. The fifty-five years since the Treaty of Rome are a blink of an eye in historical terms, she said on another occasion. No one could guarantee that Europe would retain its peaceful, stable order. Or, as she told the Bulgarian Prime Minister, Boyko Borisov, more in jest than earnest, no one has a divine right to be the leading power. Even the Mayas died out eventually. And Angela Merkel didn't want Europe to die out. She wanted to achieve great things for Europe. Yet at the same time she set herself a modest goal: no one should be able to accuse her of playing an active part in the downfall of a whole continent.

The British Problem

Keep Them in

On 11th November 2012, Angela Merkel flew to London for dinner. On the agenda was an informal meeting with David Cameron. This is the sort of occasion that she far prefers, because she is free of the demands of protocol and has an opportunity to learn something about the other person. So, while in Germany the period of Carnival – what Rhinelanders refer to as the "Fifth Season" – was just about to start, Merkel walked through the shiny black door of 10 Downing Street and into what might have been another world.

German visitors are always enchanted by the mystery that hovers around the British Prime Minister's official residence. Although Number Ten is essentially just a terraced house, all the power and authority of the nation's long history seem to radiate from its façade. Germans, who have often overturned their own history, admire the British sense of tradition. Yet the mystery soon evaporates when, as is likely to happen, you go in search of the guests' lavatory to the left of the front door and see a bottle of bleach and a toilet brush under the sink.

Merkel's small entourage were promptly led away into the depths of the building, and soon lost their bearings among the maze of narrow corridors and staircases that were more reminiscent of a dog kennel than the heart of a national government. One member of the delegation was utterly bewildered when they were taken through a kitchen where the pots and pans didn't seem to have changed since Churchill's day. But their surprise reached its apogee when, before the meeting started, their host, David Cameron, asked them to gather round and introduced himself as the sole performer. With the help of an aide and a laptop he gave a lively and entertaining presentation that explained the relationship between his country and the European Union, including subtle references to the upcoming arguments over the budget.

Merkel, who can be quick-witted and amusing herself, much appreciates this self-deprecating side of David Cameron's character. She once affectionately said that he loves to hog the limelight. She likes the sort of political interchange that is found in the British tradition of debates, the Prime Minister's weekly confrontation in the House of Commons that gives a clear, critical edge to political discussions – perhaps because she doesn't have a reputation as an orator herself, at least not among her domestic audience.

Whatever the case, the 11th of November 2012 would go down in the history of Anglo-German relations as the day the Chancellor got to know and understand the British Prime Minister. Of course, she didn't always agree with Cameron's interpretation of events, but at least what emerged was a kind of personal relationship without which nothing can be achieved in the political elite. But most of all it managed to heal several wounds that Cameron had inflicted in the past.

Merkel likes British politics. One reason for this is that Britain's view of the United States is similar to her own. And she speaks

English; as an East German Protestant she feels closer to Anglican sensibilities than to the Roman Catholicism of southern Europe; in her previous life in the GDR she admired the unambiguous stance taken by the British and Americans towards the Socialist regime. And although she has never forgotten Margaret Thatcher's convolutions over German reunification, that did nothing to lessen her liking for British understatement, the country's understanding of sovereignty and its deeply rooted democratic ideals.

She greatly admired Tony Blair when he was Prime Minister. He was the one who introduced her into the international political milieu when she became Chancellor, and helped her take her first steps at the European Parliament. As we have seen, immediately after her election in 2005, Merkel dispatched her newly appointed head of the Chancellery, Thomas de Maizière, to London, where he could learn the business of government from Blair's staff. Admittedly, the British Prime Minister had been damaged and politically weakened by the war in Iraq. Not dissimilarly to George W. Bush, Blair was keen to be seen as being close to the new German Chancellor, who could enhance his standing – and who if nothing else had the advantage of not being Gerhard Schröder. But after eighteen months their ways parted. If Blair had had hopes that Merkel might help him crown his career by securing a job in Brussels, then he was to be disappointed. Merkel is too much of a pragmatist for that, and knew that the Iraq affair had left Blair toxic – at least for her audience at home in Germany.

For three years Merkel's opposite number was Gordon Brown, someone whose personality greatly resembles her own. Like the

Chancellor, Brown is a hard-working, analytically minded politician, shaped by his upbringing in a Scottish manse. Like Merkel, he is also hard to read and only very occasionally confides in people. When the Lehman Brothers crisis reached Europe in the autumn of 2008, it was Brown who organized a meeting of the world's twenty leading economies in London. And it was Merkel who plagued the British Premier with her ideas for regulation until he incorporated the relevant passages in the final document. When he called a general election for the spring of 2010, Brown had no hope of being re-elected. So it was very much a personal gesture on the Chancellor's part when, a few weeks before he left office, she visited him at Chequers.

Barely six months later, Merkel was back at the British Prime Minister's official country residence, this time as a guest of David Cameron and accompanied by her husband, Joachim Sauer. When it comes to Merkel's positive attitude towards the British, Sauer isn't without influence. The professor has accompanied her on a great many of her visits to the United Kingdom – not something he does with every country. He once flew to Heathrow with Merkel and promised to join her for dinner with the Prime Minister later. When the German Embassy offered him the use of an official car, he politely refused. He said he preferred the Underground. And with that he headed for the Piccadilly Line and set off to visit a fellow academic.

Although on a personal level Merkel thinks very highly of the British, her professional view of its policy towards Europe is much more complex. In her opinion it was Tony Blair who sowed the seeds of the dilemma with which Cameron is now faced, by laying the foundations for a referendum. Although on his trips to the Continent Blair always showed a very positive attitude towards the EU, this opinion wasn't reflected in British domestic politics. He twice promised a referendum – if Britain were ever to consider joining the euro, and over the adoption of the European Constitution – but it never happened. The European Constitution had already been rejected by voters in France and the Netherlands, so Blair didn't dare put it to the test.

Britain's tendency to keep a distance from Europe reflects its traditional attitude towards the Continent. As Henry Kissinger wrote in his book *Diplomacy*, Great Britain is the only European power whose national pragmatism always prevents it from demanding expansion. In this respect its relationship with Europe and thus the European Union is diametrically opposite to that of Germany, which after two World Wars and with a dominant position in the centre of Europe that it is unable to shake off, is crying out for closer union between states. So while Merkel tries to find a perfect institutional framework for Germany, the euro and ever-closer European integration, according to the rigorously analytical opinion of the Chancellor's advisers, Britain has never made the leap from the European Community to the European Union.

Initially, however, Merkel's disagreement with Cameron was over something much more straightforward. Early in 2009, Cameron withdrew the seventy-one Tory MEPs from the European People's Party in protest at its "federalist" policies and its criticism of the British desire to hold a referendum. This decision made Merkel's blood boil. She foresaw that it might massively weaken the conservative faction in the European Parliament. It sent a very clear signal to the other parties of the centre-right alliance, as the British vote was very important to the EPP. Their departure put wind in the sails of other Eurosceptic Parties, which could develop into a veritable storm at the next European elections. European versions of the US Republican Tea Party can be found all over the Continent. Merkel regarded Cameron's decision as short-sighted and motivated by domestic politics – an opinion that she would reiterate as Cameron's European problems grew.

Merkel reacted in the same way as any party leader would. She got straight in touch with the London branch of the Konrad Adenauer Foundation, whose director had the best network of contacts within the Conservative Party, and let Cameron know by way of various channels that this definitely wasn't a good move. Cameron didn't react, but three days after being elected in May 2010 he flew to Berlin, where the personal relations between the two immediately improved.

Yet the EPP episode was only a foretaste of the problems that Germany would encounter over British policies towards Europe under Cameron's leadership. From Berlin's perspective, Britain's party-political debate about a referendum paled into insignificance beside the problems in the Eurozone that Merkel had been trying to solve since 2010. Yet two very dangerous situations looked set to collide at any moment: the euro crisis and the British desire for reform, including a demand for treaty change, would hold the EU in a double lock.

Merkel saw Cameron's problems over Europe as entirely of his own making and avoidable. And even if the Chancellor didn't presume to pass judgement on the Tories' internal squabbles, she nonetheless regarded Cameron as being hostage to his party. Tactical errors, constant concessions to the Eurosceptics, poor timing and above all else the lack of any clear, convincing direction – in his Europe policy, Cameron had not shown a jot of statesmanship.

Merkel's reaction to people in a weak position is to give them a form of electric-shock treatment: she kept pushing Cameron to play more of a part in European affairs, so he wouldn't be dragged along in the slipstream of the anti-Europe faction in his country. "We want him to get more involved," was the word in the Chancellery, which in relation to the EU budget meant: Germany was on his side when Cameron insisted that the Commission's budget couldn't be allowed to increase. It would have been the easiest thing in the world to give in to the demands of the southern European countries and leave Cameron isolated. But it was in Merkel's own interests and a fundamental concern of hers that Britain should remain in the European Union. "Constructive involvement" was the murmur that went round Berlin, or "involvement for the sake of your own interests" – dealings with London were taking on an almost disciplinary tone.

Admittedly, these electric-shock tactics also had another target: Merkel had no desire for the anti-Europe faction in Britain to start feeling emboldened and believe that all it took was a few steps and the rebate champions in London would surrender and even be pushed towards the exit. No, Merkel wanted to keep the British in the EU. Any other outcome would shift the balance of power in the EU to Germany's disadvantage, and would paralyse the Continent. Hence her key objective: Great Britain had to remain in the EU – but not at any price.

The haggling over this price began in the middle of the euro crisis in November 2011, when Merkel wanted to set up the fiscal compact but Cameron refused to join. The Chancellery made it quite clear to the Prime Minister's office that this agreement would not prevent national governments from keeping to their own financial models and introducing legislation to balance their own budgets, and that it was actually in line with Britain's decision to pursue a strict austerity policy. Since the other non-Eurozone countries all supported the idea, it seemed odd from the German viewpoint that Cameron should baulk in this way. And when he made last-minute demands in order to protect the special interests of the City, this only increased his isolation.

In Germany's view, a similar miscalculation lay behind the speech on Europe that Cameron made in January 2013. Cameron had used their dinner on 11th November 2012 to confide his thoughts and ideas to Merkel and explain the dramatic situation. The Prime Minister made two important observations. The first was that the single currency had fundamentally changed the entire Europe project. Without the euro the European Union had been inclusive, in other words oriented towards the member states. Several countries needed more time to adopt many of the constituent parts of this Europe, or else they wanted to be exempt from its regulations. At the same time the single market was becoming too weak to bind the different countries together. The single currency had now thrust itself forward to centre stage as the most important European project, thus changing the very nature of Europe. The Continent was divided between countries who used the euro and those who didn't. Cameron then asked a direct question: what was most important to her – the single market or the single currency? What he really meant by this was that Europe had to give serious thought to the relationship between the countries in the Eurozone and those outside it.

His second argument was this: Merkel had to understand how a promise of a referendum was likely to be received in Britain. He tried to impress on her that it wasn't simply a matter of placating his Eurosceptic backbenchers, but that it lay at the very heart of the British understanding of democracy.

Put in these terms, Cameron's speech almost appeared to be a nod to Merkel and Germany. Not only that, Cameron had only just missed stirring up a hornet's nest, because he had originally planned to give the speech on 22nd January – which, of all days, was the fiftieth anniversary of the signing of the Élysée Treaty between France and Germany. To mark the event, the French and German parliaments would hold a joint session in Berlin, while the two cabinets met symbolically round the same table. This High Mass of national reconciliation was thus also a form of celebration of the birth of the European project. If Cameron had delivered his speech on this particular day, then the snub could not have been more exquisitely timed. Amazingly, however, no one in Downing Street was apparently even aware of this, and it was only after a last-minute panic that the danger was averted.

Someone who had been involved in the writing of the speech commented that it was clearly aimed at two different audiences: the British public, particularly the Tories, and the German Chancellor. It was no coincidence that Cameron had mentioned it to Merkel beforehand, nor was it a coincidence that the key theme was that competitiveness lay at the heart of the European project.

The speech was supposed to pacify the Eurosceptics in Cameron's Party – the promise of a referendum after the next general election in exchange for a truce between now and then. Yet, in Merkel's opinion, Cameron was making two mistakes. First of all he was taking an enormous risk for the sake of short-term political gain at home. A referendum is no small matter and can have unforeseen consequences. Merkel would never leave herself at the mercy of such uncontrollable political forces. And secondly, it was naive to expect that the promise of a referendum would silence the critics. In fact it had the opposite effect: Cameron had played his trump card, but was still subject to coercion. And the need for a fundamental debate on the subject was clearly not satisfied by the simple announcement of a deadline. On the other hand, Cameron had managed to silence the people who had been calling for a referendum, as they now felt that they had got what they wanted.

For Merkel there were a couple of practical questions: the speech reminded her that in Cameron she had an ally in her central issue – the warning about a declining Europe. Cameron shared her view that Europe either had to improve its competitiveness or fall behind in the global race. Yet Merkel had to make a practical decision, which was how far she would go along with Cameron's demand for a repatriation of powers to the United Kingdom. She had no desire whatsoever for treaties to be reopened. So her warning to Cameron was this: only if treaties had to be renegotiated could there be a vote on them. And a vote was likely to turn out badly – of that Merkel was certain.

Merkel also had another fear: Cameron might misread her signals and take advantage of the hard line that she was adopting with the crisis-hit countries, as well as her sympathy for his demand for a repatriation of powers. If the British Prime Minister insisted too much on these demands, then ultimately she might be the only one who would be able to keep Britain in the EU. Cameron might exploit the fact that the Germans wanted to keep Britain in the EU at any cost, because it suited their interests. But Merkel doesn't like veiled threats. If it reached that stage then she would decide whether the price was too high, and if in doubt she would decline.

And then there was a third concern – the scenario that in Berlin was always described using an English expression: "accidental exit". Hopes of a referendum might be too high, there could be a backbench revolt, an unexpected result at the next general election, and then a country that was unable to handle the consequences. At which point the situation would be beyond saving.

Among the vast array of other problems faced by the European Union, therefore, Merkel was keen that her British counterpart should get the right message: Cameron should not overestimate his position, he should not count on her being too accommodating. The German government saw some serious contradictions in Cameron's logic: it wasn't possible to speak of the single market as if it were a form of Holy Grail and at the same time demand to be treated as an exception to its rules and regulations. As much as Merkel supported the principle of subsidiarity and felt that too much of the political decision-making had been transferred to civil servants and the European Commission, she would never overestimate her own power and demand that treaties be changed unless she were absolutely certain that she could achieve what she wanted.

So no, there wouldn't be a new British rebate, not even in the form of symbolic treaty changes. If treaties did have to be changed, it would only happen if it were required by the EU's new institutional structure, or by the creation of a banking union within the Eurozone. From the epicentre of the euro crisis, things looked quite different to how they seemed from Downing Street. And so in Berlin there is always a note of sympathy in people's voices when they talk about Great Britain and its romantic view of a world that has long since changed.

The Prospects for Merkel?

The Post-Political Chancellor

As yet, no clear verdict can be given on Angela Merkel's policies. The crisis has taken Merkel prisoner, and events are still racing ahead. It will be a long time before the misery comes to an end in Greece and Spain. The markets are still nervous. France is only just embarking on its most difficult phase of self-discovery since the end of the Second World War. In Germany, the election year of 2013 will be dominated by anxiety about the euro.

Only when the crisis has abated will we know what part of the rescue – or the collapse – of the euro can be attributed to Merkel. Those around her say, "If it goes wrong we will know at once, if it goes well then it might be appreciated in twenty years' time." This is classic modesty. Nonetheless, the Chancellor has risked a great deal, although she could have made things easier for herself. She prescribed a drastic remedy for the whole continent which Germany itself might not have survived. Not only that, there is a school of thought that says that the more the crisis affected the weaker nations of Europe, the more Germany benefited – from low interest rates, from its strong economy, its attraction as a place for highly quali-fied people to come and work. On one hand this gave her a powerful position in Europe. On the other, it laid her open to attack and increased the risks for herself. If Merkel does fall, it will be a heavy fall.

In private, the Chancellor has said how much she dislikes having to play the part of an economic hardliner. She does not like being portrayed as a cold-hearted person, obsessed with economics. When she visited Portugal, Greece or Spain she was greeted with swastika flags, demonstrators burned effigies of her, her face was shown with a Hitler moustache painted on it. None of this leaves Merkel unmoved. She is constantly at odds with herself over the right way out of the crisis, she weighs up all the different arguments again and again – and yet she always comes to the same conclusion: no one has yet been able to show her a better way. Should she have agreed to throw money at Greece at the start of the crisis? To provide funding from the European Central Bank without imposing conditions? To introduce Eurobonds, or a shared pooling of debt? Aside from the legal and domestic difficulties, Merkel thinks not: if she had done so, then any incentive for reform would have been lost. Eurobonds that were not controlled by the European government would be a serious flaw in the system. On its own, Germany would have been unable to bear the enormous burden of debt that weighs on the countries of the Eurozone – "Our powers have limits," she repeated again and again in 2012. And if it is unable to compete on a global level, Europe's economic system would collapse: of that she is firmly convinced.

Make cuts and reform – or protect people from every hardship and take on an ever-increasing amount of debt? Merkel never accepted that alternative; it is not the way she works. She has only one commandment – or, as she would say, only one axiom: the euro must be protected. And, since she is a systematic person, from this axiom derive several corollaries. For instance: the euro must be protected – and when the crisis is over, it must be stronger than before. Or: the euro must be protected, if possible with the agreement of all members of the Eurozone. She has continually said: "I would like Greece to stay in the euro," but not: "Greece will stay in the euro come what may."

She keeps her options open. Greece could indeed leave the single currency. If that happens, Merkel will at least want to have arguments demonstrating why she had to support Greece for so long, and why, of all the possible options, its eventual exit from the euro was the best choice for the rest of the Eurozone. For if Greece is unable to remain in the Eurozone, then at least it has to be possible to control the consequences for the euro. Among the labyrinthine complexities of her decisions, this is how Merkel defines her aim: she always wants to have more arguments on her side than there are on the side of those who disagree with her. She wants to play safe.

For all her outward self-confidence, Merkel has always been prone to doubts. In spring 2012 she was described in the most glowing terms; *Bild* praised her to the skies. It gave the impression that the crisis was under control. That summer, she welcomed the European Central Bank's announcement that when conditions were right it would buy an unlimited number of government bonds. But this was too much good news. She immediately felt that efforts were beginning to relax in the crisis-hit countries. For six months, Greece haggled over the details of an austerity programme that had long been decided and accepted in principle. New debts were mounting up. Once again, Merkel realized that the euro would not be rescued simply by a fiscal compact or a reconstruction plan. The euro would survive or fall with little Greece. In the autumn of 2012 she was accused of not facing up to the truth: Greece would never be able to repay its debts, and the wealthier European nations, Germany first and foremost, would have to foot the bill. Nonetheless, she didn't want to agree to a new cut in those debts – at least not at that stage. Because what incentive would that be – not only for Greece, but for the other troubled countries? If the pressure was relaxed there would be no European economic governance.

Merkel has sometimes wondered why she is credited with such omnipotence. Because during all the years of crisis, she has been subject to endless constraints: German domestic politics, the Federal Constitutional Court, election dates, changes of government, her coalition partners, extremely unstable alliances in the EU – she has always had to depend on her allies. Perhaps the biggest problem in the third phase of the crisis was the change of president in France. Merkel had been strong in Europe for so long, partly because she had an ally in Nicolas Sarkozy. Nothing could be done politically in Europe against the combined power of Germany and France.

But then the situation changed. François Hollande became French President. Suddenly she lacked the necessary weight to impose her political will on Europe. During the French election campaign she had made the mistake of supporting her friend Nicolas Sarkozy. It was something that Hollande wouldn't forget in a hurry. More significant, however, was that the new President was caught in a web of election promises and the political expectations of his supporters. His ideas about how to resolve the crisis were diametrically opposed to Merkel's. For some months, the

Chancellor spoke of him among her inner circle only as "her counterpart". The tensions were palpable.

Merkel doesn't share the political convictions of her father figure, Helmut Kohl. He always said that a German Chancellor does well to bow twice to the Tricolour. Merkel had no wish to bow. She was too confident of her own analysis of the crisis for that – and if she wanted Europe to continue competing with China and South-East Asia, if she didn't want it to sink into economic and demographic hibernation, then she couldn't fall in with what Hollande wanted. This is her real motive, the rationale behind all her initiatives. Europe, which represents nine per cent of the world's population, produces twenty-five per cent of its GDP, and also accounts for fifty per cent of its public expenditure. But for how much longer?

Yet should she have courted Hollande more assiduously? One thing is certain: Merkel is not given to Kohl's Rhineland joviality. She prefers to play her now familiar game: weighing up the pros and cons, making demands, exerting pressure and finally making concessions if she has gained something in return. She pins her hopes on time, which has become her closest ally. Hollande will also realize the value of time when the markets show him how little prospect there is for his economic policy.

Yet despite Merkel's rational approach, there is also anxiety. Where is all this logic leading? What do calculation and counter-calculation achieve? Among all the weighing-up of risk, has she missed a decisive, shining opportunity that she might have enjoyed shaping – or which she could have used as a launch pad? The crisis is wearing people down; few events in post-war history have tried public patience for so long. There must be an end to it at some point, but, as a stoic, Merkel is making no promises. She asks for more patience, more endurance. At some stage the public will either sense that there is a price to be paid, or will demand a firm decision. People are getting uneasy. But Merkel is not a Chancellor to take things lightly; she is the antithesis of Schröder, and thus lacks the impulsive, emotional approach that can make crises of this kind more bearable. She may overreach herself, play poker a little too long when she ought to have already made a decision – perhaps to give Greece the thumbs-down.

Someone who is close to Merkel and understands her well has said that the Chancellor is the perfect post-political politician. It was meant as a compliment, because there are a great many post-political politicians. To be post-political means not committing yourself, letting yourself drift, having few or no convictions, always being flexible, waiting for the right moment. In an overly regulated system that rips up its ideologies, these are no bad qualities to possess.

Merkel initially leaves critical matters to other politicians: reform of the armed forces? That was Guttenberg's job. The Libya debacle? Westerwelle was landed with that. Her government's aggressive policy of selling arms abroad? That was taken up by the Federal Security Council, whose members are sworn to secrecy. Merkel prefers links to her not to be too strong and, where they do exist, such as with Israel, she likes to be able to withdraw gently. When Prime Minister Benjamin Netanyahu began going too far with his settlements policy, Merkel gave him the cold shoulder. In November 2012, when the Palestinians managed to raise their status at the United Nations, Germany turned away from Israel.

Seven years as Chancellor in an atmosphere where the crises came in unusually swift succession can wear down even a woman with an iron constitution and an inexhaustible appetite for work. Merkel has become lonely in office, even more so than Helmut Kohl and Gerhard Schröder at the same point in their Chancellorship. She tends to reject external advice; she has had too many bad experiences. She circumvents Party hierarchies and prefers to communicate directly with the grass roots. The middle ranks of the CDU feel marginalized, the party is short of promising senior members. There are no strong characters, no one with a will of their own to take over from Merkel. Instead, she surrounds herself with people like herself: rational, technocratic, analytical. All of them master tacticians. Post-political politicians. Broad-brush strategists with big mouths have no place in the Chancellor's world.

A Swiss observer once accused Merkel of representing the state of experts, the politics of predictability. She satisfies the German longing for consensus – no squabbling please, we like harmony. As an observation this is not wholly inaccurate, seeing that the Opposition gave Merkel a free hand in the crisis, and even on the difficult subjects of war and peace supported the policies that she initially drafted with them. This makes German foreign policy a matter of uniformity, as if it were a civic duty to observe a truce in difficult times. Or is it that Merkel carries everyone with her? Is there perhaps no alternative to her way of doing things? Because the truth is that all sides fear the euro monster at the gates. They are all afraid of the moment when citizens will have to be told what their share of the bill is. The rational Merkel fears this too, but she hopes that by that time the figures will be sufficiently in her favour for her to be able to say: I did my best, all the alternatives would have been worse for the country.

Merkel's style forms the basis for Merkel's power. And yes, Angela Merkel is deeply conscious of power. She knows exactly who will not go along with her system. She demands no ideological loyalty, because she herself, as the archetypal post-political politician, does not make ideology a criterion of power. Instead she demands acceptance of her ideas, participation in her world of logic and counter-logic, of rational calculation and superior arguments. If she is faced with a strong argument she immediately looks for a stronger one – or uses her opponent's to bolster her own. Vladimir Putin has adopted this method. It is the only challenge to her authority that Merkel will accept. Anyone who wishes to get the better of her ideologically or boorishly will come up against a hard, slippery surface. Merkel doesn't indulge in such confrontations.

This is the secret of her power: Angela Merkel will only get involved in an argument if she knows that she will win in the end. Those who undermine the state while boasting of their invulnerability – like any number of bankers during the financial crisis – will incur her wrath. She then turns her mind to revenge. It won't be felt immediately, perhaps not until many years later. But you can be certain that Merkel won't accept being belittled. Nor will she accept being pressurized, especially not in her own camp, whether by the party or her Cabinet. If a minister is unable to do what his or her position demands and, after having made great promises simply offloads it onto her, then their time is up. This is what Wolfgang Tiefensee discovered when he was Minister of

Transport, Construction and Urban Development and wanted to dump the European Galileo satellite project, which was incurring higher and higher costs, on EU heads of government.

Blatant demonstrations of power are not Merkel's style. She doesn't shout: she speaks quietly. She doesn't bang her fist on the table; she would rather work late for a couple of nights and wear down her opponent. She considers a vote of confidence in the Bundestag a sign of weakness. If she were forced to ask for one, then she would know her time had come. However, when the coalition government denied her a majority in the last major vote on the euro in the summer of 2012, she didn't lose any sleep over it. Thanks to the opposition she had the necessary numbers, in this case a two-thirds majority. Had it been extremely close, those in the CDU who didn't vote with her would have been asked to reconsider their position. The most important thing was that the consensus held the parties together – anything else was secondary.

The euro crisis is the greatest challenge to her power. Merkel cannot really get a grip on her opponent. There are too many incalculable factors, too many players who have an influence on the game. She knows that it is events and personalities that will decide her fate – perhaps the FDP, over whose success in the 2013 general election she has only limited influence. Or the Greek Cabinet, or the Spanish Prime Minister, or the financial markets when the next French government bond is issued. Her day of reckoning will come when she least expects it – she knows that too. But what will she leave behind?

With her hardline policy during the crisis, Merkel has managed to create a new role for Germany. Isolated in the centre of Europe, the country is encountering more hostility than at any other time in more than half a century of communally constructed European history. And yet it is also much admired. This doesn't make Merkel a popular figure in many parts of Europe. The France of Hollande has moved away from her – out of weakness, because of its inability to introduce reforms, while ignoring major global trends. All this mitigates in favour of Germany and its Chancellor, yet the unequal distribution of power in Europe is still dangerous. If Merkel wants to build a new Europe, with a strong, joint economic government, with supervision of the banks, with better democratic controls, then she will have to make it clear to the German people that they will be subject to a new system, one that will react as mercilessly to them as to anyone else if they break the rules.

Above all, the other European countries have to be confident that a new, independent power has not suddenly emerged in their midst, one that requires a counterbalance. The new Europe cannot be a German Europe – that would never work. Merkel would be doing the continent and her own country no favours by preaching only productivity, low labour costs and getting up early. But the continent must also realize that its welfare, freedom and security will be endangered if the jointly agreed rules are broken.

Merkel seems surprisingly relaxed in her familiar, daily rounds. Her conscience is clear. She has led Germany for longer than anyone ever expected. The fact that she has managed to govern the country in the first place was something that was by no means certain on the eve of the 2005 election. And she lives in the knowledge that eight years as Chancellor is a respectable achievement. Several of her predecessors didn't last that long. Her ambition is for a third term – that would be like ennoblement. But from the first day after re-election she would also be burdened with the knowledge that time is running out. Merkel is enough of a realist to know that. Years of crisis have taken their toll. The business of government wears out those who take it on.

Merkel has accumulated much political capital. She is aware of that. At some point she might be tempted to give it up, to take a risk, stake everything on a single card. At some point – perhaps when she is faced with a major obstacle. Or perhaps it will remain just a temptation – Angela Merkel will always be Angela Merkel – tactical, cautious, ready to take risks only when these have ceased to be risks.

So what remains? The extraordinary fact that the girl from Templin became an international stateswoman – perhaps the strongest and certainly the most powerful that the Federal Republic has ever known. Angela Merkel will have the satisfaction of knowing that she has not only seen the world, as she wanted to do in her childhood dreams, but has understood it and changed its course a little.

And at some point voters will tire of her style and her party will rebel – that was what happened to Helmut Kohl. Then it will be clear that Angela Merkel's time as Chancellor is over. The zeitgeist changes and time runs out.